THE BEACH IN ANGLOPHONE
LITERATURES AND CULTURES

The Beach in Anglophone Literatures and Cultures

Reading Littoral Space

Edited by

URSULA KLUWICK
and
VIRGINIA RICHTER
University of Bern, Switzerland

ASHGATE

Published by
Ashgate Publishing Limited
Wey Court East
Union Road
Farnham
Surrey, GU9 7PT
England

Ashgate Publishing Company
110 Cherry Street
Suite 3-1
Burlington, VT 05401-3818
USA

www.ashgate.com

British Library Cataloguing in Publication Data
A catalogue record for this book is available from the British Library

The Library of Congress has cataloged the printed edition as follows:
  The beach in Anglophone literatures and cultures : reading littoral space / edited by Ursula Kluwick and Virginia Richter.
     pages cm
  Includes bibliographical references and index.
   ISBN 978-1-4724-5753-0 (hardcover : alk. paper)—ISBN 978-1-4724-5754-7 (ebook)— ISBN 978-1-4724-5755-4 (epub)
   1. English literature—English-speaking countries—History and criticism. 2. Beaches in literature. 3. Beaches in art. 4. Beaches in motion pictures. 5. Beaches—Psychological aspects. 6. Beaches—Social aspects. 7. Beaches—Environmental aspects. I. Kluwick, Ursula, 1977– editor, author. II. Richter, Virginia, editor, author.
   PR9080.5.B43 2015
   820.9'35820946—dc23
                                                                                            2014043574
ISBN: 9781472457530 (hbk)
ISBN: 9781472457547 (ebk – PDF)
ISBN: 9781472457554 (ebk – ePUB)

MIX
Paper from
responsible sources
FSC
www.fsc.org
FSC® C013985

Printed in the United Kingdom by Henry Ling Limited, at the Dorset Press, Dorchester, DT1 1HD

Contents

List of Illustrations

Notes on Contributors

Neal Alexander lectures in twentieth-century literature at Aberystwyth University. He is the author of *Ciaran Carson: Space, Place, Writing* (Liverpool UP, 2010); co-editor of *Poetry & Geography* (Liverpool UP, 2013) and *Regional Modernisms* (Edinburgh UP, 2013); and an editor of the peer-reviewed e-journal, *Literary Geographies*.

Tobias Döring holds a Chair of Literature in the English Department of Ludwig-Maximilians-Universität Munich. His research interests are Postcolonial Studies and Early Modern Literature. His monograph *Caribbean-English Passages: Intertextuality in a Postcolonial Tradition* was published by Routledge in 2002; a Routledge collection entitled *Edward Said's Translocations: Essays in Secular Criticism*, co-edited with Mark Stein, is currently out in paperback.

Julika Griem is Professor of English Literature at the Goethe University in Frankfurt am Main. Her publications include monographs on Joseph Conrad and the aesthetic and anthropological productivity of apes and simian figures. She has also published on narrative theory, intermediality, animal studies, literature and space, urban crime fiction and questions of genre. Her current research encompasses seriality, figurations of the whole and the oeuvre of John Burnside as well as theories and methodologies of research on contemporary literature.

Ursula Kluwick is Lecturer in English Literature and a Swiss National Foundation Marie Heim-Vögtlin Fellow at the University of Bern, Switzerland. Her research interests include postcolonial and postmodern literatures, non-realist forms of writing, Victorian literature, the representation of nature and ecocriticism. She is the author of *Exploring Magic Realism in Salman Rushdie's Fiction* (Routledge, 2011), and she is currently working on a study of representations of water in Victorian literature.

Christiana Payne is Professor of History of Art at Oxford Brookes University. Her publications include *Toil and Plenty: Images of the Agricultural Landscape in England, 1780–1885* (Yale University Press, 1993), *Where the Sea meets the Land: Artists on the Coast in Nineteenth-Century Britain* (Sansom and Company, 2007), *John Brett, Pre-Raphaelite Landscape Painter* (Yale University Press, 2010), and *The Power of the Sea* (Sansom and Company, 2014, co-edited with Janette Kerr). She is currently working on a study of the role of trees in British landscape painting, c. 1760–1870.

Katharina Rennhak is Professor of English Literature at Wuppertal University, Germany. Previous positions include a visiting assistant professorship at the

University of Texas at Austin and an interim professorship at the Ludwig-Maximilians-Universität Munich. She is especially interested in the link between literature and culture around 1800 and around 2000, in narrative theories, in theories of identity, power and relevance and in the relationship between British and Irish literary cultures and histories. Her publications include edited collections on *Revolution und Emanzipation: Geschlechterordnungen um 1800* (with Virginia Richter; Böhlau, 2004) and *Women Constructing Men: Female Novelists and Their Male Characters, 1750–2000* (with Sarah S.G. Frantz; Lexington, 2010). Her latest monograph, *Narratives Cross-Gendering* (Wissenschaftlicher Verlag Trier, 2013), analyses the construction of masculine identities in British and Irish women writers' novels around 1800.

Virginia Richter is Full Professor of Modern English Literature at the University of Bern. She has published widely on Darwinism, literature and science, literary animals and Victorian to contemporary fiction. Her latest monograph is *Literature after Darwin: Human Beasts in Western Fiction 1859–1939* (Palgrave, 2011). Currently she is co-editing, with Pieter Vermeulen, a special issue of the *European Journal of English Studies* on 'Modern Creatures'.

Meg Samuelson is Associate Professor of English at the University of Cape Town. She has published widely on Southern African literatures, including the book *Remembering the Nation, Dismembering Women? Stories of the South African Transition*. Her current research focuses on thinking from the Cape, oceanic Africa, and coastal cultures. She is involved in collaborative research projects on land, sea and city in South African literatures, African textualities and world literary debates and visual culture in Indian Ocean Africa and has recently co-edited a special section of the *Journal of African Cultural Studies* on the South African surfing film *Otelo Burning*.

Alexa Weik von Mossner is Assistant Professor of American Studies at the University of Klagenfurt in Austria and an affiliate at the Rachel Carson Center for Environment and Society in Munich. She is the author of *Cosmopolitan Minds: Literature, Emotion, and the Transnational Imagination* (U of Texas P, 2014), editor of *Moving Environments: Affect, Emotion, Ecology, and Film* (Wilfrid Laurier UP, 2014), and co-editor of *The Anticipation of Catastrophe: Environmental Risk in North American Literature and Culture* (with Sylvia Mayer; Winter, 2014).

Anne-Julia Zwierlein holds the Chair of English Literature and Culture at the University of Regensburg. She is the author of *Majestick Milton: British Imperial Expansion and Transformations of Paradise Lost, 1667–1837* (LIT, 2001), and *Der physiologische Bildungsroman im 19. Jahrhundert* (Winter, 2009). She is editor of *Unmapped Countries: Biological Visions in Nineteenth-Century Literature and Culture* (Anthem, 2005) and *Gender and Creation: Myths of Creativity, Authority, and Authorship* (Winter, 2010), and co-editor of *Innenwelten vom Mittelalter zur Moderne* (with C. Olk; WVT, 2002), *Plotting Early Modern London: New*

Essays on Jacobean City Comedy (with D. Mehl and A. Stock; Ashgate, 2004), *Interdisciplinary Perspectives on Aging in Nineteenth-Century Culture* (with K. Boehm and A. Farkas; Routledge, 2014) and *Gender and Disease in Literary and Medical Cultures* (with Iris M. Heid; Winter, 2014). She is currently engaged in a project on Victorian oral and print mass cultures.

Acknowledgements

This book has now made port, and we wish to express our gratitude to the many people who have ensured its safe passage. Ann Donahue, our wonderful editor at Ashgate, lit an early beacon to guide us into the right harbour, and we would like to thank her for her advice, patience and support, and above all for her sustained enthusiasm for our project, which was fundamental to bringing it to fruition and securing our safe arrival. Equally heartfelt thanks go out to Patricia Häusler-Greenfield, whose expertise prevented us from foundering in the rip currents of English academic style. Always ready to answer those 'quick questions', she pointed the way to firm linguistic ground. Her professional guidance was made possible by contributions from the Swiss National Science Foundation and, through Julika Griem, from the Technical University of Darmstadt, for both of which we are very grateful. Julika Griem initially set out to map the terrain with us, providing invaluable input in the earlier stages of this voyage. We are also much obliged to our anonymous reader for Ashgate for alerting us to many reefs and shoals along the shore, which we would otherwise have missed. Last but not least, David Schönthal, with his two nimble-minded helpers, Ettore Trento and Claudine Bollinger, caulked, tarred and polished our vessel until it was fully shipshape. For his meticulous inspection of any leaks and his efficient repairs, we would like to express our sincere thanks.

We gratefully acknowledge permission to use the following illustrations:

'Pegwell Bay, Kent – a Recollection of October 5th 1858', 1858–60?, William Dyce © Tate, London 2014.

'Ramsgate Sands (Life at the Seaside) 1852–54', William Powell Frith (1819–1909). Royal Collection Trust © Her Majesty Queen Elizabeth II, 2014 / Bridgeman Images.

'Four Fishwives', 1881, Winslow Homer, Scripps College, Claremont, CA; Gift of General and Mrs. Edward Clinton Young, 1946.

'A Morning amongst the Granite Boulders', 1872–1873, John Brett. Private collection.

Introduction
'Twixt Land and Sea:
Approaches to Littoral Studies

Virginia Richter and Ursula Kluwick

The Deepwater Horizon oil spill in the summer of 2010 shocked the whole world. Any attempt to downplay its impact was thwarted by the proximity of the coast, which gave the lie to the reassuring remoteness suggested by the oil drilling rig's name. As beaches in the Gulf of Mexico became contaminated with oil, visual evidence of the extent of the ecological catastrophe was broadcast by the international media. The damage was not confined to the beaches close to the source of pollution but also affected the vulnerable ecosystem of the Mississippi delta. Rare plants, birds and amphibian creatures as well as the fisheries and tourist industries of the states bordering the Gulf of Mexico suffered from the estimated 4.9 million barrels of oil escaping over three months from the rig's underwater leak. This ecological disaster not only highlighted the dangers of offshore drilling and the ecological vulnerability of our shores; it also showed how interconnected various littoral spaces – coastal waters, beaches and their immediate hinterland, river deltas and marshlands as well as the settlements on and close to the shore – are, and how interdependent their various human, animal and botanical denizens prove to be. Moreover, the Deepwater Horizon disaster underlined the ways in which a relatively local occurrence in the littoral ecotone not only has an impact on geographically distant regions but is in turn caused, dealt with and represented by actors with little or no direct connection to the locale in question: global companies, national governments, international media and, in the end, the lifestyles of consumers all over the world that make offshore drilling profitable in the first place. For all these reasons, the BP oil spill had an affective impact that went beyond the usual muted sympathy with the victims of ecological disasters.

Similarly, when a devastating tsunami wreaked havoc in large parts of South Asia's coastal regions right after Christmas 2004, the ensuing media reporting, including the many private recordings distributed through the new media, bore witness not only to the extensive damage but also to the intense shock experienced by potential tourists worldwide at the sight of holiday resorts turned into sites of destruction. The symbolic impact of these images was enhanced by the peculiar conjunction of time and place: for Western TV audiences and internet users, the peace of the festive season and the dreams of escape to a tropical paradise in the bleak mid-winter were shattered, literally within minutes, by the uncontrollable forces of nature. While major natural disasters always cause dismay, the Christmas tsunami of 2004 was experienced as exceptionally personal and traumatic even by those who witnessed it only vicariously. This particular impact can be explained not only by the scale and unexpectedness of the devastation, and by the instant availability of visual representations, but also by the psychological investment many people have in the beach as a vacationscape.

The Deepwater Horizon oil spill and the 2004 tsunami are two particularly prominent recent events that draw our attention to the fact that, as a real place, the beach is a contested site, claimed both by land and sea and symbolically construed by various, often contradictory, interests, practices and desires. The beach demarcates the precarious boundary between land and the sea, as well as between nature and culture. As a site which is claimed by various human communities and different aquatic, amphibian and terrestrial species, the beach is a contact zone where a broad array of interactions, from hospitality to hostility, are performed. Encounters here are not always peaceful but, more often than not, are conflicted and dangerous.[1] From early colonial encounters to the ecological anxieties of the twenty-first century, as a working place, as a contested habitat and as an arena for holidays, hedonism and leisure, the performativity of contact has been a crucial element in the socio-cultural as well as the political significance of the beach.

The Beach in Anglophone Literatures and Cultures sets out to investigate this polyvalent site from the point of view of the humanities. Our main concern is to analyse the generative role littoral space plays for cultural production. Conceptualising the beach as a creative trope and a socio-cultural site, as well as an aesthetically productive topography, the volume examines its multiplicity of meanings and functions: as an ecotone (a transitional zone where different ecosystems overlap and that is shared by their various characteristic species); as a natural environment engendering both desire and fear in the human imagination; as a social space inspiring particular codes of behaviour and specific discourses; as an historical site of contact and conflict, in particular in the colonial and postcolonial context; as a vacationscape – a place of regeneration and of withdrawal from everyday life, which is in turn the result of processes such as industrialisation and the rise of a modern leisure and health culture – and as both a setting and a subject for literature, film and art.

Depending on their chosen object of study and approach, the authors of the essays in this collection provide different definitions of the beach and look at different topographical zones, from the beach in the narrow sense – the strip of land on the margin of the sea – to littoral space in a more extended sense, which includes the adjoining geological and ecological zones in the sea and on shore. As studies of littoral space tend to stress, the beach is a liminal zone. On the most basic

---

[1]   According to Pratt, the term 'contact zone' denotes 'the interactive, improvisational dimensions of colonialist encounters' (7). The beach, often the site of first encounters, is a contact zone in this sense. The rules of engagement have to be negotiated by both parties; the outcome is unforeseeable; and the meaning of the event in question is interpreted differently by those who approach from the sea and those who watch their arrival from the land. Perhaps the most famous instance of such a conflicting interpretation of a landing concerns the events leading to the death of Captain Cook (see Thomas 384–7).

level, its topography is determined by its shifting boundaries, the imaginary lines which divide the sea from dry land. As the tides advance and retreat, the shore is alternately claimed by, and indeed becomes, the land and the sea; it is impossible to determine where the beach begins or ends. This shifting and elusive topography, with the conceptual liminality, instability and transitoriness contingent upon it, has been captured in one of the most recent studies on the topic:

> The beach is an ambiguous place, an in-between place. It is a place where for much of the time nothing much seemingly happens: the tide comes and goes; people arrive to pass time in leisure activities; occasional ships anchor there. But at the same time, the beach is a place where everything transformational in the cultures of coastal peoples begins and ends. The tides create a shifting boundary between sea and land. Their effect is to emphasize the liminality of the beach as parts of it are successively revealed and then swamped by tidal action. The boundary between sea and land alters on a daily basis. It is a neutral space, neither properly terrestrial nor yet thoroughly maritime, awaiting a metamorphic role. (Mack 165)

This oscillating quality of the terrain also affects its symbolic dimension: just as the material spaces denoted by the terms 'the beach' and 'the littoral' vary and shift their shape, so do their conceptualisations and sociocultural functions. In the following, we explore some of the possible approaches to littoral space in scholarly studies as well as in creative representations.

Conceptualisations of Littoral Space

It is not surprising that both the beach and littoral space more generally are currently the focus of a good deal of attention. As Gillis has claimed, coastal populations have increased worldwide by thirty per cent in the past thirty years; in the United States, fifty-three per cent of the population live in the coastal areas (fifteen per cent of the US land area), and similar trends can be observed in Australia, South America, Europe and Asia (1). As a consequence of this shift, symbolic geographies and the relationship between territorial 'centres' and coastal 'rims' are being transformed: 'We are all now creatures of the edge, mentally as well as physically. Having experienced one of the greatest physical migrations in human history, we are in the midst of a cultural reorientation of vast significance' (Gillis 1). Various fields such as historiography, social anthropology and archaeology have recognised the importance of this dynamic and consequently argue for a reconfiguration of their disciplines, shifting from a terrestrial focus – often organised around the nation state – to an orientation towards 'the seas as globalized transnational spaces' (Mack 20), to maritime travel routes and littoral contact zones, island cultures and coastal sites of arrival and departure (see also Denning, DeLoughrey and Finamore).

This claim is echoed by Cohen, who underlines the importance of sea fiction for a historical and methodological reconfiguration of literary studies and stresses its constitutive function for modern literature (2). However, Cohen's comprehensive overview of English sea fiction since the eighteenth century also shows that while the sea has already gained recognition as an important locale for literary studies, the beach has not yet received similar attention. Due to the publication of a number of groundbreaking works over the past decade or so, maritime cultural studies is now a thriving field, and it provides an important thematic and methodological impetus for our own work on littoral space. But so far, the littoral remains a largely neglected site in publications on the sea, which have concentrated on the specific characteristics which distinguish maritime from landlocked texts. Cohen's focus lies on fictions about seafaring, life on board ship and related nautical themes, and the beach is mentioned mostly in connection with shipwrecks. Similarly, two collections edited by Klein, and by Klein and Mackenthun, provide 'perspectives on the ocean' in British literature and culture and so focus on the high seas rather than littoral space (though Smith's contribution on the beach as a site of 'passing' in the collection by Klein and Mackenthun constitutes an important exception). So far, therefore, the littoral has mainly been considered under the more general rubric of a broader maritime space. Rostek's study on the sea in contemporary Anglophone fiction, for instance, looks at the beach as one among many maritime topographies, such as the deep ocean and islands. Our present collection, then, builds on the seminal work done by Gillis, Mack, Denning, Cohen, DeLoughrey, Klein, Mackenthun, Rostek and others but highlights the specificity of the littoral. While the sea and the beach are closely connected, and the one can hardly be thought of without the other, the focus of interest of this volume is explicitly on the zone *between* the sea and the land, the beginning and end of which are indeed hard to define and which is constantly reconfigured in a material as well as a symbolic sense, depending on whether it is approached from the sea or the land.

Existing book-length studies on littoral space either address literary and visual representations (Corbin, and Anderson and Tabb), or focus on particular historical aspects, such as the history of seaside tourism (Hassan, Lenček and Bosker, Walton, and Walvin). In his chapter dedicated to the beach, Mack attempts a broader approach, bringing together literary and ethnographic examples; however, this is part of a comprehensive cultural history of the sea and hence of necessity selective. A recent collection of essays addresses the importance of the sea and the beach in modernist culture (Feigel and Harris): this volume looks at a broad range of genres and material objects – from seaside architecture to picture postcards – but its geographical focus is clearly limited to the British coast. One of the contributors to the present volume, Christiana Payne, has written a seminal study of nineteenth-century British visual culture and the beach – *Where the Sea Meets the Land: Artists on the Coast in Nineteenth-Century Britain*. Other studies look at specific usages of the beach, for example in the context of nudist culture (Douglas, Rasmussen and Flanagan, *The Nude Beach*). The connections between national identity and coastal geography are explored in a cultural studies context in Perera's recent book, *Australia and the Insular Imagination: Beaches, Borders, Boats, and Bodies*. A recent collection by Klooss addresses fiction on the coast and the sea from a didactic perspective: *Writing Coast and Sea*.

As this brief survey suggests, littoral studies is profiting from the momentum generated by the recent maritime turn in the humanities. The present collection seizes this moment in order to situate the emerging field even more prominently by exploring some of the most central conceptualisations of littoral space. The beach is a contradictory and unstable signifier: what it denotes depends on the beholder's position and aims: it can offer scientific insight, sensual experience, regeneration, pleasure, sustenance and shelter, but it can also appear as a place of segregation and as a closed border.

Scientific Perspectives on Littoral Space

Organic life on earth originated in the sea; the transition from aquatic to terrestrial life forms marked a momentous step forward in evolution. For nineteenth-century naturalists, the various geological sections of littoral space – beaches, cliffs, eroded rocks, submarine forests – provided important material for their radical reconceptualisations of the natural world. The pioneering geologist Charles Lyell devoted several chapters of his *Principles of Geology* to littoral phenomena such as silting and the effects of tides and currents. His observations, as well as the fossils found in coastal strata, prepared the ground for Charles Darwin's theory of evolution. In Kingsley's *The Water Babies*, written in direct response to Darwin's *On the Origin of Species*, the river is described as a conduit from the land to the sea, and from death to renewed life, while the beach is a site of transformation and regeneration. In Darwinian nature, generation and death, evolution and extinction are always closely connected. For many Victorian observers, the beach is a privileged site on which to observe this entanglement. Even an opponent of evolution theory, Philip Henry Gosse, one of the most important popularisers of the seaside, established a connection between its teeming life, mortality and moral and intellectual improvement. In his widely read books such as *A Naturalist's Ramble on the Devonshire Coast* and *Tenby: A Seaside Holiday*, he described both the pleasures of a carefree seaside trip and the improving effects of active observation of the geology and the flora and fauna of the beach. In typically Victorian fashion, his description moves from children's play to a contemplation of death:

> It is in the middle of the day, when the tide recedes at that hour, and when the wind is moderate, the air warm, and the sun bright, that these sands are seen to advantage. The gay dresses and many-hued parasols of the ladies are dotting them over by scores; little boys and girls are scampering hither and thither, picking up shells and sea-weeds, throwing pebbles into the sea, and flying with affected fear from the advancing wave, or digging with their wooden spades moats and pits in the soft sand, as thoughtless of the next tide which will sweep all their works away, as their elders are of the scythe of Time, who, with like industry, 'heap up riches, and know not who shall gather them'. (Gosse, *Tenby* 10)

This passage exemplifies the contradictory responses the Victorians, and to a lesser degree later generations of visitors, too, showed toward the beach: delight in the pleasant surroundings, leisure activities and the display of the latest summer fashions; the children's games that seem to prefigure Gosse's own more serious and learned interest in 'shells and sea-weeds'; but also the contemplation of mortality. Gosse's studies of littoral flora and fauna were geared to his theological views. In accordance with the paradigm dominant in the early nineteenth century, Natural Theology, he considered the study of the Book of Nature to be in complete accord with revealed religion, set down in the Book of Books. Accordingly, the beach functions as a pedagogical space: through its sensual pleasures, the visitor is ideally induced to look beyond the ephemeral to the eternal. Paradoxically, the invigorating, relaxing and educational effects of a visit to the beach ultimately derive their impact from an awareness of the futility of human striving induced by observing the inexorable movement of the tides.

For Darwin's supporter Thomas Henry Huxley, by contrast, the littoral functions as an epitome of a seemingly chaotic nature, in which the man of science can discern nature's underlying causality:

> If one of these people [Darwin's adversaries] … should be within reach of the sea, where a heavy gale is blowing, let him betake himself to the shore and watch the scene. Let him note the infinite variety of forms and sizes of the tossing waves, out at sea; or of the curves of their foam-crested breakers, as they dash against the rocks. Let him listen to the roar & scream of the shingle as it is cast up & torn down the beach, or look at the flakes of foam as they drive hither & thither before the wind, or the play of colours, which arouses a gleam of sunshine as it falls upon their myriad component bubbles; surely here, if anywhere, he will say that chance is supreme, and bow as one who has entered the very penetralia of his divinity. But the man of science knows that, here as everywhere, perfect order is manifested and that there is not a curve of the waves; not a note in the howling chorus; not a rainbow-glint in a bubble, which is other than a necessary consequence of the ascertained laws of nature; and that with a sufficient knowledge of the conditions, competent physico-mathematical skill could account for & indeed predict every one of these 'chance' events. (79)

As Huxley suggests here, for the nineteenth-century man of science the beach calls for close observation since it offers evidence of the ways in which nature works, both in a synchronic and in a diachronic sense. Moreover, for someone trained in the art of scientific observation, this evidence is apparently easily accessible on the beach – although, as the example of Gosse shows, completely contradictory readings of it are possible. But if the beach functions as a trope of phenomenological clarity for Huxley, contemporary science finds it more difficult to disentangle 'the laws of nature' from human impact in its assessment of the beach. When trying to determine the vulnerability of coastal systems to anthropogenic climate change, the 2007 Intergovernmental Panel on Climate Change (IPCC) Assessment Report foregrounds the 'strong interactions both within and between the natural and human subsystems in the coastal system' (Nicholls et al. 318), conceding that the 'direct impacts of human activities on the coastal zone have been more significant over the past century than impacts that can be directly attributed to observed climate change' (319). But even leaving aside the human element, the beach here features as a site of scientific uncertainty that contrasts strikingly with Huxley's rhetorical gesture, which dispels chaos in the name of scientific self-confidence. As the IPCC Report stresses, it is precisely the 'natural variability of coasts' that 'can make it difficult to identify the impacts of climate change' (318). Given the complexity of littoral change, the IPCC Assessment Report denies any easily discernible correlation, even between changing sea levels and beach erosion: 'there is not a simple relationship between sea-level rise and horizontal movement of the shoreline' (324). With the 'sufficient knowledge of the conditions', which Huxley celebrates, 'competent physico-mathematical skill' might perhaps be able to 'account for & indeed predict every one of these "chance" events' involved in littoral change, but the awareness of the great interplay of global and local, natural and human factors makes the beach a difficult site to navigate for contemporary scientific empiricism.

The Beach as Vacationscape

The subtitle of Lenček and Bosker's classic book on the beach is *The History of Paradise on Earth*, and indeed, the conceptualisation of the beach as vacationscape, which seems to dominate modern Western ideas of the beach, is deeply connected with the vision of the beach as paradisiacal. First constructed in travel reports and Enlightenment texts such as Diderot's 'Supplément au voyage de Bougainville' (written in the early 1770s but published only in 1796), the trope of the beach as a (tropical) paradise – already denoting easily accessible sexual fulfilment – has lost little of its force. Together with the resultant desire for the perfect beach, it continues to circulate in various popularisations, such as the film versions of the *Mutiny on the Bounty*, the romantic film *The Blue Lagoon* and, more recently, the novel and film *The Beach*, as well as through advertisements and travel brochures.

Pristine beaches, however, are increasingly hard to find. The densely populated coasts of continental seas such as the Mediterranean have been undergoing anthropogenic alterations since antiquity. Though they have been marked by long histories of human habitation as sites of work, religious practice, imperial conflict and cultural production, what such beaches tend to render most visible nowadays is the high investment in the beach as vacationscape. Today, only a few stretches of coastline resemble 'wild nature'; rather, the almost unbroken skyline of the Adriatic is prototypical of architectonic patterns along the shoreline. Not even the surface of the beach is given: sandy beaches need to be 'nourished' – the sand lost by erosion needs continually to be replaced – to maintain their resemblance to the ideal beach constructed in film and advertising (see Alvarez). In areas frequented by tourists and day-trippers, the beach offers various kinds of infrastructure to its users: showers, toilets, deck chairs and sun shades for rent, and kiosks selling refreshments and souvenirs. Often, the beach is differentiated according to access regulations, activities, sartorial rules and groups of users: there are communal and semiprivate areas allocated to hotels; clothed and nudist beaches; beaches demarcated for families, volleyball players and surfers; doggy beaches. While beach culture in the 1960s denoted surfing, parties and sex as part of the lifestyle revolution of those years, today the beaches once famous for this kind of hedonistic freedom, in California and southern France, are heavily regulated and policed.[2]

The paradisiacal beach might persist as the vanishing point of the modern traveller's desire, but even 'dream beaches' in Thailand and on the Maldives cannot escape the impact of international tourism and commercialisation, and the reality is, more often than not, a scene of overcrowding, of sunbathers lying towel-to-towel. Commonplace as these images have become today, the beach as a holiday destination is a fairly modern invention. The negative perception of the beach, as a site of chaos and mortal danger, only began to change with the slow advent of seaside health resorts from the seventeenth century onwards. As Corbin has shown, the beneficial effects expected from treatment by the sea were built on a conceptualisation of the maritime environment as vitalising precisely because it was exacting. In other words, the older denotation of the seaside as a frightful place, inspiring repulsion rather than admiration, was not, at least not for some time, replaced but rather revalued. Basically, it was proximity to the sea as a piece of untamed and challenging nature that constituted some of the new appeal of the seaside:

> This explains how the paradox developed on which the fashion for the beach
> is based: the sea became a refuge and a source of hope because it inspired fear.
> The new strategy for seaside holidays was to enjoy the sea and experience the
> terror it inspired, while overcoming one's personal perils. Henceforth, the sea
> was expected to soothe the elite's anxieties, re-establish harmony between body
> and soul, and stem the loss of *vital energy* of a social class that felt particularly
> vulnerable through its sons, its daughters, its wives, and its thinkers. (Corbin 62;
> emphasis in original)

Far from invoking scenes of idleness and sensual enjoyment, the early seaside holiday was much more akin to a battle: against the elements, against one's own constitutional weakness, against the temptations of the flesh. Stays at seaside resorts – mostly in an invigorating, northern climate rather than in the sensuous south – were prescribed for health reasons. The social rituals surrounding 'taking the waters' were rigid and, from today's hedonistic perspective, rather forbidding: stoical valetudinarians were driven into the sea in bathing machines in which they changed, then were 'dipped' into the cold water by professional bathing women. This practice remained in place well into the nineteenth century, long after seaside resorts had been transformed from places of self-inflicted torture in the service of health into fashionable meeting places for the higher classes, where activities

---

[2]   For example, the following restrictions are imposed on visitors to Long Beach, California: 'No Smoking; No Alcohol; No Nude (or topless for women) sunbathing; No Pets of any kind (except Rosie's Dog Beach); No driving on the beach; No Camping or sleeping; No Fires or barbecues (except where fire pits or barbecues are provided); No Fireworks; No Amplified music; No Littering' (Deioma).

other than bathing provided the grounds for their attraction: social events such as promenades, exhibitions and balls 'enabled the gentry and bourgeoisie to profit from each other's company, with social, nuptial and commercial objectives in mind' (Hassan 17).[3] The late eighteenth century and the Regency saw the rise of English seaside spas under the patronage of royalty and the aristocracy. In the course of the nineteenth century, a socially differentiated map of seaside resorts developed: from Brighton, the favourite coastal residence of the Prince Regent, later George IV, to up-and-coming places such as Margate and Blackpool, patronised by wealthy merchants and manufacturers. With the advent of the railway and the offer of cheap day trips, the seaside became accessible for the working classes. In fact, 'the working-class seaside visitor was a phenomenon of the railway age' (Walton 26), a phenomenon that transformed the character of seaside holidays in the last quarter of the nineteenth century just as today cheap long-distance flights have changed the shores of Mallorca, the Dominican Republic or Turkey beyond recognition. The history of the beach as vacationscape, therefore, is characterised by the gradual displacement of the very features which rendered the seaside attractive in the first place.

Contact Zone and Place of Segregation

The beach is often represented as a contact zone where incongruent social elements meet and mix. To a degree, social distinctions are suspended. In Eduard von Keyserling's *Wellen* (*Waves*), for example, the divorced countess Doralice von Köhne-Jasky, who would be 'cut' by polite society in the city and on the Baltic gentry's country estates, strikes up an acquaintance with the aristocratic von Palikow family. Rambles along the seashore make casual encounters inescapable; under these circumstances a rigidly enforced exclusion of the social sinner would appear ridiculous even to the defenders of old-fashioned morality. Similarly, in Colm Tóibín's short novel *Brooklyn*, set in the 1950s in New York, the beach on Coney Island figures as a synecdoche of the melting-pot: a site easily accessible to the various population groups of New York where, by virtue of the proximity necessitated by overcrowding, they are forced to mix and to mingle. And while such mixing might be fairly provisional and temporarily restricted on the beach when it functions as vacationscape, Tracy Chevalier's neo-Victorian novel *Remarkable Creatures* describes a more sustained form of contact between different classes, which is enabled by the beach as a place of work and study. The novel follows the history of famous nineteenth-century fossilist Mary Anning, sketching her life as a discoverer, restorer, and seller of fossils. Mary's occupation provides the livelihood for her family, but it also creates social tension. As a palaeontologist, Mary spends her days on the beach either on her own or else in the company of middle-class amateur fossil hunters or, more importantly, professional natural

---

[3] On the history of seaside resorts, see also Anderson and Tabb, Lenček and Bosker, Walton, Walvin, and Corbin.

historians. As such, she is in constant contact with middle-class men and, hence, is at odds both with her own working-class background, as well as with notions of female propriety. While her work on the beach grants her an immense sense of freedom, it also leads to social ostracism.

As the example of *Remarkable Creatures* shows, it is precisely because social intercourse is potentially unrestricted on the beach – be it in the form of vacationscape, working place or site of scientific observation – that the beach is not exempt from surveillance and attempts at segregation. In Chevalier's novel, Mary's movements on the beach are never hidden from the eyes and ears of the town for long, and her 'goings on' in her littoral workshop, the various places on the beach in which she finds and excavates fossils, render her socially suspicious. In *Brooklyn*, by contrast, the beach is depicted as a site that is overtly free from surveillance: precisely because it is overcrowded, individual misdemeanours go unnoticed. For the protagonist Eilis, a recent immigrant from Ireland, the trips to Coney Island constitute a process of hybridisation, a mixing of American, Italian (via her Italo-American boyfriend Tony) and Irish practices. The beach allows her to experiment with different codes of behaviour, to acquire sexual experience and, finally, to achieve a new sense of self-confidence and identity.

Implicitly, this liberating effect only works for white visitors. The presence or absence of New York's black population on Coney Island is not mentioned. This blind spot can be put down to Eilis's lack of awareness of racial issues in US culture. Historically, however, it is a central issue, severely compromising the positive conceptualisation of the beach as a 'free' space where classes and races mix without restraint. On American beaches, racial segregation was widely practised, at least unofficially, until well into the second half of the twentieth century. The online *Encyclopedia of Chicago* describes incidents that occurred when the idea of the beach as a space accessible to all was taken at face value by the city's black citizens:

> The fight between public and private interests over the lakeshore included racial divisions that resulted in the segregated use of the beaches and waters of Lake Michigan. Through the first decades of the twentieth century African American children were not welcome at most of the bathing beaches in the city. In 1912 an African American child was attacked for attempting to bathe at the 39th Street Beach. As a mob grew, the police responded and quashed the riot. Racial tension soared again in 1919 over a similar incident. On a hot summer day in July at the 29th Street Beach white beachgoers threw rocks at an African American teenager who crossed an invisible line in the lake that extended from the racially segregated beaches. The black teenager drowned, igniting a race riot in the city that lasted for seven days. Though the beaches in Chicago were never officially designated by race, racial segregation continued along the lakeshore for much of the twentieth century. ('Shoreline Development')

In many countries, invisible – and sometimes visible – lines divide the beach and regulate access according to unforgiving social rules. Anti-Semitic segregation was practised in German seaside resorts well before the Nazis officially came to power in 1933. As early as 1900, hotels, resorts and entire islands on the Northern and Baltic Seas were advertising themselves as *judenfrei* (free of Jews), a policy that was officially implemented by the Nazi government in 1935 (see Bajohr). Official race segregation, regulated by the 'Reservation of Separate Amenities Act', Act No 49 of 1953, was practised on South African beaches until the end of Apartheid (see Samuelson's contribution in this volume, and also Booth xix–xxii). These examples show that the Western conception of the beach as an innocent, paradisiacal space, as a space where social distinctions and conventional fetters dissolve as visitors shed their clothes in the sun, can always turn into a political nightmare. The freedom one hopes to experience on the beach is deeply subjective and might well be regarded by others as an infringement of their own licence to enjoy themselves. Indeed, a particular person's mere presence on the beach might already be felt to be just such an infringement. Whether in the context of American segregation, South African apartheid or First-World prosperity, the rights of access to beaches are as strictly regulated as they are contested. In this respect alone, littoral spaces are, of course, not unique. The peculiarity of the seaside in this context lies in the tenacity of its association with pure freedom, even while it functions not only as a social and racial frontier but also as a border for countries situated on the coast.

Border Zone and Non-Lieu

The beach may be a contact zone, but it is also a space of demarcation: a strip of land that separates *terra firma* from the sea, belonging to neither; a border that is policed, where strangers – such as Odysseus when found by Nausikaa – may receive a warm welcome but, more often than not, are refused entry, provided they even make it to the shore alive. In our day and age, the beaches of the Mediterranean have increasingly become a repository for such human debris. Thousands of Africans, trying to escape from the poverty in their home countries, cross the *Mare nostrum* – construed by the European Union as 'our sea', rather than as a space connecting its European, African and Levantine shores (see Braudel) – and endeavour to reach the Spanish, Maltese or Italian coasts, the liminal zone 'twixt land and sea that is a holiday destination for others. The European coastline has become a border zone policed by Frontex, the EU agency created to patrol its external frontiers. For the migrants crossing the Mediterranean in unseaworthy boats, littoral space either becomes a site of detention or, in fact, the site where their dead bodies are washed up on the shore. At the time of writing, news reports are coming in covering one of the deadliest shipwrecks in recent history: in autumn 2013, close to Lampedusa, the Italian island that is nearest to the African coast, 296 Eritrean refugees perished in their attempt to reach European territory. The survivors, who, by the very fact of being rescued and brought to shore by Italian fishermen and the coast guard, had infringed the country's law against illegal immigration, were automatically placed under investigation (see Kington). While this most recent disaster was particularly shocking, it is by no means a unique event.[4]

Even if they reach the shore safely, migrants taking the sea route experience littoral space not as a site of hope and hospitality but, rather, as a non-place (*non-lieu*) in the sense of Marc Augé: 'a space which cannot be defined as relational, or historical, or concerned with identity' (77–8). The non-place, while part of an international mobility grid, is in fact a place of stasis for those who are not considered legitimate participants in that mobility: 'Non-places, often spaces of transit, refer to other places without taking you there' (Cresswell 244). This is literally true for those whose northbound journeys come to a stop on the European coastline. For them, littoral space is not a destination but a zone of deferred transition, of suspension, of waiting. Dislocated and uncertain about their future, those stranded in the reception centres of Southern Europe experience a complete loss of agency and an erasure of social identity which brings them close to the condition described by Giorgio Agamben as 'bare life', a form of existence defined by exclusion from the *polis* (Agamben 11), that is, the loss of political entitlement. Lampedusa's euphemistically named *centro di primo soccorso e accoglienza* (early assistance and reception centre) is chronically overcrowded; detainees regularly sleep on the floor or in the open. Psychological support is insufficient, and conflicts between various groups are frequent. Deprived of their status as citizens, the inmates of the reception centre are treated as criminals rather than refugees: following a fire incident in September 2011, seven hundred men waiting for repatriation 'were handcuffed with plastic cuffs and kept below deck [of three ferryboats appropriated for the purpose], without any external associations, lawyers or doctors allowed access to them. Their mobile phones were confiscated to stop them communicating with people outside' (Maccanico 1). As a result of the European Union's refugee policy, the local authorities are logistically and financially unable to offer adequate solutions and to treat the African refugees in a humane way. In consequence, news reports on the refugees' plight, and images of hundreds of coffins lined up in Lampedusa's harbour jarringly contrast with the symbolic investment in the beach as a vacationscape: in the consciousness of European TV audiences (and potential paying visitors), places like Lampedusa are transformed from popular holiday destinations to areas branded by mass detention and death. As these regions are dependent on the tourist industry, their inhabitants, not among Europe's richest populations to begin with, are in danger of losing their own means of sustenance as they are left by European governments to shoulder the burden of poverty-driven migration.[5] While the experience of dislocation and

---

[4]   According to the latest UNHCR report, the number of refugees peaked in 2011, with more than 58,000 people crossing the Mediterranean sea and more than 1,500 drowning or going missing in that period (see 'Mediterranean'). Despite this death toll, there are no indications that the flow of refugees may be slowing down in 2013. On the refugee situation on Lampedusa, see also Reckinger.

[5]   According to the Italian daily *La Stampa*, tourist numbers fell off by sixty per cent in 2011 as a result of the influx of refugees following the Arab Spring (see Geremicca).

depersonalisation is certainly not unique to detainees in littoral space, it is precisely the contrast between the connotations of the beach as a site of regeneration, pleasure and freedom, an economy dependent on this positive construction, and the bleak reality of detention camps that epitomises one of the most dramatic conflicts about the meaning, use and control of littoral space at present.

This list is by no means exhaustive, but the concrete examples given here illustrate some of the vital issues raised by littoral space. Whether we consider the beach from the vantage point of affluent consumers in the West, of local residents affected by the geographical and climatic changes wrought on the coasts or of participants in globalised mobility, the zone 'twixt land and sea has become a highly visible, contested territory. The present volume offers new perspectives on cultural representations of this space and thus hopes to stimulate a debate about one of the most fascinating spaces on our planet.

The Beach in this Book

Contributions to this volume come mainly from literary studies, as well as from art history, film studies and cultural studies, and they focus on cultural objects such as literary prose fiction, non-fiction, poetry, painting, documentary and feature film and photography. One of our objectives is to demarcate areas of future exploration, and consequently the analytical focus of the individual essays varies. While some of the chapters of the present volume provide overviews, others take the form of case studies, concentrating on the oeuvre of a single author or on thick descriptions of single works. In order to reflect on the polyvalence of littoral space, they choose a variety of theoretical approaches, drawing on fields as diverse as marine ecology and Kristeva's concept of the abject. Despite this breadth, however, the essays are interlinked by an interest in the beach and the littoral as an aesthetic and culturally productive terrain; as a liminal space between nature and culture; as a social space that can function as a contact zone or a site of closure and separation; and as a site of intersection between postcolonial and ecocritical concerns.

Throughout the volume, there is an ongoing conversation between classical Western visions of the beach and postcolonial perspectives. Geographically, the contributions consider seaside beaches in various climatic zones, from the Northern and Irish Seas to the beaches of the Caribbean, South Africa and the Pacific Rim; they highlight distinct social and historical problems related to these particular littoral landscapes. Viewed together, they tell a story that explores the variability of the littoral across global geographical and cultural space. At the same time, our contributors also share a strong interest in the significance of the beach as natural environment – as a site which promises a connection with nature or as a specific ecosystem in itself. They consider forms of interaction between humanity and nature and between different species and they view the littoral as a particular landscape which enables cultural expression. Some of the essays foreground formal qualities and concentrate on the rhetorical and poetic characteristics of littoral texts. They share a primary interest in the aesthetic aspects of the beach as a trope, and they address questions of genre, intertextuality and the imaginary. Though keenly aware of how aspects of class and cultural tradition influence a person's access to and aesthetic appreciation of littoral space, the authors approach such issues through analyses of literary, cinematic and artistic form. They show how aesthetic responses to the beach as a natural and social space represent a complex cultural terrain in which contact between coloniser and colonised, humanity and nature, and between social groups and individuals is not only staged and negotiated but also creatively transformed into a starting point for cultural work. Others approach these matters from a more context-oriented perspective and focus on engagements with the social and historical aspects of littoral space. They continue to engage with formal elements but shift their focus to the social practices that determine cross-cultural and cross-species relations on the beach. They turn their attention to the manner in which littoral space is shared between classes and social and cultural groups and across geographically removed regions. In most of the chapters, the emphasis is on conventions of inclusion and exclusion, as well as on the social, cultural, ecological and global interconnectedness of littoral space. As regards the temporal scope of this volume, some of the contributions have a focus on the nineteenth century, but most essays concentrate on contemporary cultural production. Many of them, however, reach back to Victorian concepts of nature and littoral space and, by considering the repercussions of nineteenth-century formulations of the beach, provide a link between the Victorian Age and the present. Since the Victorian period, the age when mass tourism on the beach first developed, the conceptualisation of the beach as vacationscape has acquired particular dominance, and many of our contributors touch on this meaning of the beach, either by making it their main concern or, more often, by using it as a foil for other conceptualisations of littoral space. In its entirety, this volume engages with and emphasises a great variety of different formulations of the littoral. In terminology as well, littoral space evokes a wealth of expressions: beach, shore, coast, seaside – these are just some of the words that spring to mind. While many of the essays concentrate on the beach, they also engage with other terms and concepts, such as shorelines and the land-sea divide. As a whole, and rather than adopting a unified terminology, the volume makes use of the advantages of a collection in that it affords an opportunity to survey and examine the terminological diversity on offer. The manner in which the contributors approach terms associated with littoral landscapes reflects the complexity and suggestiveness of the littoral both as a topos and a trope.

Christiana Payne opens our collection with a discussion of the beach as a social space that in nineteenth-century England acquired new meanings as a realm in which class and gender boundaries started to become permeable. Payne, curator of a number of influential exhibitions related to the beach, offers a comparative analysis of four mid- to late Victorian paintings. Highlighting the particular resonance which seascapes and the seashore hold for the British, she shows how the paintings analysed in her essay negotiate a great many conceptualisations of littoral space, among them the beach as contact zone, as a subject of scientific and aesthetic reflexion and as a space of work. Payne shows how the particular aesthetic choices the artists make allow them to fuse a variety of paradigmatic meanings of the Victorian beach in their representations and to turn them into documents typical of their period.

From painting, we turn to poetry. Katharina Rennhak covers a broad spectrum in her piece, which ranges from the Victorian period to contemporary literary production. She analyses Matthew Arnold's classic beach poem 'Dover Beach' and pursues its literary, philosophical and theological afterlife through a focus on Dover beach as an aesthetic and cultural contact zone. In reading a variety of prose and lyrical texts that are intertextually related to Arnold's piece, Rennhak traces the aesthetic development of the Dover beach trope in English, Scottish and Black British pre- and post-Arnoldian poetry which hinges on the topographical positions of their narrators and speakers in relation to the shore. She suggests that in order to oppose Arnold's liberal politics, lyrical subjects need consciously to choose a location on or relating to the beach which does not repeat Arnold's perspective and vantage point. This is particularly pertinent to poems which, by voicing the position of the cultural other from a location on this most famous of English beaches, point to differences not from the outside but from within Britain itself.

Like Rennhak, Anne-Julia Zwierlein is concerned with the dialogue between the nineteenth century and the present in her investigation of the land-sea divide as an existentialist and ecocritical trope in contemporary British and Irish fiction. She links scientific and aesthetic perspectives on littoral space by observing how Victorian perceptions of evolutionary deep time led to the questioning of human uniqueness and by examining the repercussions of this re-evaluation of humanity's position in contemporary novels which set their negotiations of human identity on the beach. Focussing on the cultural symbolisms of the land-sea divide, Zwierlein reads the littoral in these texts as a catalyst for human relationships. In addition, the beach offers a stage on which the position of humankind is examined from an ecological perspective. In all of the novels discussed in this essay, scenes of coastal erosion underline the precariousness, as well as the possible meaninglessness, of human existence. At the same time, Zwierlein demonstrates how the coastal setting also emphasises the tenacity of life, partly by foregrounding the Darwinian closeness of humans and animals in their struggle for survival. Nature and natural processes, here, do not merely serve as backdrops for the unfolding of human stories but crucially influence human fates, and call into question the sovereignty of the human species.

Neal Alexander turns to shorelines as physical and metaphorical border zones. He analyses the poetry of Michael Longley and Robert Minhinnick, two poets of place, as test cases for the possibilities and shortcomings of ecocritical analysis. The manner in which both writers revisit the same Irish and Welsh littoral spaces in the course of their poetic production lends itself to a questioning of the Heideggerian concept of dwelling. Alexander foregrounds the fact that, for Longley and Minhinnick, sense of place is not secure and comforting but always unstable and unsettling. In the two poets' disorientation of dwelling, the seashore as a characteristic locus of contingency and fragility becomes a crucial element on their poetic agenda. Furthermore, their poetic constructions of the beach allow them to challenge a nature-culture dualism which separates the human from the non-human and to show instead how people and human traces are integral parts of littoral landscapes.

Julika Griem, in the next chapter, reads Scottish writer John Burnside's littoral landscapes as liminal zones which generate aesthetic reflexion about being in and speaking about the world in ways which echo some of the concerns of Alexander's contribution. Burnside's continued revisiting and rewriting of littoral spaces endows his beaches with a multiplicity of metaphorical and symbolic meanings which trigger reconsiderations of the relationship between questions of literary form and of environmental conflict. With the help of spatial theory, Griem systematises Burnside's littoral and maritime motifs and identifies differences in his engagement with the beach in his poetry and in his prose. She teases out the relations between Burnside's littoral topographies, the political commitment of his writing and his eco-philosophical project.

Similarly concerned with littoral landscapes as creatively fertile sites for cultural production, and continuing the discussion of intertextual relations while moving to another cultural and geographical setting, Tobias Döring focuses on literary traces left on Caribbean beaches. Conceptualising littoral space as a cultural contact zone, he analyses the particular form of creativity that develops from the gathering of lost wreckage and debris and its reassembling as a bricolage. For Döring, Caribbean beaches are important sites for processes of creolisation. Focussing on the poetic oeuvre of Derek Walcott, Edward Brathwaite, and others, Döring explores the beach as an enabling trope for Caribbean literary production. Reading the cultural practice of beachcombing as a metaphor for literary creation, he suggests that a poetics of fragmentation and recycling forms an essential constituent of contemporary Caribbean writing and its engagement with tradition and newness. Hence the literary sea and beach emerge, in a Caribbean context, as crucial spaces for autopoetic reflexion.

If the beach in Döring's essay features mainly as a place in which various people and cultures meet and intermingle, Meg Samuelson addresses a diametrically opposed function of the beach by analysing it as a site of segregation. Directing our attention to South Africa, Samuelson seeks to recover the beach as a significant locale of South African literature, which, she argues, has been marginalised due to the way in which it complicates binaries and boundaries. Samuelson encourages us to reconsider the beach as a site which enables the narrativisation of the various encounters that have crucially shaped South African history. Like Payne's chapter, Samuelson's essay is historicist, and she traces the function of the beach as a cultural contact zone in a survey of South African literature stretching from the period of colonial exploration and expansion, through the apartheid regime to the post-apartheid present. Both as a setting and as a figure, Samuelson suggests, littoral space encourages the imagination of alternative positions that challenge the national story of South Africa.

The next two essays in our collection are more specifically concerned with the relationship between humans and animals and with the manner in which they coexist in coastal spaces, or perhaps even share them. Ursula Kluwick's analysis of the representation of sharks and shark attacks in popular science books and film investigates the complex dynamics between beach and shore. Kluwick discusses how shark attacks challenge conceptualisations of the beach as vacationscape, and she explores the shore as a thanatoscape with ambivalent alliances to humanity, artifice and nature. Popular renditions of shark attacks examine the relationship between humanity and nature on the beach through a combination of cultural and scientific visions of littoral space. Kluwick interprets the voyeuristic pleasure inspired by sharks and their victims in terms of abjection and examines how the cultural mediation of shark attacks turns littoral landscapes into spaces where divisions collapse, prompting interrogations of what it means to be human, in relation to nature as well as to other humans.

The marine creatures in Virginia Richter's essay have an entirely different cultural meaning. Taking whales as exemplary figures of inter-species contact, Richter compares three postcolonial works: Witi Ihimaera's novel *The Whale Rider*, Niki Caro's film *Whale Rider* and Linda Hogan's *People of the Whale*. The focus of this essay is on coastal communities whose members dwell and work in littoral space and, thus, on changing social practices such as indigenous whale hunts and the rescue of stranded whales. The beach functions here as a contact zone in a very specific sense: not only as a meeting ground between human groups with different cultural backgrounds, and between human and non-human species, but also as a space in which different ethical stances towards nature are negotiated. The aesthetic mode employed in the novels, magic realism, allows a perspective on littoral space that foregrounds its potential as a nature-culture continuum as well as a realistically depicted human working environment. The comparison with Caro's film gives insights into the repackaging of these themes for international consumption.

In the final contribution to this volume, Alexa Weik von Mossner shifts the focus to the disappearing beach. Like Kluwick, Weik von Mossner distinguishes between the beach and the shore, but, in tune with the ecologically informed orientation of her essay, her definitions of these sites are influenced by geography and marine science. She considers beach and shore as specific natural environments in which various perspectives, such as the scientific, the local and the global, can come into conflict or can be productively combined. Applying Rob Nixon's concept of slow violence to Briar March's documentary *There Once Was an Island*, Weik von Mossner examines the ways in which the future existence of the tiny Pacific atoll of Takuu hinges not only on local but also on global developments. Due to rising sea levels, the vanishing beaches of Takuu are losing their protective function as border zones. As a result, the inhabitants of Takuu are faced with the gradual submersion of their island home, which also entails the loss of their traditional Polynesian culture and autonomy, as the Bougainville government already treats them as refugees in need of relocation. Highlighting both the collaborative aspects of the film, which brings together local and scientific knowledge, as well as the interactive notion of space with which it operates, Weik von Mossner presents March's documentary as an eco-cosmopolitan project reaching out to new forms of solidarity.

The scope of the essays included here demonstrates that some of the most pressing concerns of our age can be articulated through an engagement with littoral space. Though our collection reflects the theoretical and methodological state of the art, more work, of course, remains to be done, and *The Beach in Anglophone Literatures and Cultures* sees itself as a critical intervention intended to stimulate further investigation of littoral topics. Beach architecture, to name but one example, would constitute another fascinating object of analysis, from the facilities offered to tourists to buildings commemorating invasions and landing operations in war, such as the memorials and information centres dedicated to the landing of the Allies on the beaches of Normandy. For researchers turning to this and related objects of study, the present volume seeks to supply a broad spectrum of model analyses and theoretical explorations which can point the way towards future engagements with the beach and establish littoral studies as a productive new field of interdisciplinary research.

Works Cited

Agamben, Giorgio. *Homo Sacer: Sovereign Power and Bare Life*. 1995. Trans. Daniel Heller-Roazen. Stanford: Stanford UP, 1998.

Alvarez, Lizette. 'Where Sand is Gold, the Reserves Are Running Dry'. *The New York Times* 24 Aug. 2013. Web. 30 Sept. 2013. <http://www.nytimes. com/2013/08/25/us/where-sand-is-gold-the-coffers-are-running-dry-in-florida.html?pagewanted=all>.

Anderson, Susan C., and Bruce H. Tabb, eds. *Water, Leisure and Culture: European Historical Perspectives*. Oxford: Berg, 2002.

Augé, Marc. *Non-Places: Introduction to an Anthropology of Supermodernity*. 1992. Trans. John Howe. London: Verso, 1995.

Bajohr, Frank. *'Unser Hotel ist judenfrei': Bäder-Antisemitismus im 19. und 20. Jahrhundert*. Frankfurt am Main: Fischer, 2003.

Booth, Douglas. *Australian Beach Cultures: The History of Sun, Sand and Surf*. London: Cass, 2001.

Braudel, Fernand. *La Méditerranée et le monde méditerranéen à l'époque de Philippe II*. 1949. Paris: Librairie Armand Colin, 1966.

Chevalier, Tracy. *Remarkable Creatures*. London: Harper, 2009.

Cohen, Margaret. *The Novel and the Sea*. Princeton: Princeton UP, 2010.

Corbin, Alain. *The Lure of the Sea: The Discovery of the Seaside in the Western World 1750–1840*. Trans. Jocelyn Phelps. Berkeley: U of California P, 1994.

Cresswell, Tim. *On the Move: Mobility in the Modern Western World*. New York: Routledge, 2006.

Darwin, Charles. *The Origin of Species*. 1859. Ed. Gillian Beer. Oxford: Oxford UP, 1996.

Deioma, Kayte. 'Beach Rules and Regulations for Long Beach, CA'. *About. Los Angeles Travel*. n.d. Web. 30 Sept. 2013. <http://golosangeles.about.com/od/losangelesbeaches/ ss/Beaches-In-Long-Beach-CA_12.htm>.

DeLoughrey, Elizabeth M. *Routes and Roots: Navigating Caribbean and Pacific Island Literatures*. Honolulu: U of Hawaii P, 2007.

Denning, Greg. *Beach Crossings: Voyaging Across Times, Cultures, and Selfs*. Philadelphia: U of Pennsylvania P, 2004.

Diderot, Denis. 'Supplément au voyage de Bougainville'. *Œuvres philosophiques*. Ed. P. Vernière. Paris: Classiques Garnier, 1990. 447–518.

Douglas, Jack D., Paul K. Rasmussen and Carol Ann Flanagan. *The Nude Beach*. Beverly Hills: Sage, 1978.

Feigel, Lara, and Alexandra Harris, eds. *Modernism on Sea: Art and Culture at the British Seaside*. Bern: Lang, 2009.

Finamore, Daniel. *Maritime History as World History*. Gainesville: UP of Florida, 2004.

Geremicca, Federico. 'Lampedusa, isola dimenticata'. *La Stampa* 8 Jan. 2012. Web. 21 Oct. 2013. <http://www.lastampa.it/2012/01/08/italia/cronache/lampedusa-isola-dimenticata-TPDKr144NzCZlOCYVs1jTL/pagina.html>.

Gillis, John R. *The Human Shore: Seacoasts in History*. Chicago: U of Chicago P, 2012.

Gosse, Philip Henry. *A Naturalist's Ramble on the Devonshire Coast*. London: Voorst, 1853.

———. *Tenby. A Sea-Side Holiday*. 1856. Memphis: General Books: 2009.

Hassan, John. *The Seaside, Health and the Environment in England and Wales since 1800*. Aldershot: Ashgate, 2003.

Huxley, Thomas Henry. 'Reminiscence of the Reception of the *Origin*'. 1887. *Darwin Online*. Transcribed by Kees Rookmaaker. Arts and Humanities Research Council, 2009. Web. 14 Dec. 2011. <http://darwin-online.org.uk/content/frameset?keywords=huxley&pageseq=1&itemID=CUL-DAR112.B77-B84&viewtype=text>.

von Keyserling, Eduard. *Wellen*. 1911. Göttingen: Steidl, 1998.

Kingsley, Charles. *The Water-Babies: A Fairy Tale for a Land-Baby*. 1863. London: Penguin, 2008.

Kington, Tom. 'Lampedusa Shipwreck. Italy to Hold State Funeral for Drowned Immigrants'. *The Guardian* 9 Oct. 2013. Web. 17 Oct. 2013. <http://www.theguardian.com/world/2013/oct/09/lampedusa-shipwreck-italy-state-funeral-migrants>.

Klein, Bernhard, ed. *Fictions of the Sea: Critical Perspectives on the Ocean in British Literature and Culture*. Aldershot: Ashgate, 2002.

Klein, Bernhard, and Gesa Mackenthun, eds. *Sea Changes: Historicising the Ocean*. New York: Routledge, 2004.

Klooss, Wolfgang, ed. *Writing Coast and Sea*. Würzburg: Königshausen and Neumann, 2013.

Lenček, Lena, and Gideon Bosker. *The Beach: The History of Paradise on Earth*. New York: Viking, 1998.

Lyell, Charles. *Principles of Geology: An Attempt to Explain the Former Changes of the Earth's Surface, by Reference to Causes now in Operation.* 3 vols. 1830–1833. Cambridge: Cambridge UP, 2009.

Maccanico, Yasha. 'Italy: Fire and Loathing on Lampedusa'. *Statewatch* Oct. 2011. Web. 17 Oct. 2013. <http://www.statewatch.org/analyses/no-154-lampedusa.pdf>.

Mack, John. *The Sea: A Cultural History.* London: Reaktion, 2011.

'Mediterranean Takes Record as Most Deadly Stretch of Water for Refugees and Migrants in 2011'. *The UN Refugee Agency* 31 Jan. 2012. Web. 20 Sept. 2013. <http://www. unhcr.org/4f27e01f9.html>.

Nicholls, R.J. et al. 'Coastal Systems and Low-Lying Areas'. *Climate Change 2007: Impacts, Adaptation and Vulnerability. Contribution of Working Group II to the Fourth Assessment Report of the Intergovernmental Panel on Climate Change.* Ed. M.L. Parry et al. Cambridge: Cambridge UP, 2007. 315–56. *Intergovernmental Panel on Climate Change.* Web. 22 Oct. 2013. http://www. ipcc.ch/pdf/assessment-report/ar4/wg2/ar4-wg2-chapter6.pdf.

Payne, Christiana. *Where the Sea Meets the Land: Artists on the Coast in Nineteenth-Century Britain.* Bristol: Sansom, 2007.

Perera, Suvendrini. *Australia and the Insular Imagination: Beaches, Borders, Boats, and Bodies.* Basingstoke: Palgrave, 2009.

Pratt, Mary Louise. *Imperial Eyes: Travel Writing and Transculturation.* London: Routledge, 1992.

Reckinger, Gilles. *Lampedusa: Begegnungen am Rand Europas.* Wuppertal: Peter Hammer Verlag, 2013.

Rostek, Joanna. *Seaing Through the Past: Postmodern Histories and the Maritime Metaphor in Contemporary Anglophone Fiction.* Amsterdam: Rodopi, 2011.

'Shoreline Development'. *Encyclopedia of Chicago.* Chicago Historical Society, n.d. Web. 14 Dec. 2011. <http://www.encyclopedia.chicagohistory.org/pages/300066.html>.

Smith, Vanessa. 'Costume Changes: Passing at Sea and on the Beach'. *Sea Changes: Historicising the Ocean.* Ed. Bernhard Klein and Gesa Mackenthun. New York: Routledge, 2004. 37–53.

Thomas, Nicholas. *Discoveries: The Voyages of Captain Cook.* London: Lane, 2003.

Tóibín, Colm. *Brooklyn.* 2009. London: Penguin, 2010.

Walton, John K. *The English Seaside Resort: A Social History 1750–1914.* Leicester: Leicester UP; New York: St Martin's P, 1983.

Walvin, James. *Beside the Seaside: A Social History of the Popular Seaside Holiday.* London: Viking, 1978.

Chapter 1
Visions of the Beach in Victorian Britain

Christiana Payne

The beach played an important role in nineteenth-century British art. In the early part of the century, Turner and Constable made repeated studies of waves crashing on beaches, in Margate and Brighton respectively. The resulting exhibition pictures showed contrasting facets of the beach: Constable focused on seaside visitors seeking health and fresh air, Turner on the darker subject-matter of shipwrecks, death and destruction. Other artists depicted the fishermen and women at work, studied rock formations or celebrated the exploits of heroic lifeboatmen. All these subjects were part of the larger category of seascapes and coastal scenes, which acquired particular resonance in British culture because of their associations with the navy, and hence with the national character and its assumed propensities for bravery, scientific enquiry, even democracy. This essay will examine four key paintings from the mid-Victorian years which exemplify these associations: William Powell Frith's *Ramsgate Sands* (1852–1854, Figure 1.1), William Dyce's *Pegwell Bay* (c.1858–1860, Figure 1.2), John Brett's *A Morning amongst the Granite Boulders* (1872–1873, Figure 1.3) and Winslow Homer's *Four Fishwives* (1881, Figure 1.4).

All these paintings focus on beaches, that is, flattish areas of sand or pebbles adjacent to the sea. In the nineteenth century the word 'beach' began to take on its modern connotation as a site for holiday-making and leisure. In tourist resorts such as Ramsgate and Pegwell Bay in Kent, the beach was a social space where people prepared to bathe, read novels and newspapers, flirted, rode donkeys, watched entertainers, collected natural history specimens or simply sat out in the open air. In fishing villages, however, the flat beach had a more utilitarian function as the place where boats were pulled up onto the sand, where their catch was unloaded and sometimes where the fish were sold to merchants and the general public. In these locations, such as Cullercoats on the north-east coast near Newcastle, the beach was a different kind of social space, one in which the relationships within a close-knit community were cemented and tested. Here, and on unfrequented rocky beaches in more remote locations such as Cornwall, images of the beach might remind viewers not of holidays but of the symbolism of the seacoast as a metaphor for the fragility of human life and the hope of immortality.

The beach was a significant topos in English literature, and there was a close relationship between visual and verbal imaginings of it in this period. Artists were well aware of the poetic symbolism which saw the beach as the boundary between life and death, as expressed by Wordsworth in 'Intimations of Immortality':

> Hence in a season of calm weather
>   Though inland far we be
> Our souls have sight of that immortal sea
>   Which brought us hither,
>   Can in a moment travel thither,
> And see the children sport upon the shore,
> And hear the mighty waters rolling evermore. (lines 166–72)

In equally well known lines, Byron had described the ocean as 'boundless, endless, and sublime, / The image of Eternity, the throne / Of the Invisible' (Canto Four, stanza 183, lines 5–7). Later in the century, Tennyson used the same idea, that of the sea representing the eternal life from which the human soul came, and to which it would return, in 'Crossing the Bar':

> Sunset and evening star,
>   And one clear call for me!
> And may there be no moaning of the bar,
>   When I put out to sea,
>
> But such a tide as moving seems asleep,
>   Too full for sound and foam,
> When that which draws from out the boundless deep
>   Turns again home. (lines 1–8)

For Christian believers, the sea was a reminder of the promise of immortality. But in an age of religious doubt, it could equally well offer a bleak vision of a world without faith, in which the waves went on beating remorselessly against the coast, death was final, and the individual was of little account. Tennyson's 'Break, break, break' suggests this chilling prospect:

> Break, break, break,
>   At the foot of thy crags, O Sea!
> But the tender grace of a day that is dead
>   Will never come back to me. (lines 13–16)

And the melancholy of the seashore is explicitly linked with the loss of faith in Arnold's 'Dover Beach':

> Listen! You hear the grating roar
> Of pebbles which the waves draw back, and fling,
> At their return, up the high strand,
> Begin, and cease, and then again begin,
> With tremulous cadence slow, and bring
> The eternal note of sadness in.
> …
> The Sea of Faith
> Was once, too, at the full, and round earth's shore
> Lay like the folds of a bright girdle furl'd.
> But now I only hear

Its melancholy, long, withdrawing roar,
Retreating, to the breath
Of the night-wind, down the vast edges drear
And naked shingles of the world. (lines 9–28)[1]

Artists were avid readers of poetry, often using lines from poems to accompany the titles of their paintings in the catalogues of Royal Academy exhibitions, and the sea habitually evoked a meditative and poetic response, both from the artists themselves and from contemporary viewers of their paintings.

The artistic interest in the sea and coast, and hence the beach, in nineteenth-century Britain was intensified by the growing popularity of the seaside holiday. Across the Western world, visiting a coastal resort to bathe in the sea and enjoy the fresh air gradually changed from being the preserve of the wealthy and of invalids, to become a pleasurable experience for the middle class and eventually for most of the population (see, for example, Corbin or Walton, passim). The mingling of men and women from different classes on the beach gave rise to social embarrassment and sexual excitement, providing a rich field for satirical humour in both visual and verbal media. Sea-bathing was a particular focus of interest: in many places, men insisted on their right to bathe naked, while women wore long shifts which were perhaps even more thrilling than nudity as they clung revealingly to wet bodies. Despite the bathing machines, and the segregation of men's and women's bathing areas, it was evidently quite possible to get more than a glimpse of bare flesh on the Victorian beach. The 'respectable' visitors constantly complained about breaches of decorum, as men and even women used binoculars and telescopes to get a better look (see Payne, *Where* 97–102).

The beach was also a place of potentially embarrassing social encounters. It was an unregulated space open to all, and this was the cause of some disquiet in the strictly hierarchical society of mid-Victorian Britain. Impecunious bachelors went to the beach to find heiresses, and a gentleman might find himself bathing in the sea next to his tailor (see Becker 47–8; and Payne, *Where* 96). Charles Dickens was one of the first to exploit the comic potential of seaside social climbing in his short story 'The Tuggses at Ramsgate' (1836). Mr Tuggs is a grocer who comes into money, so the family decides to give up their business and go to Ramsgate, where they try to pass themselves off as upper-class. They are set up by confidence tricksters who flatter them by remarking on the similarities in their appearance to that of various titled personages – and eventually manage to swindle them out of a considerable part of their new-found fortune. The Tuggses find crowds of people on the beach, and Dickens describes it as a place of constant activity, where human foibles are revealed:

The sun was shining brightly; the sea, dancing to its own music, rolled merrily in; crowds of people promenaded to and fro; young ladies tittered; old ladies talked; nursemaids displayed their charms to the greatest possible advantage, and their little charges ran up and down, and to and fro, and in and out, under the feet, and between the legs, of the assembled concourse, in the most playful

---

[1] See Rennhak in this volume.

and exhilarating manner. There were old gentlemen, trying to make out objects through long telescopes; and young ones, making objects of themselves in open shirtcollars; … and nothing was to be heard but talking, laughing, welcoming, and merriment. … The ladies were employed in needlework, or watch guard making, or knitting, or reading novels; the gentlemen were reading newspapers and magazines; the children were digging holes in the sand with wooden spades, and collecting water therein. (333–5)

The Tuggses are initially embarrassed as they watch the bathers in the sea, but this does not stop them from using their telescopes (336–7).

The pretensions, vanity and hypocrisy of seaside visitors were satirised in the graphic arts by Dickens's friend John Leech, whose cartoons in *Punch* mined a rich vein of comic imagery throughout the 1850s and early 1860s, familiarizing the public with stock characters: the hideous bathing woman, the long-suffering *paterfamilias*, the beautiful young lady who inadvertently reveals her charms in the wind, the ugly older woman who likes to think that the young men are looking at her, the overdressed 'swell' whose one aim is to flirt. Leech's cartoons gave visual form to some of the characters and incidents noted by Dickens. He also made fun of seaside fashions, such as the bonnets which came so far over women's faces (to protect them from sunburn) that they looked like the hoods of bathing machines. Both Dickens and Leech took holidays at the seaside, where they had plenty of opportunity to observe amusing behaviour. In 1849, they rented houses not far from each other on the Isle of Wight, and one can imagine them sitting on the beach together and pointing out particular types to one another (see Houfe, 83).

Leech was also a friend – and seaside holiday companion – of the artist William Powell Frith, whose painting *Ramsgate Sands, Life at the Seaside* (Figure 1.1), was one of the sensations of the Royal Academy exhibition of 1854. It was based on Frith's own summer holiday in Ramsgate in 1851, where he said 'the variety of character on Ramsgate Sands attracted me – all sorts and conditions of men and women were there' (Frith 243).[2] To eyes accustomed to the modern beach, the painting is extraordinary. The figures crowd together, rather than seeking out their own spaces; they wear an enormous amount of clothing, the faces of the women shaded from the sun by large bonnets and umbrellas; and many of them stand or sit stiffly, as if they are attending a formal social event rather than relaxing in the open air. The crowd dominates the picture space, and their surroundings are those of town rather than country, with the natural elements confined to a narrow strip of sea in the foreground and a rock face in the right background. The viewpoint is contrived and not entirely logical. As observers, we feel very close to the figures, as if we are standing in the shallow waves; but at the same time, we can see over their heads, which gives a panoramic effect usually associated with map-making and with a sense of knowledge and control. The holiday-makers are presented to our gaze like specimens in one of the aquaria that were the popular craze of the time (Payne, *Where* 117–9).[3]

---

[2]   Frith and Leech holidayed together in Ramsgate in 1852 (Houfe 83).
[3]   Philip Henry Gosse's classic text *The Aquarium* came out in 1854.

Fig. 1.1   'Ramsgate Sands (Life at the Seaside)', 1852–1854, William Powell Frith (1819–1909). Royal Collection Trust © Her Majesty Queen Elizabeth II, 2014/ Bridgeman Images.

This painting was probably the most influential visual image of the beach produced in nineteenth-century England. It was reproduced as an engraving, and the original painting was bought by Queen Victoria and hung in her seaside home, Osborne House on the Isle of Wight. Ironically, she herself had retreated to the Isle of Wight to escape the crowds on the beach in Brighton. In 1845, she had found them 'very indiscreet and troublesome' (Gilbert 107). Possession of Frith's painting enabled her to study her 'people' in detail without any risk of being jostled or pestered by them – or worse. After the 'year of revolutions' in 1848 had toppled monarchs across Europe, Queen Victoria was well aware of the importance of popular support in maintaining the constitution, and also of the dangers of the mob. Frith's painting focuses on families and children and shows people from different social classes coexisting happily, two further characteristics that would have appealed to Queen Victoria. The figures are shown sandwiched between symbols of Britain's military and naval strength – the crescents named after Nelson and Wellington in the background and the sea in the foreground. The obelisk commemorates George IV's departure from Ramsgate on his visit to Scotland in 1821. In 1851, in his dedication to his first book of poems as Poet Laureate, Tennyson had praised Queen Victoria's wise rule, which kept her throne unshaken, unlike those of so many of her European counterparts, because it was 'Broad-based upon her people's will, / And compassed by the inviolate sea' (Tennyson, 'To the Queen' lines 35–6). Frith's painting can be seen as an illustration of that declaration. Ramsgate is a port that looks across to France, and the thin strip of sea functions as a defensive barrier, a symbol of the Channel that had saved Britain from invasion during the Napoleonic Wars.

The critical response to the painting indicates some of the ways in which contemporary reviewers would have interpreted it. They looked closely at the figures and wove stories around them, surmising that the widow on the right was proposing to 'the young man with an apologetic moustache' seated behind the chair, or that the four sisters to right of the centre were worrying their father for the list of marriages in the newspaper (*Art Journal* 161–3). In front of this group there is an itinerant entertainer who has let out his performing mice onto the sand, but the young ladies behave with commendable restraint and he kneels deferentially, suggesting a stable social hierarchy. One critic thought that this family (the most prosperous looking on the beach) had carved out a space for themselves, despite their proximity to their neighbours:

> That family at the centre are remarkable for their exclusiveness; at Peckham, their garden wall is higher than that of everybody else; and here they turn their backs upon everybody, living as it were within a ring-fence. … There is another 'Happy Family' behind, but they are not so well fed; it is therefore in a social point of view an interesting fact, that they do not dine on each other. (*Art Journal* 161)

This last remark is rather cryptic, but the critic seems to be suggesting that the painting shows how rich and poor can share the same space peacefully – that human society is different to the aquarium, where the more powerful creatures literally 'dine on' those lower down the food chain. The reviews do not mention bathing, which, in the painting, is alluded to in a very subtle way. The only bare flesh revealed is in the legs of the little girl who stands in the waves in the left foreground, but, as Arscott (162) has shown, Frith incorporates discreet references to the voyeurism of the seaside. The man and child with telescopes on the left and the two men on the extreme right are both looking towards the part of the beach that was reserved for bathers, while the women avert their eyes.

Middle-class tourists also walk on the beach in William Dyce's *Pegwell Bay, Kent – a Recollection of October 5th 1858* (Figure 1.2). Unlike Frith's *Ramsgate Sands*, this painting aroused little comment when it was shown at the Royal Academy in 1860, but it has become very famous in modern times, as it seems to sum up perfectly the mood of the decade that saw the publication of Darwin's *Origin of Species*. It was recently shown in an exhibition that marked the bicentenary of Darwin's birth and 150 years since the publication of *Origin of Species*. In the catalogue, Rebecca Bedell related it to the 'new geological vision of an ancient, dynamic, constantly evolving earth' that was the foundation for Darwin's theory of evolution (49; also see 62–4). Following Pointon's classic account of the painting ('The Representation'), Bedell suggested that Dyce was troubled by the threats to religious belief represented by the new discoveries. The painting dates from the same decade as Arnold's 'Dover Beach' and matches its mood of melancholy contemplation at sunset.

It is a very personal painting. The figures in the foreground are Dyce's wife Jane, her sisters Isabella and Grace, and Dyce's son William, who was about seven at the time. In the middle distance, on the extreme right, Dyce represents himself, with his painting equipment, looking up at the sky, where Donati's comet is just visible. The painting was bought by the artist's father-in-law, James Brand (see Melville 44). Dyce was an artist with strong interest in both science and religion – he had studied medicine and theology before deciding to become an artist. Pegwell Bay was a resort just down the coast from Ramsgate, where Dickens' Tuggs family went for donkey rides, but in Dyce's painting the emphasis is on the elements rather than the holiday-makers. The pebbles and rocks on the beach, the crumbling chalk cliffs and the beauty of the luminous sky dominate the composition, and the human beings seem relatively insignificant, like ants crawling over the surface of a planet surrounded by millions of miles of interstellar space.

Many modern observers have noted a sense of dissociation between the figures and the landscape, particularly evident in the foreground figures, none of whom look at or interact with one another. This effect may be partly due to Dyce's use of photography (Pointon, *William* 171). But it also reflects the fact that the activity in which they are engaged – collecting shells and other natural history specimens – was meant to evoke religious contemplation. Many handbooks for collectors of seaside specimens were published in the 1850s, and most of them saw the beauty and intricacy of marine creatures and shells as proof of the existence of a benevolent Creator (see Payne, *Where* 117–21). The small boy and the woman in the striped cloak particularly express this effect, as they look out of

Fig. 1.2   'Pegwell Bay, Kent – a Recollection of October 5th 1858', 1858–60?,
William Dyce (1806–1864). © Tate, London 2014.

Fig. 1.3   'A Morning amongst the Granite Boulders', 1872–1873, John Brett. Private collection.

the picture towards something that the viewer cannot see, the open sea with all its symbolic connotations. The gaze of the little boy is uncannily reminiscent of Sir Isaac Newton's description of himself as being 'like a boy playing on the seashore, and diverting myself in now and then finding a smoother pebble or a prettier shell than ordinary, while the great ocean of truth lay all undiscovered before me' (Brewster 407). Newton meant that his scientific discoveries were relatively insignificant, when compared with the greater truths of religion. The anecdote had been published in 1855, in a book by Sir David Brewster, a good friend of Dyce's. Recently, Melville has supported this interpretation of the painting, adding that for Dyce 'the great 'ocean of truth' was an understanding of the wonder of Nature, not as a denial of religious truth but as physical proof of it' (44).[4] The association of the painting with religious doubt may well be a modern misreading of a painting that actually affirms Dyce's religious faith. Nevertheless, the painting eloquently conveys some of the aspects of the beach that could encourage religious doubt amongst contemporary or modern observers. On this beach, we are reminded of the vastness of time and space, the processes of erosion that are gradually destroying the cliffs and the isolation of the individual human being – themes which resonate both in Victorian writing and in recent fiction, as Zwierlein demonstrates in her contribution to this volume.

The relationship between science and religion is also an issue raised by the coastal scenes of John Brett. Brett, like Dyce, was an artist who was deeply interested in both science and religion, but in Brett's case the conflict between them led to him abandoning conventional religious practices in the 1860s or 1870s. *A Morning amongst the Granite Boulders* (Figure 1.3) is one of the many large seascapes and coastal scenes he exhibited at the Royal Academy in the 1870s, 1880s and 1890s. It is based on sketches he made at Whitesand Bay, north of Land's End in Cornwall. Brett was regarded as the leader of the Pre-Raphaelite school of landscape painting, and painting on the spot was an important part of his practice.[5] However, by this stage in his career he was painting small sketches out of doors and executing his exhibition pictures – which, like this one, were usually seven feet wide – in his studio in London. Nevertheless, his coastal scenes faithfully represent the character of each location, and he paid particular attention to the movements of the waves, the cloud formations in the sky and the textures of the rocks.

A Morning amongst the Granite Boulders was widely praised for its accuracy, but one reviewer, F.G. Stephens, also described it as 'a noble painting, replete with sadness' (*Athenaeum* 634). Here, in contrast to the paintings by Frith and Dyce, the viewpoint is low: this reflects Brett's actual viewpoint as he sat and sketched on the sands, but it also means that the observer imagines him- or herself as situated right down on the beach, vulnerable to the incoming waves. The human element has been cut to a minimum, and at first sight it looks as if it is entirely absent, a vision of the earth before (or after) humankind; but then the viewer sees tiny distant boats, battling against the waves, and footprints in the sand, destined to be

---

4   See also Smith 75–7.
5   For Brett's career, see Payne, *John*.

obliterated by the incoming tide. It must be for this reason that Stephens found it full of sadness, thinking, perhaps, of poems like Tennyson's 'Break, break, break'.

This is not the kind of beach, one would think, that would accommodate many visitors or provide safe sea-bathing. The rocks dominate the composition, and they are made of uncompromising granite, at the opposite extreme from the chalk in *Pegwell Bay*. Brett had a particular interest in geology. As a young man he had read and admired Volume 4 of John Ruskin's *Modern Painters* (1856) which argued that God deliberately made the hardest rocks the most beautiful because they are exposed to humankind's view on the high mountains – and also, of course, on the seacoast. Ruskin had written that granite decomposes into the purest sand or clay 'the sand often of the purest white, always lustrous and bright in its particles', while 'the sea which washes a granite coast is as unsullied as a flawless emerald' (143–4). The name of the beach, Whitesand Bay, evidently refers to this effect. In the 1850s Brett had been devoutly religious, and his later work retains a sense of the allegorical meaning of features of the natural landscape, when the specific beliefs that underlay this meaning have vanished. In this he may be compared with Swinburne, whose poetry repeatedly uses the sea as a symbol of death, even when his themes are explicitly anti-Christian, as in the 'Hymn to Proserpine':

> Fate is a sea without shore, and the soul is a rock that abides;
> But her ears are vexed with the roar and her face with the foam of the tides.
> …
> All delicate days and pleasant, all spirits and sorrows are cast
> Far out with the foam of the present that sweeps to the surf of the past. (lines 41–8)

Swinburne's imagery is of the rugged coastline of Northumbria and the cold, grey North Sea, while Brett's usually draws on the intense blue seas of the south-west.

Cornwall had become popular as a location for discerning seaside visitors who wanted to escape the crowds and social mixing of the beaches of south-east England. Once the railway was connected to Penzance in 1859, it was easier to access, though still relatively remote and unspoilt. John Brett regularly spent summer holidays on the coasts of Cornwall, South Wales and the west of Scotland, throughout the 1870s, 1880s and 1890s. With his common-law wife Mary and his growing family (he eventually had seven children) he would take a house for three or four months, from July through to early October, spending each day sketching, bathing and boating. For a short period in the 1880s, the family took their annual holiday on their own yacht, the *Viking*, which served as a floating studio for the artist. In 1880, he was thinking of buying land near Land's End on which to build a bungalow, regarding it as a good investment since they had 'done a great deal to make Cornwall known and popular in [their] own world' (Brett, 'Memoranda').[6] He was successful in selling his paintings to private collectors in London and Birmingham, where the broad horizons and fresh air of Cornish beaches must have seemed particularly appealing in the later years of the nineteenth century.

---

[6] For John Brett's holidays in Cornwall, see Brett, Hickox and Payne.

By 1896, when he wrote a long letter to his brother Arthur about the different characteristics of various parts of the British coast, Brett was less enthusiastic about the unspoilt nature of Cornwall, at least as a place to settle for good. 'Cornwall has fine places but they are too remote except for excursions, and generally there are no houses and no grub' (Brett, 'Letter') Like many of his contemporaries, Brett was disparaging about the crowded beaches of the south-east coast: 'all the scum of the earth gravitate to the sea coast, so that, on the whole, none of it is fit for decent people. … Margate and Ramsgate are out of the question although healthy. A pig could not survive for a month by reason of the human swine' ('Letter'; emphasis in original). He was equally unimpressed by the fishing villages that other artists found picturesque: 'The west of Scotland is crowded with lovely coast places but the natives so defile them that you cant walk near the sea [*sic*]' (Brett, 'Letter').

The emptiness of Brett's coastal scenes appealed to those who were horrified by the kind of scene depicted by Frith, and to scientists who could admire his conquest of the difficulties involved in painting moving waves and atmospheric effects. They also provided a space onto which exhibition visitors and picture buyers could project their own thoughts, like the sea itself.

However, other artists were going to the coast with the explicit aim of studying the 'natives' of the fishing villages – that is, the fishermen and women who saw the beach as a place of work rather than pleasure or contemplation. The American artist Winslow Homer spent some eighteen months living and working in the village of Cullercoats, near Newcastle on the north-east coast, between March 1881 and November 1882. His watercolour, *The Four Fishwives* (Figure 1.4) is typical of the work he produced there. Fisherfolk were greatly admired in nineteenth-century Britain. Both in non-fiction and in novels such as Sir Walter Scott's *Antiquary* (1816) and Charles Reade's *Christie Johnstone* (1853), the strong women of the self-sufficient, independent-minded fishing communities were celebrated for their beauty and for their stoicism in the face of the constant dangers involved in fishing from small boats. The bare arms, relatively short skirts and healthy complexions of Homer's four 'fisherlasses' made them picturesque subjects for painting. Their woollen skirts were of a pattern that was distinctive of the village. Three of them have on their backs the 'creels' which they used to carry the fish when they went into the local town – in this case, Newcastle – to sell the catch. Fisherwomen were notoriously strong, carrying many hundredweight of fish on their backs and walking many miles, in all weathers, to sell them. In some villages, they even carried their menfolk out to the boats so that they would not get wet (see Gray 90). In *The Antiquary*, Sir Walter Scott famously described the 'gynecocracy' of the Scottish fishing villages, whereby the women managed the households, their husbands being away at sea for long periods of time (208, 346).

It has been suggested that it was Homer's reading of Reade's novel, *Christie Johnstone*, which encouraged Homer to come and settle in Cullercoats – an episode in his life which has never been satisfactorily explained (see Cikovsky and Kelly 176). The heroine of the novel is a fisherwoman from Newhaven, near Edinburgh, another village where the fisherfolk wore distinctive regional costume. She is

Fig. 1.4   'Four Fishwives', 1881, Winslow Homer. Scripps College, Claremont, CA; Gift of the General and Mrs Edward Clinton Young, 1946.

described as naturally healthy and beautiful, and she falls in love with an artist, Charles Gatty, an Englishman who believes in painting out of doors. Christie is a strong character, a fine singer and storyteller, who has saved up a considerable sum of money as a result of her work in selling fish. She is skilled in operating boats and brave enough to rescue her lover from drowning. Before going to Cullercoats, Homer had produced many paintings and illustrations of fashionable women, and he seems to have relished the chance to depict the contrasting characteristics of the sturdy women of Cullercoats. At least one reviewer, seeing his Cullercoats watercolours in the United States, felt the same:

> Look from these women of Homer's, sturdy, fearless, fit wives and mothers of men, to the dolls which flaunt their millinery all around the walls and you are no man yourself if you do not find rising within you a sentiment of personal regard and admiration for the artist who can honor woman so by his art. (Johns 105)[7]

In the watercolour of *The Four Fishwives*, the surroundings, however, suggest another type of subject – those which dealt with the devastation of shipwrecks and the bravery of those who went out in lifeboats. The threatening sky and the groups of women waiting on the shore for the boats to come in are echoed in other watercolours by Homer which specifically address this theme, such as his series entitled 'the perils of the sea'. Another likely reason for his stay at Cullercoats was the village's association with new forms of lifesaving (see Payne, *Where* 164–5). The little boats, seen in silhouette on the right-hand side of the painting, look frail and insubstantial as they are tossed about by the wind. It is very likely that Homer would have known Charles Kingsley's poem 'The Three Fishers', which was very popular in the later nineteenth century and was often quoted by artists in exhibition catalogues. It describes three fishermen who go out fishing in the evening and the three wives who sit up waiting for them to return, with a tragic denouement:

> Three corpses lay out on the shining sands
>   In the morning gleam as the tide went down.
> And the women are weeping and wringing their hands
>   For those who will never come home to the town;
>   For men must work, and women must weep,
>   And the sooner it's over, the sooner to sleep;
>   And good-bye to the bar and its moaning. (lines 15–21)

Homer's painting is not an illustration to the poem – he depicts four fishwives rather than three – but it clearly reflects its spirit, with the wives expressing a sense of camaraderie as they walk across the wet sands towards the men returning from the sea, grateful that on this occasion, at least, they are safe.

As this essay has shown, literary sources were very important to the artists, and to their viewers, both in suggesting subjects and in determining the response

---

[7]   Johns quotes from an unsourced press cutting of Homer's from 1883 in the collection at Bowdoin College Museum of Art, Brunswick, Maine.

to the paintings. I would also like to suggest that the converse is true: that writers of novels and poetry would have been affected, often unconsciously, by the images they had seen, especially when particular themes from Royal Academy paintings were repeated in prints and journal illustrations. Ideas of the beach as a place for social interaction, for scientific and religious contemplation, for a consciousness of the sadness of death and separation, would all have been intensified by the exploration of such themes in the visual arts. The four paintings discussed here were typical of their period. Frith's *Ramsgate Sands* was the prototype for many paintings and illustrations that focus on the humorous embarrassments associated with the holiday beach. Dyce's *Pegwell Bay* shows a more serious side to the experience of visiting the beach, when the rocks and sea-creatures would remind visitors of the current debates over religion and evolution and inspire thoughtful contemplation. Brett's *A Morning amongst the Granite Boulders* responds to a new demand for unspoilt beaches, while Homer's *Four Fishwives* avoids the tourist beach in favour of an even more serious acknowledgement of the stoicism and bravery of those who made their living from the sea.

Works Cited

Arnold, Matthew. 'Dover Beach'. *The Poems of Matthew Arnold*. Ed. K. Allott. London: Longmans, Green & Co, 1965. 239–43.

Arscott, Caroline. '*Ramsgate Sands*, Modern Life, and the Shoring-up of Narrative'. *Towards a Modern Art World*. Ed. B. Allen. New Haven: Yale UP, 1995. 157–68.

Art Journal, 1 June, 1854.

Athenaeum, no. 2377, 17 May 1874.

Becker, Bernard H. *Holiday Haunts by Cliffside and Riverside*. London: Remington, 1884.

Bedell, Rebecca. 'The History of the Earth: Darwin, Geology and Landscape Art'. *Endless Forms: Charles Darwin, Natural Science and the Visual Arts*. Ed. Diana Donald and Jane Munro. New Haven: Yale UP, 2009. 49–79.

Brett, Charles, Michael Hickox and Christiana Payne. *John Brett: A Pre-Raphaelite in Cornwall*. Bristol: Sansom, 2006.

Brett, John. 'Letter to Arthur Brett'. 5 February 1896. Private Collection.

———. 'Memoranda of the Early Travels of our Children, written for them by John Brett and Mary Brett on alternate Sundays commencing in the autumn of 1879 at Penally'. Typescript prepared by Charles Brett. Private Collection.

Brewster, David, Sir. *Memoirs of the Life, Writings, and Discoveries of Sir Isaac Newton*. Vol. 2. Edinburgh: Thomas Constable and Co, 1855.

Byron, George Gordon, Lord. 'Childe Harold's Pilgrimage'. *The Poetical Works of Lord Byron*. London: John Murray, 1859. 1–61.

Cikovsky, N., and F. Kelly. *Winslow Homer*. New Haven: Yale UP, 1995.

Corbin, Alain. *The Lure of the Sea: The Discovery of the Seaside in the Western World 1750–1840*. Trans. Jocelyn Phelps. London: Penguin, 1995.

Dickens, Charles. 'The Tuggses at Ramsgate'. *The Dent Uniform Edition of Dickens' Journalism: Sketches by Boz, and other early papers, 1833–39.* Vol. 1. Ed. M. Slater. London: J.M. Dent, 1994. 330–341.

Frith, William Powell. *My Autobiography and Reminiscences.* Vol. 1. London: Richard Bentley, 1887.

Gilbert, Edmund W. *Brighton: Old Ocean's Bauble.* Hassocks: Flare Books, 1975.

Gray, Malcolm. *The Fishing Industries of Scotland, 1790–1914: A Study in Regional Adaptation.* Oxford: Oxford UP, 1978.

Houfe, Simon. *John Leech and the Victorian Scene.* Woodbridge: Antique Collectors' Club, 1984.

Johns, Elizabeth. *Winslow Homer: The Nature of Observation.* Berkeley, Los Angeles: U of California P, 2002.

Kingsley, Charles. 'The Three Fishers'. *Poems: Including The Saint's Tragedy, Andromeda, Songs, Ballads, &c. Collected Edition.* London: Macmillan & Co, 1878. 212.

Melville, Jennifer. 'Faith, Fact, Family and Friends in the Art of William Dyce'. *William Dyce and the Pre-Raphaelite Vision.* Ed. Jennifer Melville. Aberdeen: Aberdeen City Council, 2006. 38–45.

Payne, Christiana. *Where the Sea meets the Land: Artists on the Coast in Nineteenth-century Britain.* Bristol: Sansom, 2007.

———. *John Brett, Pre-Raphaelite Landscape Painter.* New Haven: Yale UP, 2010.

Pointon, Marcia. 'The Representation of Time in Painting: A Study of William Dyce's *Pegwell Bay: A Recollection of October 5th, 1858*'. *Art History* 1.1 (1978): 99–103.

———. *William Dyce 1806–64: A Critical Biography.* Oxford: Clarendon P, 1979.

Ruskin, John. *Modern Painters*, Vol. 4. 1856. *The Works of John Ruskin.* Vol. 6. Ed. E.T. Cook and A. Wedderburn. London: George Allen, 1903–1912.

Scott, Walter, Sir. *The Antiquary.* 1816. Edinburgh: Robert Cadell, 1841.

Smith, Jonathan. *Charles Darwin and Victorian Visual Culture.* London: Cambridge UP, 2006.

Swinburne, Algernon Charles. 'Hymn to Proserpine'. *Algernon Charles Swinburne: Selected Poems.* Ed. L.M. Findlay. London: Carcanet, 2002. 59.

Tennyson, Alfred, Lord. 'Break, Break, Break'. Tennyson, *The Poems.* 24.

———. 'Crossing the Bar'. Tennyson, *The Poems.* 253–4.

———. *The Poems of Tennyson.* Vol. 2. Ed. Christopher Ricks. Harlow: Longman, 1987.

———. 'To the Queen'. Tennyson, *The Poems.* 464.

Walton, John K. *The English Seaside Resort: A Social History 1750–1914.* Leicester: Leicester UP, 1983.

Wordsworth, William. 'Intimations of Immortality'. *Poems in Two Volumes.* London: Longman, Hurst, Rees and Orme, 1807. 297.

Chapter 2
Dover Beach and the Politics and Poetics of Perspective

Katharina Rennhak

Matthew Arnold's 'Dover Beach' and Ian McEwan's *Saturday*

If there is a paradigmatic 'beach poem' that draws on the 'liminality, instability and transitoriness' of the beach and uses this 'contradictory and unstable signifier' (Richter and Kluwick 5 in this volume) in order to negotiate not only philosophical and religious issues but also questions of human relationships, it is, of course, Matthew Arnold's 'Dover Beach', which has been the object of renewed attention in recent years. This current interest was certainly triggered by the central position occupied by the poem in the plot of Ian McEwan's *Saturday* (2005). McEwan's novel is set in post-9/11 London on 15 February 2003, the day of the great London anti-war march. On that day, the London house of the novel's protagonist Henry Perowne, a neurosurgeon, and his family is invaded by the violent lower-class Baxter who seeks revenge for a humiliating confrontation between himself and Perowne earlier that day. Inside the family home, Baxter breaks the grandfather's nose, slashes an expensive sofa, holds a knife to the throat of Perowne's wife, and forces his daughter, Daisy, to undress herself. After threatening Daisy with rape, he asks her, a young and aspiring poet, to read one of her poems out loud. Daisy pretends to do so, but recites Matthew Arnold's 'Dover Beach' instead. Her recitation saves the day: Baxter relaxes, 'his posture … suggests a possible ebbing of intent' (McEwan 221) and the reader witnesses a 'transformation of his role, from lord of terror to amazed admirer [of Daisy and her poetry]' (McEwan 223). So, in McEwan's novel, Arnold's poem 'precipitate[s] a mood swing' (221) which helps to put an end to an aggravated burglary that is represented as equivalent to a terrorist attack.

The first reaction to McEwan's intertextual deployment of Arnold's 'Dover Beach' was exasperated disbelief. For Hadley, Arnold and his poem are touchstones of a Victorian liberal humanism that is ideologically suspect as it combines a pre-Foucauldian belief in the self-conscious, self-present and holistic individual subject as agent with universal truth claims and patriarchal and imperialist assumptions. As a consequence, she interprets McEwan's intertextual reference to 'Dover Beach' as 'an indication of [the author's] belief that the problems of the contemporary age can be faced with Arnold's version of 'liberalism's social aesthetic, a certain fantasy of an elegant, cognitive agency' [Hadley 95]' (Gunning 106).

More recently, Hillard has challenged Hadley's argument and the many rather unsympathetic reviews that read '*Saturday* and 'Dover Beach' alike as triumphs of personal intimacy and withdrawal from the world, maneuverings of liberal individualist agency' (187). She argues that McEwan does not simply reinstate Arnold's 'Dover Beach' but presents various re-readings of the poem and demonstrates that its interpretation is dependent on the context and on the particular perspective of its (diegetic) reader. Hillard speaks of various 'telescoping positionalities' through which Arnold's poem is presented, and claims that '[t]hese telescoping positionalities indicate McEwan's concerted attempt to 'hack' – to infiltrate gender, genre, and periodization' (200).

This may well be the case, and Hillard's emphasis on the question of positionalities is certainly of great relevance in any discussion of the politics of 'Dover Beach' and other literary works which refer to Arnold's canonical poem. However, the attempt to oppose Arnold's liberal humanist ideology through a reinsertion of 'Dover Beach' into a fictional world must inevitably be fraught with difficulty, as it cannot but re-establish the Arnoldian text and must thus also repeat its politics.[1] Gunning assumes that any mere quotation of Arnold's poem in narrative fiction, while it may 'demonstrate the inadequacy of the Arnoldian vision … seems unable to offer an alternative' (106). Successful attempts at countering Arnold's liberal project, I want to argue, must certainly encounter his poetry on the same territory and lyrically imagine Dover beach differently.

In what follows, I will look at a number of pre- and post-Arnoldian Dover beach poems and demonstrate that the politics of these poems is very much dependent on how and where exactly the speaker (or focalising subject) is physically and lyrically, literally and metaphorically positioned in relation to the beach. While the liberal humanist ideology of Arnold's and other 'Dover Beach'-poetry certainly introduces questions of religion, gender, age, race and nation, I will focus on negotiations of the identity categories 'race' and 'nation'. Readings of pre-Arnoldian poetry by Dinah Maria Mulock Craik, William John Courthope, William Lisle Bowles, and Philip Bourke Marston will help to demonstrate how Arnold builds on what could be called a poetical tradition of fashioning subjectivities and political subject positions vis-à-vis Dover beach and how he cleverly fuses a number of different Dover beach topoi so as to convincingly establish his well-known liberal humanist vision. Analyses of Iain Crichton Smith's and Daljit Nagra's late twentieth-century and early twenty-first-century poems show how exactly contemporary poets try to rewrite Arnold's canonical 'Dover Beach' poem.

---

[1]   There is a long tradition of quoting Arnold's poem in the novel. Among the best-known examples are Bradbury's *Fahrenheit 451* and Heller's *Catch 22*. See Roberts for an analysis of a number of American science fiction writers who 'assert their kinship to high art, to Arnold, and to his valorisation of "culture" as literature through their appropriation of "Dover Beach"', on the one hand, while they 'expos[e] its assumptions about gender and culture' (255), on the other.

Thus, while (and by) also referring to a concrete geographical location, 'Dover beach' pre-dominantly functions as a trope in this article and in the poetry analysed. Unlike the Caribbean beach in Döring's interpretation, this trope of 'Dover beach' does not conceptualise a 'specific rhetorical *plot*' (Döring 110 in this volume; emphasis added) but, rather, establishes a number of topoi[2] – most importantly: England and its colonial other; the cliffs and the shifting ground of the beach; an inward turn of the main subject; as well as issues of human communication, and the function of poetry – which are used to lyrically negotiate the question of how an individual subject can stabilise his (hardly ever: her) subject position when faced with the uncertain and the unknown.

Fixing Identities in Late Eighteenth- and Nineteenth-Century Dover Poems

Dover is not just any English seaside town, of course, but lies at the extreme south-east corner of Britain, where it faces France across the narrowest part of the English Channel. Because of its proximity to France, the town has always been of great strategic importance to Britain. Many Englishmen have left their native land from Dover in times of war and peace, and the seaport town therefore figures in a fair number of patriotic poems of the eighteenth and nineteenth centuries. 'The Last Look of England' by Dinah Maria Mulock Craik, the Victorian author who is best known for her bestselling novel *John Halifax, Gentleman* (1881), serves as a good example.

Craik's short poem, which consists of five four-line stanzas, does not elaborate in any great detail on the topography of Dover, the sheer white cliffs and the beach, or on the military importance of the port, but it clearly draws on the traditional image of Dover, as a sublime site well established in the collective national imaginary ever since Shakespeare's *King Lear*. It begins with the lines 'The last look of England – as the ship in full sail / Glides past Dover pier in the moon-set so pale', positions a young English sailor-boy offshore in a ship that is leaving England and focuses on his thoughts and feelings as he departs. As the ship sails past Dover, however, the boy's look does not linger on the port town but seems to be invited by the view to turn inward and look 'a dozen miles inland' (line 5), and he sees in his mind's eye his mother in 'a hop-covered cottage and three hives of bees' (line 6). Passing Dover, Craik's sailor-boy looks within, as it were, and there finds the mother he cherishes whose picture and, by implication, whose moral standards he will carry with him wherever he goes. 'Mother' and 'England' are one and the same in this patriotic piece, where the brave boy is allowed to shed a tear over his departure from mother (and) England without compromising his

---

[2]   I use the term as it is known from classical rhetoric where it designates '"intellectual places (tópoi)" or very general patterns and ways of grasping or seizing something intellectually and in speech' (Eikeland 226). Also see Spranzi who emphasises that 'for Greek commentators …, as well as for Latin authors, "topoi" serve as tools both for finding arguments, that is for invention, and for justifying conclusions' (31).

masculinity, because the heartfelt promise to his mother, "'I'll be good, I'll be brave, / and I'll never forget the last kiss that you gave",' (lines 11–12) ensures that he will act as a true Briton abroad.

> Not a bit of a coward is the sailor-boy true,
> With his bright open eye and his jacket of blue,
> He can work like a Briton, fight too, if needs be,
> Yet his last look of England is a sad sight to see. (lines 13–16)

The sailor-boy's eponymous 'last look' at Dover is, importantly, followed by a 'first sight' of the same scene in the last stanza of Craik's poem which envisions a future that will bring him

> back after years four and five
> …
> As the white Dover cliffs gleam afar on his lee,
> Oh, the first sight of England is a glad sight to see. (lines 17–20)

What this poem with its engaging rippling rhyme and meter implies is, of course, that after the sailor-boy has spent some years abroad in the British Empire, he will have grown up and turned into an even braver, stronger, more experienced and very probably financially better-off Englishman. But he will not only profit personally by gaining experiences and riches. During his journey, the poem suggests, he will also disseminate his mother's English ideals throughout the world and, thus, help to build the Empire. In Craik's poem, then, the position of the focalising subject towards Dover establishes the British Isles as the English nation, and the English nation as a firm, secure and stable entity which helps to stabilise the sailor-boy's personal identity by providing him with a patriotic ethic that directs and redirects his journey from and to England.

The same principles are at work in many other Dover poems of the eighteenth and nineteenth centuries, in which Dover with its white cliffs also represents home and stability. William John Courthope's 'Song', for example, works similarly even though it shifts the sailor's focus from mother to lover:

> **Farewell**, white cliffs of Dover!
> Dear heart, don't weep for me:
> The seas must bear thy lover
> From country and from thee.
> The soldier must not tarry,
> When honour points the way;
> When danger calls, my deary,
> You would not have me stay. (lines 1–8; emphasis in original)

By focusing on the shifting ground of the beach rather than on the 'white cliffs', Arnold's later 'Dover Beach' certainly problematises this self-confident representation of England as a home that guarantees security and moral stability. Still, he and later authors of Dover beach poems contribute to a renegotiation of these topoi of 'the English nation and its other'. It will also become evident that 'the subject's inward turn' as established in patriotic nineteenth-century Dover poems becomes a recurring topos.

Other pre-Arnoldian poets, such as William Lisle Bowles, who contributed to the sonnet revival during the Romantic period, or the Victorian Philip Bourke Marston, Dinah Maria Mulock Craik's godson and an intimate friend of Dante Gabriel Rossetti and Algernon Charles Swinburne, neglect the patriotic aspect of Dover in favour of a depiction of the awe-inspiring and sublime cliffs of Dover, in the case of Bowles, or a melancholic meditation, in the case of Marston. Unlike Arnold's and Marston's lyrical subjects more than half a century later, the speaker of or subject addressed in Bowles's Romantic sonnets 'Dover Cliffs. At Dover, 1786' and 'Dover Cliffs' is still confident that a trust in God and the Christian virtue of charity can help to overcome personal despondency and depression.[3] This confidence and moral mastery is very much dependent on the fact that Bowles's speaker is standing 'On these white cliffs, that calm above the flood / Uprear their shadowing heads' ('Dover Cliffs' lines 1–2). Bowles's subject can either look down into the abyss and despair or enjoy the elevated position on top of the cliffs that presents him with a full view of the sublime scenery which he seems to be able to partly master from his location high above. Only there can he successfully repress the fearful and melancholy thoughts triggered by the sound of the 'surge that has for ages beat' down below on the beach (line 3). On top of the cliffs only 'the lifted murmur [meets] his ear' (line 4). The insecurities and uncertainties associated with the beach experience can be dealt with by the subject who is securely located on the cliffs and who – in Bowles's poems – does not, like some of his friends (lines 8–9), intend to leave England and change this position. Ultimately, the position high above the beach empowers him to lift his gaze further upwards, as it were, and to realise that 'his God [is] his Guide' – to quote the last words of 'Dover Cliffs'. Everything depends on how you focus on Dover beach; everything depends on the perspective you adopt. By standing in the right, that is to say an elevated, place and by looking in the right direction, Bowles's subject can gain self-presence and become a moral agent, able to feel with and even charitably approach the 'many' others who are stranded on the beach below

---

[3]   William Wordsworth's Dover poems, by some regarded to be the 'chief sources' of Arnold's 'Dover Beach' (O'Gorman 312) – for example, 'After Landing – The Valley Of Dover, November 1820', 'At Dover', 'Composed in the Valley near Dover, on the Day of Landing', 'September 1802, Near Dover' – certainly deserve more careful exploration elsewhere. This article focuses on Bowles's poems because here the Romantic negotiation of the 'Dover beach' trope builds more rigorously on reflections of specific Dover topographies than Wordsworth's poems, which tend to abruptly change the perspective from Dover vale, valley or town to the sea or ocean and, thus, to neglect the very borderlines represented by the beach or the cliffs. An article on Wordsworth's Dover poems could also take into consideration 'It is a beauteous evening, calm and free' which provides an interesting contrast to Arnold's 'Dover Beach' not only because, with its speaker positioned at Calais, it provides the perspective from the other side of the English Channel.

and of whom we learn that '[t]ossed on the surge of life … [they] sink' – literally and metaphorically ('Dover Cliffs. At Dover 1786' line 8).

In contrast, the melancholy speaker of Marston's sonnet 'Parting with Summer: On Dover Beach' finds himself right down on the beach 'By this still sea' (line 3) where he and 'the summer say / Our long farewell' (lines 3–4). The perspective of the subject positioned on the beach is limited and imperfect, and Marston's speaker is far from mastering the view that presents itself. For him 'sea and sky are of one pensive gray' (line 6). Sea and sky become indistinguishable and impenetrable. For the subject on the beach there is neither a God, nor any transcendental power, nor even a benign or invigoratingly sublime nature. Marston's nature only ever mirrors the melancholic mood of the subject by whom it is perceived: 'The small waves seem to sigh about the Bay' (line 7). While summer is followed, in Marston's sonnet, by an 'Autumn [which] will mock us for a little space / With Summer's semblance' (lines 9–10) and 'the wild Winter winds that blow / The sea-foam, like tumultuous banks of snow' (lines 12–13), spring, the season that conventionally signifies new life, is totally omitted and thus seems to lie beyond the speaker's horizon. The only alternative to the bleak and disempowering view which the external world offers is the solipsistic inward turn suggested in the last line: 'And in our hearts Summer's remembered grace!' Unlike the sailor-boy who departs from and returns to Dover in Craik's patriotic poem 'The Last Look of England', Marston's speaker does not see before his mind's eye an emblem of the nation and its values that helps him construct a stable national and class identity, but only a personal experience of summer which is not specified at all. Rather than looking at the reassuring solidity and fixity of the cliffs, like Craik's sailor-boy, Marston's speaker standing on the beach only observes the constant inconstancy of the waves and a greyness which makes it impossible to even distinguish between sea and sky. 'Parting with Summer' thus presents a subject whose mastery and agency is vastly diminished. If there is a trace of the Victorian liberal ideology in this sonnet, it is to be found in the speaker's belief in himself as a self-conscious, self-present and holistic individual. Still, Marston's 'lyrical I' is not an agent who interacts socially in any way but a disempowered, asocial subject who finds himself imprisoned within his own subjectivity.

Arnold's 'Dover Beach': Positioning the Liberal Subject Towards the Beach

A look at how Arnold's predecessors and contemporaries deal with the politics and poetics of Dover beach by assigning different perspectives to their speakers or focalising subjects helps to demonstrate the complexity of position(ing) s and perspectives in Arnold's canonical 'Dover Beach', this 'deeply affecting melanchol[ic] poem … [which] is the poetical record of a crisis of 'Faith' — … of Arnold's and his culture's faith in religion, in nature, and in civic institutions' (Furr n.p.). What becomes apparent is that Arnold is able to establish a position from which the liberal subject can defend itself against falling prey to the overwhelming and debilitating dangers of scepticism and doubt, and against absolutely succumbing to despair, by having recourse to three closely interrelated strategies that all involve position(ing)s and perspectives.

Most importantly, his poem blends different perspectives which the speaker is shown to be able to assume simultaneously by carefully making a distinction between the sense of sight and the sense of hearing. The first eight lines of Arnold's 'Dover Beach' present the traditional, reassuring trope of Dover beach. 'The sea is calm to-night' (line 1), 'the moon lies fair / Upon the straits' (line 2–3) and the cliffs are represented as the ever reliable, beautiful backbone of the nation: 'the cliffs of England stand, / Glimmering and vast, out in the tranquil bay' (lines 4–5). Since no other sense is mentioned, one automatically assumes that the speaker describes what he sees from behind the 'window' (line 6) which overlooks Dover bay. At first *sight*, the world seems peaceful and quiet to the Victorian observer who (like Bowles's subject) looks at the scene from above. This impression changes as soon as the speaker and, presumably, his addressee listen to rather than look at Dover beach.

> Listen! you hear the grating roar
> Of pebbles which the waves draw back, and fling,
> At their return, up the high strand,
> Begin, and cease, and then again begin,
> With tremulous cadence slow, and bring
> The eternal note of sadness in. (lines 9–14)

By concentrating on what he hears, Arnold's speaker homes in on the transitory, daunting and dispiriting beach experience. Focussing on the sounds of the sea as it endlessly and randomly moves the pebbles on the strand, he finds himself engulfed by the 'liminality, instability and transitoriness' of the beach (Richter and Kluwick 5 in this volume). As 'now [he] only hear[s] / [the sea's] melancholy, long, withdrawing roar' (lines 24–5), the masterful position as observer behind the window, which enables him to assume 'an Olympian perspective versus the eddying existence of the darkling plain' (Gibson 31), is undermined (even though it remains available). Listening to the sounds of the beach leaves the subject alone with 'the vast edges drear / And naked shingles of the world' (lines 27–8), which signify a universe that is devoid of meaning and 'certitude' (line 34).

If one takes the speaker's conflicting positions – with his beloved behind the window and, simultaneously, lost in the beach experience – and the closely related contrast between the visual and the audible (stressed in lines 9, 24 and 29–30) seriously, it becomes clear how the situation of utterance, which the poem constructs, contributes towards protecting the Arnoldian subject from the dangers of an insecure world and from despair. Certainly, the acoustic experience of the beach's liminality is accompanied by an irretrievable loss of faith in a well-ordered, peaceful universe, but, by addressing his beloved again in the first line of the last stanza, the speaker tries to regain his agency. He re-establishes his position within the room that overlooks Dover beach even as he feels drawn into the 'darkling plain / Wept with confused alarms of struggle and flight / Where ignorant armies clash by night' (lines 35–7). The (in)famous 'Ah, love, let us be true / To one another!' (lines 29–30) at the beginning of the last stanza clearly signals his turn away from a disheartening contemplation of cruel nature towards human society. The address, 'Ah, love', points to the undiminished and continuing desire and struggle for and, ultimately, the 'belief in the liberal subject's ability to seek out a private space of thoughtful emotion, of human intimacy, where subjects alienated in mind or body can become fully authentic and intentional in relation to themselves and to each other, in spite of the chaotic world without' (93), which Hadley criticises so harshly in her reading of McEwan's *Saturday* and its references to Arnold's 'Dover Beach'. One could also say that, while the position behind the window, precarious as it has become, points to the speaker's potential aloofness from the world of constant change, his very voice as he addresses another empowers the Arnoldian subject even more. Through his communicative act, which as such represents the continued search for meaning and happiness, he counters the noisy sound of the beach with human language. The fact that his voice only claims to be universal and dialogic but is, in fact, clearly monologic, gendered and English (see, for example, Gibson, or Hadley) further contributes to the project of defending the liberal humanist subject's position in the world even in the face of the speaker's otherwise unrelenting Victorian doubt.

While the success of this attempt to secure the liberal subject's agency remains doubtful on the level of content, Arnold's poem 'Dover Beach' stands as proof of the poet's cultural agency in so far as it presents a clever intertextual engagement with the Western literary tradition from Sophocles[4] to Shakespeare's *King Lear* and from Coleridge's 'conversational poems' to Wordsworth's 'Lines: Composed a Few Miles above Tintern Abbey' and 'At Dover',[5] which – here as elsewhere in Arnold's œuvre – serves to fend off the beach experience of anxiety, insecurity and doubt. Many critics have demonstrated that Arnold's 'Dover Beach' is a self-consciously poetic attempt to deal with the crises its speaker reflects upon and that, as such, it can be read in the context of that one belief – and liberal humanist credo - which Arnold does not doubt but, rather, helps to write into existence, namely, that 'More and more mankind will discover that we have to turn to poetry to interpret life for us, to console us, to sustain us … most of what now passes with us for religion and philosophy will be replaced by poetry' ('The Study' 161–2).

Destabilising Fixed English Identities in Late Twentieth- and Twenty-First-Century Dover Poems

In this final section, I will focus on the Dover beach poems of a late twentieth-century Scottish and an early twenty-first-century Asian-British poet: Iain Crichton Smith's 'At a Poetry Reading' and Daljit Nagra's collection of poetry

---

    [4]   'Sophocles long ago / Heard it on the Ægæan, and it brought / Into his mind the turbid ebb and flow / Of human misery' (Arnold, 'Dover Beach' lines 15–18).

    [5]   Also see footnote 3 above.

entitled *Look We Have Coming to Dover!* from 2007.[6] Iain Crichton Smith, one of Scotland's most admired twentieth-century men of letters, novelists and poets, has famously described himself as "a linguistic double man' who speaks a dialect of 'Highland English" (Wickman 105)[7] and has aptly characterised his work as being suspended 'between Lewis and Wittgenstein' (Smith, 'The Double Man' 145), between 'a Hebridean home place and linguistic constructivism' (Wickman 101). In his collection *Ends and Beginnings*, Smith tackles the liberal ideology of Arnold's English 'Dover Beach' from a specifically Scottish perspective or, to be more precise, from the perspective of two Scotsmen who find themselves on an anglicised British Isle in a poem whose very title 'At a Poetry Reading' points to its meta-poetical aspect and alerts the reader to its intertextual thrust right from the beginning.

> After I'd recited my poems in Folkestone
> you came to speak to me.
> You were from Lewis. (lines 1–3)

The speaker of this poem is clearly a poet persona of the Scottish author Crichton Smith, who grew up on the Hebridean island of Lewis. The very first stanza situates two Scotsmen – the said poet-persona and someone who listened to his poetry reading and who is also from Lewis and far from home – in Folkestone, a town in Kent which is very close to Dover. Since references to Dover itself abound in what follows, this repositioning of the subjects from Dover to Folkestone is certainly significant: Smith seems to emphasise that he is not quite writing another Arnoldian 'Dover Beach'. His poem assembles what we can by now call the conventional elements of a Dover beach poem but presents them from the perspective of Scotsmen in England. Once again, there is, firstly, Dover's proximity to the continent:

> Near Dover they're digging the Channel Tunnel
> through miles of water.
> …
> During the war shells from Calais travelled
> towards this land of stockbrokers. (lines 6–10)

---

[6] It should be stressed here that it is the page limit rather than a lack of relevant modernist and post-war Dover beach poems which forces me to skip a whole century within the confines of this article. W.H. Auden's well-known 'Dover' must at least be mentioned in this footnote. For an analysis of Robert Frost's 'lifelong conversation with Matthew Arnold' see George Monteiro's article on 'Robert Frost's Liberal Imagination', which also demonstrates that 'the Matthew Arnold of 'Dover Beach' [and twentieth-century American liberal critics who were his followers, such as Lionel Trilling, Randall Jarrell, Carl and Mark Van Doren] became the touchstone for the key concept of American liberalism at mid-century', which sought to 'replace … dogma and ideology by human feeling and relations as the guiding principles for moral behaviour' (104).

[7] Wickman quotes from Crichton Smith's 'The Double Man' (137, 139).

There is also, secondly, the inward turn of the speaking subject, which brings into view an emblematic national entity and the values and characteristics attached to it: 'My island, you are a distant diamond in my consciousness' (line 15). The geographic entity (and with it the social community) envisioned in Smith's Dover beach poem is explicitly not England, which is said to be 'another country, richer than us' (line 17), but the Scottish Lewis 'far in the north' (line 21), which is clearly opposed to the prosperous, mercantile British Isle: Lewis is rougher and rural, characterised by 'the sparse climate of peasants' (line 18); it is 'an affair of thistles' (line 22). Here Smith obviously draws on stereotypical Scottish and English national binaries. The main thrust of the poem is, nevertheless, about some kind of approximation or even convergence of the English and the Scottish – even if lines 11–12 suggest that the only thing that England and Lewis may 'perhaps' have in common is the sea: 'The sea is perhaps the same around Lewis and here. / It is a salt ring of blue'. The sea, this potential common denominator of the British Isles, and Arnold's 'Dover Beach' are the topic of the last lines of Smith's poem.

> And all that unites us is the sea,
> resonant, indifferent, estranging,
> where Arnold for a moment forgot his chalk
> and pierced the heart with absence. (lines 28–31)

Smith's poem here constructs an Arnold whose poem 'Dover Beach' enables an experience of absence – an absence of faith, trust and certainties but also of unity and community. Although by pointing to Arnold's well-known poem, Smith's 'At a Poetry Reading' ends on this same Arnoldian note of absence, it clearly attempts to counter Arnold's absences by reinserting and emphasising the precarious presence of something else, something Northern and Scottish that has always existed on the island that is Great Britain; a presence, moreover, which has not only coexisted with the English on the same island, but also helped to defend their land:

> I think however it's possible
> that some of our villagers might have been drowned here,
> defending the white cliffs made of chalk. (lines 24–6)

In this context, the combination of adjectives in line 29, which describe the sea as 'resonant, indifferent, estranging', gains relevance. While 'indifferent' and 'estranging' unequivocally sound an Arnoldian note, 'resonant' – which can be read as just meaning 'melancholy' – does not only point to the similarities between Arnold's English world and Crichton Smith's Great Britain. It also introduces a difference between the two poets' visions. Especially in relation to 'places', the *OED* explains that *resonant* means '[r]esounding or echoing *with* [something]' and 'Filled or imbued *with*; strongly suggestive or reminiscent of a particular thing' (4. a, b; emphases in original). The Arnoldian absence can thus be said to point to an obscured and precarious presence: the presence in England of the Scottish dead.

Moreover, the situation of utterance in 'At a Poetry Reading' mirrors the dialogic situation of Arnold's poem (where a speaker talks to a second person who does not answer) and with it takes up the theme of 'self and other' and the question of how to interact socially in a world which is – in Smith's poem and in Arnold's 'Dover Beach' – dominated by the sea. While Arnold's 'Dover Beach' tries to counter the loss of faith and security by constructing the unity of yet another pair characterised by its (gender) differences, the situation of utterance in Smith's poem imagines a community of Northerners who seem to be united by their consciousness of the obscured presence of the Scottish in England and of the precarious unity of the British Isles rather than by a nationalistic English or Scottish identity. In other words, Crichton Smith's poem gives the Scottish villagers a presence not only by memorialising the forgotten and drowned but also by firmly positioning a culturally active Scottish community in England. An important integrative force is, of course, assigned to the (Scottish) poet and his poetry which he reads in England and is presented as being part of a larger European cultural tradition. 'The Arts Centre' of Folkestone not only houses the poetry reading of the Scottish author but also 'speaks of Brecht, Pinter, [and the Irish] Shaw' (line 13). Smith thus neither locates his speaker on the 'ground of absence' that is Arnold's Dover *beach* nor in a twosome, heterosexual seclusion behind a window. Rather, he repositions Dover and Dover beach by perspectivising it through the poetical representation of a communication that takes place between a Scottish poet and another Scotsman after a poetry reading in Folkestone, Kent, England.

A look at two poems from Daljit Nagra's celebrated collection of poetry entitled *Look We Have Coming To Dover!* shows that Arnold's paradigmatic beach poem and the liberal ideology which it has come to represent are still being tackled afresh in intertextual poetic repositionings today. In what follows, I suggest that the prize-winning title poem 'Look We Have Coming to Dover!' and the last poem in the collection, entitled 'Singh Song!' can be regarded as complementary and that only taken together do they formulate the early twenty-first-century Asian-British poet's answer to Arnold's 'Dover Beach'. The two poems perspectivise Dover or Dover beach differently in two significant ways. Firstly, they geographically locate the speaking subject differently towards Dover. Secondly, they reconstruct the Arnoldian situation of utterance.

In 'Look We Have Coming to Dover!', immigrants on a ferry and 'hutched in a Bedford van' (line 10) approach an England which they, unlike Craik's sailor-boy, have never entered before. The epigraph, which cites Arnold's 'So various, so beautiful, so new', refers both in Arnold's 'Dover Beach' and in Nagra's poem to 'a land of dreams' (Arnold, 'Dover Beach' line 31). However, for Nagra's migrants this 'land of dreams' that is 'revealed as a falsehood in Arnold's poem is real and they "swarm" to possess this imagined Britain' (Gunning 106). Even though 'the vast crumble of scummed / cliffs' and the 'thunder [that] unbladders / yobbish rain and wind' (lines 8–10) do not give them a particularly heartfelt welcome, the migrants cling to their dream of a land which they envision as 'various, beautiful, ... new'. From their perspective, crossing the border into England, which will 'passport us to life' (line 19), is envisioned as a 'hoick[ing] ... for the clear' (line 20), a passage from the dark into the light, into freedom.

The depiction of this moment of crossing the border into a dreamland suggests that the migrant subject's agency is one which – unlike Arnold's – inevitably involves taking sides and making decisions. Nagra's poem also demonstrates that the migrants' entry into Britain at Dover does not result in a stabilisation of their identity. Nagra's Dover differs from Craik's Dover in this respect. As soon as the speaker and his love find themselves 'Blair'd in the cash / of our beeswax'd cars, our crash clothes, free' (lines 22–3) or inside Britain, they begin to register differences between Britain and the East like, for example, 'unparasol'd tables' (line 24). Even more importantly, their 'lingoes' (which seem to always already be in the plural) become 'flecked by the chalk of Britannia' (line 25). As they pass and enter Dover, a new colour, the white chalk of the cliffs, seems to be added to the plural and flexible spectrum of their migrant identities.

It is also remarkable that the binary pairing of 'my love and I' is opened up in Nagra's poem to include 'our sundry others' (lines 21–2). As Gunning notes, '[t]he restricted intersubjectivity of the source text is [replaced]. … The couple echo the figures in the original poem but the intimacy is displaced by the unspecified multitude' (107). Thus Nagra's repositioning of the speaker towards Dover points to a social ethics that is much more inclusive than the bourgeois domestic morality of Arnold's 'Dover Beach'.

However, Nagra's lyrical Dover beach story does not end here. At the end of the poem 'Singh Song!', a newly wed I and his beloved wife are located behind a window through which they, like Arnold's lovers, look 'at di beaches ov di UK in di brightey moon' (line 50). Unlike the migrants in 'Look We Have Coming to Dover!', this couple has arrived and is firmly settled in Britain. The male speaker, Singh, is very probably a second generation Asian-British citizen, and he has – like his father and so many of his fellow Asian-British – chosen a proverbially British profession, that of a shopkeeper. For him and his wife, the Arnoldian 'land of dreams' is still a very real presence. Britain does not seem to have disappointed them. For there certainly is 'joy', 'love' and 'light' (Arnold, 'Dover Beach' line 33) – the attributes which Arnold's world lacks – in this couple's life. Moreover, the ending that allows them to view all 'di beaches ov di UK' (line 50) from an Olympian perspective suggests that what Arnold's speaker can only hope for has, in a way at least, become true for the Singhs: their union gives them the faith and strength to master the social realities they are confronted with.

Another significant difference between Nagra's couple behind the window and Arnold's lovers is that 'Singh Song!' allows the reader a glance into the private life of the couple who are, thus, depicted as being much more approachable than Arnold's speaker and his love, who totally shut themselves off from the world. The male speaker and his wife in 'Singh Song!', moreover, both interact with the world beyond the shop. While the speaker serves his customers, he hears 'Above [his] head high heel tap di ground / as [his] vife on di web is playing wid di mouse' (lines 18–19). Again Nagra rejects Arnold's vision of a 'restricted intersubjectivity' and stresses that the heterosexual couple of his poem is embedded within a larger community, which includes the virtual multitudes (potentially incorporating relatives in India) connected through the internet. This social embeddedness, in turn, is again shown to contribute significantly to the construction of their migrant identity or, to use Mishra's term, their 'hyphenated' Asian-British identity (433; also see Gunning 99–100).

Nagra's two Dover beach poems are not just complementary because they look at Dover beach from opposite vantage points, from without and from within Britain but also because they are written in different languages, as it were. 'Look We Have Coming To Dover!' adopts a very British literary style. 'Singh Song!', in contrast, is performed in an extremely colloquial 'Punglish'. It is especially interesting to note that the localisation of the speaking subject in space – his relation to Dover – and the language or idiom he uses are at cross purposes in both poems. While the subject of 'Look We Have Coming to Dover!', with his restricted perspective from without the UK, is as yet a rather powerless subject, his sophisticated vocabulary and complicated syntax certainly draws level with the English of Arnold's canonical poem (without denying the speaker's hyphenated migrant identity which is performed through a language that is strangely at odds with any standard use of English). In 'Singh Song!' it is exactly the other way round: here the speaker's Punglish stands in stark contrast to the Olympian mastery his view over the whole of 'di beaches ov di UK' (line 50) suggests. In both cases, this crossing of spatial and linguistic position(ing)s counters Arnold's attempt to overwrite the despair and disempowerment triggered by the limited perspective which only ever sees the endless and endlessly inconstant movement of the waves with a masterful poetic language. Nagra does not substitute the one spatial or linguistic position for the other. His characters must forever negotiate various positions, cultures and different languages. In doing so they are not only shown to be defined by an inevitably precarious, multifaceted and *per se* contradictory identity, but also demonstrate, firstly, that such an identity entails an agency that does not strive to withdraw and master, but to include and connect; and that, secondly, such an agency can momentarily, at least, empower Asian-British subjects and give them the impression that they can be the masters of their own lives.

Conclusion

To conclude, it should have become apparent that poems about Dover from around 1800 until the early twenty-first century can be said (if in the case of pre-Arnoldian poems only with hindsight) to establish a recurring 'Dover beach' trope which – by drawing on a number of recurring topoi – negotiates the question of human agency. In all the Dover beach poems discussed, the politics and poetics of the respective poem are absolutely dependent on the position(ing)s and perspectives the subject assumes with regard to Dover beach. Those (focalising or speaking) lyrical subjects who are (literally or metaphorically) located on the cliffs or focus on the shore and the land assume a much more powerful subject position than those who find themselves on the shifting ground of the beach. The overview of a long tradition of Dover beach poems should also have demonstrated that there is a clear difference in how position(ing)s and perspectives are handled in pre-Arnoldian and post-Arnoldian poems. While the pre-Arnoldian poem assumes rather unambiguous perspectives and thus creates seemingly stable (national, religious, moral and gendered) identities, Arnold's liberal human politics is an attempt to save, at least, the faith in the subject's self-presence and to thus endow it with a fixed identity in the face of 'the vast edges drear / And naked shingles of the world' (lines 27–8) symbolised by his representation of Dover beach as 'the darkling plain' (line 35). If he succeeds in doing this, the success depends on a clever blending of various perspectives which the one speaker is shown to be able to assume simultaneously, thanks to his different senses and to his manly, poetical voice. The idea that there is no vantage point that can guarantee the individual subject its self-presence and mastery over its various environments is central to the Dover beach poems by Iain Crichton Smith and Daljit Nagra – two poets who comment on British culture from positions of the cultural other, a cultural other that is not located elsewhere, out of England as it were. Rather, Smith, Nagra and their lyrical subjects are located (literally and/or metaphorically) on the most significant of English beaches, just as their English predecessors were. They speak from a position which also points to differences within Britain. But even though they still find themselves confronted with the Arnoldian beach experience of ever-shifting ground and endless insecurities, their cultural investments in poetry and song end on a much more confident and socially inclusive, and in Nagra's case even cheerful, note.

Works Cited

Arnold, Matthew. 'Dover Beach'. *Victorian Poetry: An Annotated Anthology*. Ed. Francis O'Gorman. Malden, MA: Blackwell, 2004. 312–3.

———. 'The Study of Poetry'. *English Literature and Irish Politics*. Ed. Robert H. Super. *The Complete Prose Works of Matthew Arnold*. Vol. 9. Ann Arbor: U of Michigan P, 1973. 161–88.

Bowles, William Lisle. 'Dover Cliffs'. Bowles, *The Poetical Works*. 12.

———. 'Dover Cliffs. At Dover, 1786'. Bowles, *The Poetical Works*. 23–4.

———. *The Poetical Works of William Lisle Bowles*. Vol. 1. Edinburgh: J. Nichol, 1855.

Courthope, William John. 'Song'. *Poems: By Novus Homo*. Oxford: Wheeler & Day, 1865. 58–60.

Craik, Dinah Maria Mulock. 'The Last Look of England'. *Children's Poetry*. London: Macmillan, 1881. 110–11.

Eikeland, Olav. *The Ways of Aristotle: Aristotelian Phrónêsis, Aristotelian Philosophy of Dialogue, and Action Research*. Bern: Peter Lang, 2008.

Furr, Derek. 'An Overview of "Dover Beach"'. *Poetry for Students*. Detroit: Gale. *Literature Resources from Gale*. LMU München. Web. 2 Jan. 2009. <http://go.galegroup.com/ps/ start.do?p=LitRG&u=lmum>.

Gibson, Mary Ellis. 'Dialogue on the Darkling Plain: Genre, Gender, and Audience in Matthew Arnold's Lyrics'. *Gender and Discourse in Victorian Literature and Art*. Ed. Antony H. Harrison and Beverly Taylor. DeKalb: Northern Illinois UP, 1992. 30–48.

Gunning, Dave. 'Daljit Nagra, Faber Poet: Burdens of Representation and Anxieties of Influence'. *The Journal of Commonwealth Literature* 43.3 (2008): 95–108.

Hadley, Elaine. 'On a Darkling Plain: Victorian Liberalism and the Fantasy of Agency'. *Victorian Studies* 48.1 (2005): 92–102.

Hillard, Molly Clark. '"When Desert Armies Stand Ready to Fight": Re-Reading McEwan's *Saturday* and Arnold's "Dover Beach"'. *Partial Answers: Journal of Literature and the History of Ideas* 6.1 (2008): 181–206.

Marston, Philip Bourke. 'Parting with Summer: On Dover Beach'. *The Collected Poems of Philip Bourke Marston*. London: Ward & Lock, 1892. 397.

McEwan, Ian. *Saturday*. London: Cape, 2005.

Mishra, Vijay. 'The Diasporic Imaginary: Theorizing the Indian Diaspora'. *Textual Practice* 10.3 (1996): 421–47.

Monteiro, George. 'Robert Frost's Liberal Imagination'. *The Iowa Review* 28.3 (1998): 104–27.

Nagra, Daljit. *Look We Have Coming to Dover!* London: Faber, 2007.

———. 'Look We Have Coming to Dover!' Nagra, *Look*. 31–2.

———. 'Singh Song!' Nagra, *Look*. 51–3.

O'Gorman, Francis. *Victorian Poetry: An Annotated Anthology*. Malden, MA: Blackwell, 2004.

Radhakrishnan, R. 'Ethnicity in an Age of Diaspora'. 1991. *Theorizing Diaspora: A Reader*. Ed. Jana Evans Braziel and Anita Mannur. Malden, MA: Blackwell, 2003. 119–21.

Roberts, Robin. 'Matthew Arnold's 'Dover Beach', Gender and Science Fiction'. *Extrapolation* 33.3 (1992): 245–57.

Smith, Iain Crichton. 'At a Poetry Reading'. *Ends and Beginnings*. Manchester: Carcanet, 1994. 106–107.

———. 'The Double Man'. *The Literature of Region and Nation*. Ed. R.P. Draper. New York: St. Martin's, 1989. 136–46.

Spranzi, Marta. *The Art of Dialectic between Dialogue and Rhetoric: The Aristotelian Tradition*. Amsterdam: John Benjamins, 2011.

Wickman, Matthew. 'Gaelic Poetry's Province of Stone: Iain Crichton Smith and the Hebridean Echoes of Paul de Man's Late Work'. *Scottish Studies Review* 6.2 (2005): 99–112.

Wordsworth, William. 'After Landing – The Valley of Dover, November 1820'. Wordsworth, *The Collected Poems*. 416.

———. 'At Dover'. Wordsworth, *The Collected Poems*. 416.

———. *The Collected Poems of William Wordsworth*. Hertfordshire: Wordsworth Editions, 1998.

———. 'Composed in the Valley near Dover, on the Day of Landing'. Wordsworth, *The Collected Poems*. 364.

———. 'It is a beauteous evening, calm and free'. Wordsworth, *The Collected Poems*. 306.

———. 'Lines: Composed a Few Miles above Tintern Abbey'. Wordsworth, *The Collected Poems*. 241–3.

———. 'September 1802, near Dover'. Wordsworth, *The Collected Poems*. 364–5.

Chapter 3

'Gripping to a wet rock': Coastal Erosion and the Land-Sea Divide as Existentialist/Ecocritical Tropes in Contemporary British and Irish Fiction

Anne-Julia Zwierlein

Coastal Erosion: British and Irish Coastlines under Threat

'Living on the Edge' (Nicolson); 'The Owners Whose Homes Are Going over a Cliff' (Fryer); 'I can't even relax in bed as I'm certain that it will go in the middle of the night' (Akwagyiram): these are just some samples from UK media coverage of the threat of coastal erosion at the onset of the twenty-first century. Through their dramatic staging of the physical processes of erosion along with their human consequences, these articles become, in a quite literal sense, what Kerridge in the Routledge *Green Studies Reader* has termed 'ecothrillers: environmental cliffhangers'. In 2010, the Environment Agency, a non-departmental public body responsible to the UK Secretary of State for Environment, Food and Rural Affairs, published new long-term predictions until the year 2110 for coastal erosion along the British and Irish coastlines, along with interactive maps which allow users to zoom in on erosion zones in their local area and watch the predicted development over three timescales (see 'Coastal Erosion Maps').

Coastal erosion is caused by factors such as the hydraulic action of waves, abrasion and attrition (see 'Coastal Erosion'). While the phenomenon had been documented throughout history, scientific investigations into erosion proliferated with the advent of nineteenth-century geology, most famously in Lyell's chapter on the 'Action of the Sea on the British Coast' from his *Principles of Geology*, and arguably, the natural process itself has recently accelerated on many stretches of the British and Irish coastline due to climate change. For a sizeable number of people who settled near cliffs once thought safe, worries over coastal erosion have become very serious indeed. In response to this, since 2001 scientists have been compiling the first detailed map of Britain's coastline, using aerial photographs, satellite pictures, and computer technology to build up a 3D model of coastal erosion – while '[t]he traditional techniques [had] involve[d] watching wooden posts falling into the sea to estimate how much the coast is eroding' ('Coastal Erosion: The First UK Map'). As Nicolson reported in *The Guardian* in 2006, 'Britain's coastline has remained more or less intact since the end of the last ice age. But as sea levels rise, erosion is accelerating and more than a million homes are now under threat'. UK government figures corroborate that 'UK coastal waters have warmed by about 0.7 degrees Celsius over the past three decades. … [T]he average sea level around the UK is now about 10 centimetres higher than it was in 1900' ('Effects').

Still Britain's most popular retirement location (see 'Seaside'), the seaside is also a symbolic boundary, which in British and Irish cases is marked by a highly visible coastline composed of cliffs and steep rocky outcrops alternating with more level areas of grassland: the land-sea divide. As part of cultural (and literary) narratives, this symbolic boundary also translates into the nature-culture divide – and, in more specifically political and ideological discourses, it also becomes synonymous with the boundary of Englishness, associated with the island status of Great Britain as described in John of Gaunt's 'famous geographical blunder of England as the "scept'red isle", the "precious stone set in the silver sea"' (Tönnies 226). Discourse about the land-sea divide, in the case of Britain, is ambivalent: on the one hand, national pride reinforces the emblematic status of what the National Trust designates as 'heritage coast', as in the 2007 plea by the then Environment Secretary David Miliband to open up the whole of England's coastline, in the form of freely accessible coastal walks, to the public: 'We are an island nation. The coast is our birthright and everyone should be able to enjoy it' ('Access'). And indeed, at present just over 1,000 kilometres, or 33 per cent, of the English coastline are designated 'heritage coast' and maintained by Natural England and the National Trust (see 'Heritage Coast'). On the other hand, the sea is the 'other' of England: it is where England stops – as Enright describes it in *The Gathering* (2007):

> And there it is: the open tang, the calling, the smell of the sea. Such a miracle, at the end of the Brighton line, with the town stacked behind me, and behind that all the weight of England, in her smoke and light, jammed to a halt here, just here, by the wide smell of the sea. (76–7)

Accordingly, the language used to describe coastal erosion in today's political and cultural discourse is often militaristic: as Nicolson maintains, '[the British] are … living in a fortress defended against the sea'. Discussions abound as to how much of that defence line Britain will be able to keep up – will the stakes be raised, or 'do we abandon what we cannot maintain?' (Nicolson). Cost-benefit analysis requires the value of property under threat to be greater than the cost of protecting it for coastal defence to be economically viable. In the 1990s, the cliff at Birling Gap in East Sussex became a well-known example of the National Trust's 'new orthodoxy of managed retreat' (Nicolson), and while 'the Landmark Trust has begun to spend £900,000 transporting the prominent folly known as Clavell Tower … just 80 feet back from the cliff edge', this 'is a luxury treatment that few other buildings will be afforded' (Nicolson). For almost a decade, spectacular cliff falls on the East Sussex coast and elsewhere have also become, rather predictably, high-scoring hits on YouTube. As Ellie Robinson of the National Trust insists: 'Cities, towns will be defended. But large stretches of the coastline are going to go. The coast is a history of process and change and that is what we all now have to understand' (Nicolson 2006). The British government's 'Shoreline Management Plan', published in 2010–2011, set out a number of possible options for dealing with the effects of erosion, from 'hold[ing] or advanc[ing] the existing shoreline position' ('Coastal Erosion Maps') to 'managed realignment' to 'no active intervention' ('Shoreline'). Indeed, if climate change and global warming are among the factors causing coastal erosion, in this case their consequences, usually too slow for ordinary human perception, can be observed in the here and now.

Victorian 'Ecocriticism': Deep Time versus Local Time on the Beach

In the light of recent ecocritical studies, the case of coastal erosion opens up other issues: the holistic ecosystems approach which sees humans as part of a changing natural environment deliberately includes instances of loss and destruction as natural and inevitable occurrences. Arguably, this perspective on nature originated in the Victorian era. More specifically and with reference to this essay's concern with the cultural symbolisms of the land-sea divide, from the middle of the nineteenth century onwards, the seaside came to figure as setting for a 'deep historical', evolutionary perspective on humankind – as indeed, according to Parham, 'ecology … represents a conjunction of natural history and evolutionary theory' (157; also see Worster). From Mary Anning's fossil finds embedded in a cliff-face at Lyme Regis which provided paleontological evidence for Hutton's *Theory of the Earth* (1788) (see Garrard) – which are also evoked in Fowles's *The French Lieutenant's Woman* (1969) – to Lyell's aforementioned *Principles of Geology*, the coastline started to open up non-anthropocentric vistas into deep time. Significantly, the subtitle to Lyell's study changed in the course of its publication history. The original 1830–1833 subtitle: *being an attempt to explain the former changes of the Earth's surface, by reference to causes now in operation*, with the 9th edition (1853) turned into: *or the Modern Changes of the Earth and its Inhabitants Considered as Illustrative of Geology*. In other words, the title page now advertised explicitly that historical changes in the distribution or phenotypes of the earth's 'Inhabitants' (that is, species of animals) could be seen as indicative of, and caused by, historical changes in their geological habitat – a concept that had been influential in the young Charles Darwin's researches during his voyage on the *Beagle* (1831–1836). Lyell's geological and Darwin's evolutionary biological visions became ubiquitous in mid- to late-Victorian literature, which questioned humankind's position in a universe thus reconceived, famously, in Thomas Hardy, whose 'cliffhanger scene' from *A Pair of Blue Eyes* (1873) can serve as shorthand for the larger issues: Charles Knight here comes face to face with fossilised beings, discovering his connection to the long-lost world of trilobites – 'Separated by millions of years in their lives, Knight and this underling seemed to have met in their place of death' (209).

There are multiple instances in Victorian culture where the land-sea divide similarly emphasises the smallness of human lives against the backdrop of evolutionary time in seaside settings where, due to the erosion of cliffs, geological strata are more immediately visible than in other natural settings. Lyell's observations on the '[a]ction of the sea on the British coast', which survey 'the eastern and southern shores of the British Islands, from our Ultima Thule in Shetland to the Land's End in Cornwall' (Lyell 507) document neutrally and scientifically the powers of tides and currents and their effects on the coastline, including both erosion and the accession of new land (524). Yet Lyell's vivid descriptions of landslips, submerged woods or churchyards laid open in eroding sea-cliffs also acknowledge that there is poetic sublimity to such natural spectacles and emphasise destruction and loss from an anthropocentric perspective, evoking the 'waste' (531), the 'havoc and ruin' (509) and 'annihilation' (534), caused by coastal erosion. Indeed, narrative methods of melodrama and sensationalism are sometimes used in order to represent the distance between the deep and the local timescale, as when Lyell offers glimpses of gravestones or disinterred skeletons protruding from cliff-faces. Numerous seaports, monasteries and churches are recorded in his pages as having been 'blotted out' (525) by the incursions of the sea so that 'no traces … are now perceptible' (535). Like the entire work, this chapter evokes visions of geological 'deep time', sometimes having recourse to living memory, quoting childhood recollections by local eyewitnesses, but more frequently gesturing towards the remote future, speculating that 'in a few centuries … future geologists will learn [about previous coastlines] from historical documents only' (534).

A comparable example of historical 'deep time' vision from pictorial art is the famous Victorian seaside painting by William Dyce, *Pegwell Bay* (1859–1860),[1] which offers a view of barely distinguishable human figures against the overwhelming natural background of its seaside cliffs. While Payne's reading of the painting in this volume argues convincingly that it may in fact convey an affirmation rather than a denial of religious faith, traditionally, 'commentators on the painting have tended to argue that humans and human life are rendered as insignificant, especially in comparison to the vastness of time (as represented by the geological strata of the cliffs) and space (as represented by Donati's Comet, visible in the sky above the cliffs)' (Smith 75). For Pointon, *Pegwell Bay* 'is a painting about time, and especially about the contrast [perhaps not necessarily a pessimistic one] between human time and deep or cosmic time' (42). Moreover, the 'shell collecting activities of the humans in the foreground', inspired by the Victorian amateur fascination with seaside studies, are closely associated, as Smith argues, with those 'lessons of geology and astronomy' (75). Impressed with the seeming insignificance of humans in the scheme of nature, George Eliot, sifting the beach at Ilfracombe in 1856 for biological specimens together with her partner, the scientist G.H. Lewes, perceives the houses of the coastal village, and the humans inhabiting them, as clinging to the rocks like 'a parasitic animal – an epizoon making his abode on the skin of the planetary organism' (Eliot 241–2). Indeed, the beach with its deposits of oceanic life often functions,

---

[1]   See Figure 1.2 in Payne's contribution to this volume.

as Corbin notes in his book on the 'discovery' of the seaside during the Romantic and Victorian eras, as an 'indeterminate place of biological transitions, [where] the links connecting mankind with the mineral, vegetable, and animal kingdoms can be seen with exceptional clarity' (223). Lyell's accounts of the transitional space of the beach, the sheer disorder created by enormous landslips, emphasise once again the huge natural forces involved; he describes 'a confused assemblage of broken strata, and immense blocks of rock, invested with sea-weed and corallines, and scattered over with shells and star-fish, and other productions of the deep' (Lyell 543). By contrast, a famous cartoon from *Punch*, John Leech's 'Common Objects at the Seaside' (1857), treats the disorder of the seaside and the blurring of the species boundary in a more humorous manner, depicting female amateur scientists at the beach looking, in their crinolines, just like the sea anemones for which they search.[2] Humorously or not, nineteenth-century literature and culture thus increasingly use the land-sea divide as a biological and geological trope which, in its strong visuality, questions humankind's uniqueness in the ecological system.

The Land-Sea Divide in Contemporary British and Irish Fiction

Taking up these cues from their Victorian precursors, a considerable number of recent British and Irish novels have staged their discussions of individual and social identity at or near the seaside, using the drama of evolutionary and geological deep time not only to reinforce symbolically the crises in their protagonists' lives but also to offer a larger, strikingly existentialist picture of the West European human condition at the turn of the twenty-first century: Iris Murdoch's *The Sea, The Sea* (1978), Graham Swift's *Last Orders* (1996), John Banville's *The Sea* (2005), Ian McEwan's *On Chesil Beach* (2007) and Anne Enright's *The Gathering* (2007), for instance. However, I will focus primarily on Margaret Drabble's *The Witch of Exmoor* (1996), Colm Tóibín's *The Blackwater Lightship* (1999), Jeanette Winterson's *Lighthousekeeping* (2004) and Graham Swift's *Tomorrow* (2007). In all these novels, the ever-shifting margin between land and sea functions as symbolic catalyst for existential situations, for the probing and unravelling of human relations. As contact zone and frontier, the coast is a 'liminal space' as defined in van Gennep's *Rites of Passage* and later by Turner. Preston-Whyte, too, argues that 'as a place of desire [liminal spaces] offer a "dreamtime" that resonates with spiritual rebirth, transformation, and recuperation. However, transitional states are also places of anxiety replete with darker images of threat and danger' (350).

One main concern of these texts, gesturing back to the scientific upheavals of the Victorian era, is the analysis of humankind's position from an ecological perspective, against the backdrop of huge geological changes taking place over the course of centuries, as described by Lyell. Murdoch, Drabble, Tóibín and Winterson all present their protagonists perched on the edges of cliffs, in houses crumbling

---

2   On this cartoon, whose title echoes 'both Wood's *Common Objects of the Sea-Shore* and Pratt's *Common Things of the Sea-Side*' see Smith 71; also see Stott 160.

into the sea due to coastal erosion, exploiting these images for their combined symbolic and ecocritical potential. All the novels, indeed, oscillate between depicting personal human tragedies and displaying larger perspectives of entropical decline or cyclical processes of birth and death. This interplay of existentialist and ecocritical tropes, I would suggest, can be analysed by inquiring into the texts' ambivalent negotiations between 'deep time' and 'local time' (see Rudwick), or, in more recent ecocritical terminology, 'deep green' and 'anthropocentric' time (Ryle 11). Graham Swift's *Last Orders* (1996), for instance, fuses a concern for the individual with a non-anthropocentric insistence on transitoriness; the famous ending has Jack's ashes thrown to the wind 'on the end of Margate Pier, [looking] across to Dreamland' (Swift, *Last* 294–5), a derelict fun park which in its very shabbiness exposes the futility of escapist seaside dreams. The merging of the human with the non-human, ash with grey sky, grey water and grey horizon, is the key theme, alluding to both Gerard Manley Hopkins's 'That Nature is a Heraclitean Fire and of the Comfort of our Resurrection' (1888) and T.S. Eliot's *The Waste Land* (1922), and the collapse of the pier, bridge between nature and civilisation, symbolically highlights nature's dominance over humankind.

In all the novels, scenes of coastal erosion serve to illustrate the haphazardness and possible meaninglessness of human lives – often re-emphasised by way of shorthand references to evolutionary theory or Darwinism, references which do not, however, amount to systematic remodellings of nineteenth-century evolutionary biology but can rather be explained as twenty-first-century popular cultural versions of what Peckham has termed 'Darwinisticism', that is to say a mixture of ideological reappropriation and rehashing of isolated clichés about Darwin's theory, such as the 'struggle for existence' or the 'survival of the fittest' (see Peckham). What unites these novels' adaptations of, or shorthand allusions to, nineteenth-century geology and evolutionary theory is a deeply felt vision of the transitoriness and possible insignificance of human lives, a vision that should not, however, be confounded with nihilism. Thus the sea's movements are seen by Banville's narrator as 'the great world's shrugs of indifference' (264), and in Tóibín, official attempts to stop erosion are mentioned in passing but declared to be futile (51). Likewise, Banville's protagonist remembers swimming 'between two of the green-slimed concrete groynes that long ago had been thrown out into the sea in a vain attempt to halt the creeping erosion of the beach' (136). The lack of insurance or government compensation for property lost due to 'chronic coastal erosion' is also mentioned by Tóibín as having unsettled the family's life plans in the past (adopting a child was impossible) – and indeed, the phrase 'chronic coastal erosion' (243–4) is also used by the insurance division of NatWest Bank (see Fryer). A recent report by the Joseph Rowntree Foundation suggests that the government's 'Shoreline Management Plan' tends to reinforce the detrimental impact of climate change on 'disadvantaged UK coastal communities' (Zsamboky et al.), and aspects of deprivation and geographic isolation feature prominently in journalistic and fictional representations. Tóibín's novel even links the lack of insurance or government compensation for lost cliff-top property with the idea of human extinction or the individual as genealogical terminus. Moreover, all the novels depict the sheer physical dangerousness of the border between land and sea. In Murdoch's *The Sea, The Sea*, for instance, getting out of the sea again after a swim is a continual challenge, life-threatening and blood-drawing. By collecting stones from rock pools and '[erecting a] border round the edge of the grass', the main character attempts, in vain, to reimpose control and create boundaries with material imported from the unruly sea (260). Finally, death by water, the annihilation of human identity, is a ubiquitous motif in all the novels; Drabble, Winterson and Enright all insist on the fact that drowned bodies are usually 'unrecognisable but for [their] teeth' (Winterson 184; also see Drabble 196, and Enright 10).

Notwithstanding, all of these novels emphasise a vision of the 'stubbornness' of life, the will to survive (Drabble 83; Winterson 6) – vindicating human beings' desire to live and transferring a 'Darwinisticist' idea of the 'struggle for existence' to the individual characters depicted while at the same time blurring the boundaries between human and animal. Charles in *The Sea, The Sea* admires the 'flowers which contrive somehow to root themselves in crannies' (Murdoch 6), and Mike in Swift's *Tomorrow*, before 'being biological' with his wife-to-be Paula, treats her to a lecture about marram grass, 'that wind-blown stuff that grows exclusively on the brows of sand dunes' (78). As Corbin states: 'By the sea, the animal nature hidden in man erupts with particular ferocity' (225), and indeed, the land-sea divide as a setting for Darwinian – or Darwinisticist – competition even among the unborn is a topic throughout: in Winterson, the protagonist's conception is imagined as '[s]hoals of babies [vying] for life. I won' (3); Enright's protagonist, leaving behind the liminal space of the shore where her brother died, feels 'the shadow of a child in me, the swoop of the future in my belly' (205); and in McEwan's novel, Edward meditates, years after the rupture with his bride on their Chesil Beach wedding night, 'what unborn children might [otherwise] have had their chances' (166). As more detailed attention to four of these novels will now reveal, the biological proximity of humans and animals, underlined by the peculiarities of the seaside setting, is depicted as both disconcerting and reassuring.

Drabble, Winterson, Tóibín, Swift: Coastal Erosion versus the 'will to grip'

The symbolism of crumbling cliffs encapsulates the precariousness of the land-sea divide in Margaret Drabble's *The Witch of Exmoor* (1996), which centres on a misanthropic, aging protagonist, Frieda Haxby, who after a successful life as a writer cuts all ties with family and society in order to retire to Ashcombe, a ramshackle former hotel on Exmoor 'about to fall into the sea' (9). Frieda has become a 'man-hater' (23) like Timon of Athens, who in his death was likewise 'entomb'd upon the very hem o'th' sea' (23; see *Timon of Athens* 5.4.66). In a text that has been described as an 'intellectual exercise' rather than a novel (Sellers; as quoted in Lorenz 58), Drabble mixes Frieda's disgust with capitalism, commercialism and pollution, and her concern for animal rights that makes her anticipate J.M. Coetzee's Elizabeth Costello in *The Lives of Animals* (1999), with philosophical meditations about the 'just society'. Drowning – whether accidentally or voluntarily – is a leitmotif in the novel, linked to the utopian wish '[t]o float free of all this, to begin again' (20).

In her isolated situation on the cliff, however, Frieda has escaped human society in order to be confronted with something more primitive and visceral: the Darwinian struggle for existence, termed by Darwin himself in his *The Origin of Species* (1859), with reference to the 'high geometrical ratio of [the] increase [of] all organic beings throughout the world' and political economy's teachings about population dynamics, 'the doctrine of Malthus, applied to the whole animal and vegetable kingdom' (Darwin 6). Writing her memoirs at the seaside, thus trying 'to salvage her own self' (69), Frieda is also, on a much more mundane level, using her natural surroundings to supply her with food. Here she is confronted by beings of a lower kind whose tenacious grip on life far surpasses her own, like Murdoch's 'flowers … root[ing] themselves in crannies' (6) and Swift's marram grass. These encounters are featured as archaic confrontations between hunter and hunted; observing the scarce 'forms of simple seashore life [that] have colonized [the stony shoreline]' (83), Frieda collects resisting, 'stubborn' (83) mussels on the seaside rocks, with bleeding hands:

> Blood and sea-salt mingle. She hacks, and curses. She has broken a mussel shell, and its living body is exposed. She pulls it away from its rock and a lump of its flesh seems to leap from its crushed dwelling place and attach itself like a leech to her bare and bleeding hand. Horrified, she tries to brush off the clinging fragment, but it sticks. It is fierce and hopeful. It will not die. Its flesh seeks a home on her flesh. She scrapes it off with the knife, and it falls vanquished on to the pale purple rock. (83–4)

Here the novel taps into the Victorian contemplation of ecocritical 'deep time' by having Frieda meditate on the laws of evolution, considering her own past life as nothing more than 'an evolutionary trick, a spasm of self gripping to a wet rock' (135):

> She thinks of the laws of living and the laws of dying, of that severed blob of orange flesh from the sea that had clung to hers. So tenacious, so unformed. And here she is, so complex, and so tired. She has lost that simple will to grip. … We were born without meaning, we struggled without meaning, we met and married and loved and hated without meaning. We are accidents. All our passions are arbitrary, trivial, a game of hazard. (135–6)

Moreover, Frieda associates her exile on the cliff with Napoleon's on St Helena – another seaside location where the ousted emperor, according to her interpretation of a Turner painting, was similarly confronted by a meaningless nature, 'staring at an ill-placed, an improbable and outsized rock limpet' (136).

Eventually, 'stick or leap' seems the only remaining alternative (260), and, like several other characters in the novel, Frieda chooses death by drowning, defiantly seeking out danger instead of shunning it. Or was it an accident – did she slip when picking mushrooms on the cliffside? In any case, her death finds a glorious parallel in an old legend about a nearby coastal headland, 'Hindspring Point', where a deer had allegedly, in order to escape its hunters, 'with three mighty leaps ... bounded down the cliff into the sea' (259). In tune with Frieda's ambiguous death, the equally ambiguous ending, set on the beach below her old mansion, presents either her grandchildren's double suicide or their courageous leap to safety and a new and better life (275–6; also see Lorenz 64).

Contrasting a Freudian death-drive, symbolically reinforced by the vastness of geological time as seen against the backdrop of the land-sea divide, with a tenacious will to survive or 'Darwinisticist' struggle for existence (which, however, is transferred to individual characters, especially the protagonist, and dissociated from the long-term perspective of species evolution), Jeanette Winterson's novel *Lighthousekeeping* (2004) similarly oscillates around the poles of fixity and fluidity, insisting on the impermanence of identity – 'My life is a trail of shipwrecks and set-sails. There are no arrivals, no destinations' (127) – but also emphasising the necessity for 'anchors' (21), for 'navigation points' (102), indeed, for lighthouses: 'The sea moves constantly, the lighthouse, never' (17). The lighthouse at Cape Wrath that served as a model was erected in 1828 by Robert Stevenson, grandfather of the late-Victorian writer Robert Louis Stevenson, whose works feature as a prominent intertext; the name 'Cape Wrath' derives from a Norse word for 'turning point', a fact whose metaphorical potential Winterson exploits throughout. The novel's present-day protagonist, named 'Silver' (5) after Long John Silver of Stevenson's *Treasure Island* (1883), lives with her mother in a house cut steeply into the cliff above the town Salts. The mother dies in the act of saving her daughter when both fall off the precipice. Silver manages, with 'bleeding fingers' (7), to 'hang ... on to one of [their] spiny shrubs ..., a salty shrub that could withstand the sea and the blast' (6–7) – again, faced with the greater capacity for survival of lower life forms. Living for a while in the lighthouse with its keeper, ancient Pew, she is stranded again when it is mechanised, 'as indeed it was in 1998' (Andermahr 146).

The nineteenth-century subplot centres around Babel Dark, a parson who has encounters with Robert Louis Stevenson and Charles Darwin. Living a double life like Jekyll and Hyde, one with his wife, one with his mistress, 'Babel Dark's split personality and his struggle between scientific and religious world views' are central to the plot (Andermahr 149). Unsurprisingly, Darwin's ideas are linked to the theme of survival, but they also gesture towards the interconnections between species, things and people, again reflected in the land-sea divide, Corbin's 'indeterminate place of biological transitions' (223), as is evident when *Lighthousekeeping* evokes the famous cliff-hanger scene from Hardy's *A Pair of Blue Eyes*, mentioned above: as he attempts to save his dog, who has fallen down a cliff, Babel is suddenly confronted, like Charles Knight, by the 'wall of [a] cave ... made entirely of fossils' (116):

> He looked at the dark sea-stained wall, but how could the sea have reached here? Not since the Flood. He knew the earth was 4,000 years old, according to the Bible.

> ... He put his fingers to his mouth, tasted sea and salt. He tasted the tang of
> time.
>   Then, for no reason at all, he felt lonely.
>   ... He had always believed in a stable-state system, made by God, and left
> alone afterwards. That things might be endlessly moving and shifting was not
> his wish. ... Darwin tried to console him. 'It is not less wonderful or beautiful or
> grand, this world you blame on me. Only, it is less comfortable'. Dark shrugged.
> Why would God make a world so imperfect that it must be continually rightening
> itself? It made him feel seasick ... knowing that the fight in him was all about
> keeping control, when his hands were bloodless with gripping so tight. (117–20)

As with Murdoch's protagonist, the 'tight grip' he tries to retain on his life is linked metaphorically to the Darwinian struggle for survival and to the coastal setting, evoking an image of humanity's hands clutching the rocks in a desperate bid for safety. Indeed, after losing his mistress and true love, Babel's psychological decline is metaphorically linked to the erosion he observes on the coast – 'the cliffs were worn away at the base' (188). Lacking the paradoxical tenacity of his fossils, he, too, finally chooses death by water. In fact, the initially comforting image from his favourite hymn of Christ's love as a 'rock' onto which his church is 'fastened' (121) is now associated first with the dead fossils fixed to the cliff, then with the sea village, Salts, clinging to the rocks in what George Eliot would have seen as a parasitical position and, finally, 'transformed into a pagan counter-image of ... everlasting torment: "Fastened to the rock. And he thought of Prometheus, chained to his rock for stealing fire from the gods"' (Onega 219).[3]

Coastal erosion, evoking the ecocritical vision of 'deep time', is the dominant metaphor of Colm Tóibín's *The Blackwater Lightship* (1999), set in Tóibín's home county of Wexford, Ireland. The action of natural forces, of currents and tides, is here depicted with a precision that evokes Lyell's *Principles of Geology*; Tóibín's long, poetic descriptive passages also share Lyell's sense of the sublime and, at the same time, of the human and historical losses involved. His plot revolves around three generations of women, estranged by hurtful events buried in the family's past and reunited in the grandmother's house on the coast because Declan, their brother, son and grandson, is dying from AIDS. As Ruth Padel in a September 1999 *Independent* interview with Tóibín has it, they are 'try[ing] and often fail[ing] to understand each other, fitfully illuminated by staring across the dark, estranging, loss-filled sea between'. The title focuses on a lightship, a permanently moored ship with light beacons, established in 1857 and 'taken out of commission by Irish Lights' in 1968; Tuskar lighthouse across the bay is still in operation and is mentioned in the novel as well (191).

Grandmother Dora's derelict house is situated perilously close to a crumbling cliff; a neighbour's house has already partly fallen into the sea. The 'walk' to the beach is rather a climb and a run: 'there was always too much loose sand at the bottom' (50), and Dora is plagued by perpetual fears about people's cars rolling over the cliff (49; 138). The Irish big-house theme is here combined with

---

3   Onega quotes from Winterson 121.

the symbolic erosion of a family. The human psyche is described in geological metaphors, as when Helen sees the hurts of the past as 'eating away at me all these years' (211). AIDS, the disease that comes in waves and erodes Declan's body, and their father's death from cancer when they were children, are likewise connected to the natural spectacle on the coast (216). The novel ends on a note of reconciliation – even though Declan's imminent death has to be accepted by all, and even though the view of the eroding cliffs and the land-sea divide, with its intimations of a prevalence of nature over culture, for a while reinforces the 'hardness in [Helen's] heart against the world' (260), yet:

> Imaginings and resonances and pain and small longings and prejudices. They meant nothing against the resolute hardness of the sea. They meant less than the marl and the mud and the dry clay of the cliff that were eaten away by the weather, washed away by the sea. It was not just that they would fade: they hardly existed, ... they would have no impact on this cold dawn, this deserted remote seascape. ... It might have been better, she felt, if there never had been people, if this turning of the world, and the glistening sea, and the morning breeze happened without witnesses, without anyone feeling, or remembering, or dying, or trying to love. She stood at the edge of the cliff until the sun came out from behind the black rainclouds. (260)

While the backdrop of eroding cliffs diminishes the importance of human experience, as Helen's more pessimistic self sees it – similar to traditional readings of Dyce's *Pegwell Bay* – the motif of erosion also acquires more hopeful connotations in the novel's metaphorical web: identified by Persson as a 'coming out novel' (150) concentrating on Declan's homosexuality and that of his friends Paul and Larry who come to watch over him at the seaside, the novel arguably confronts the nuclear family model of 'middle-class suburbia' (160), 'the very foundation of Catholic Ireland' (161), with other life models. The seaside thus also functions as the setting for 'confessions'; here 'the characters share crucial memories from their past: Paul talks about his relationship, Helen about her father's death and Lily remembers the story of Tuskar Lighthouse and the Blackwater Lightship' (Persson 166). The liminal space of the land-sea divide facilitates more intense (and perhaps more honest) self-analyses, as the protagonists are reduced to an existentialist mode dissociated from the professional routine of their urban lives. Paul's work for the European Commission and Larry's profession – he is an architect – are, likewise, perhaps too obviously, symbolic; according to Persson, 'new structures can be built inside or on top of old ones. Furthermore, a sense of change is strongly felt in the repeated references to ... erosion ... [T]he landscape ... is bound to change, as are attitudes' (Persson 166). At least according to this reading, erosion here becomes a symbol for the crumbling of prejudices, for a positive process of change.

The land-sea divide and its reduction of the human in scale and importance in Graham Swift's *Tomorrow* (2007), my last example, likewise allows for more hopeful connotations: the sea is life-threatening but also a place of new beginnings. The novel is told in a monologue by Paula, mother of two, lying in bed awake before a crucial day of revelation. Focusing on the family secret of artificial insemination about to be revealed to the twins, now sixteen, she meditates, like Drabble's Frieda, on nature's indifference, the sheer haphazardness of existence in terms of the evolutionary scale: 'nature is colossally wasteful. For every life that makes it, a staggering number of potential lives are lost. There may be millions of us walking around, but we are all extraordinary little exceptions' (98). She opposes to this the paradoxical fact that her children 'were really *meant*' (98; emphasis in original), contrasting, as far as her husband Mike is concerned, biological with spiritual parenthood. He may have a low sperm count, but he has been a father to his children, and he is, coincidentally, editor of a biology magazine called *The Living World*.

Indeed, the land-sea divide, catalysing eruptions of 'the animal nature hidden in man … with particular ferocity' (Corbin 225), had been a leitmotif of their life together: Paula and Mike's relationship started by the sea in Brighton – 'The ship of our future … was launched that day (43) – and later Mike proposed to Paula in the dunes near Craiginish during sexual intercourse, another moment of primitive ritual initiation which aligns them with the animal world on the beach and which is catalysed by the proximity of the land-sea divide: 'Second birthdays definitely occur, lives begin all over again' (44).[4] The novel's central and most highly symbolised instance of a 'second birthday' takes place in Cornwall a few years later, when their children, hiding in a little cave at the end of a line of rocks leading out into the sea, are surprised by the tide coming in. In danger of drowning, they have to be rescued by Mike, and the novel's testing of biological versus spiritual paternity seems to be resolved: 'how could that man not have been your father?' (195). Moreover, this 'second birth' had been prepared earlier when Paula remembered thinking that the twins' birth was like their escaping from 'some hidey-hole together' (208), anticipating the seaside cave that nearly cost them their lives. The blood drawn from the twins' shins and knees when they are pulled up out of the water by their frantic mother also evokes their biological birth – and the Darwinian or rather 'Darwinisticist' struggle for existence, once more transferred from the diachronic scale of species evolution to the individual lives at the centre of the novel's plot. Still, there is an even more fundamental connection at this climactic moment between the symbolic 'birthing' process and the 'will to grip' of primitive life forms which the family encounter as they are clinging to the rocks' edge: 'under the lip of the ledge, just beneath the glinting waterline, there were clusters of barnacles, little clenched, packed shells, tresses and twirls of swaying seaweed, a whole world of gripping life' (213). Again, as in the other novels surveyed here, the liminal space between water and land offers a vivid picture of the instinct for survival shared by humans and animals, and thus it also evokes evolutionary deep time, embedding the concerns of local time and individual fates in a much larger picture.

---

[4]   See the echo in Paula's exclamation '"Yes", I said. "Oh yes, yes, yes"' of Molly's concluding words in Joyce's *Ulysses* (1922), recalling her acceptance of Bloom's marriage proposal.

Conclusion

While not qualifying as 'environmentally oriented work[s]' on all the counts of Lawrence Buell's checklist, first and foremost among these being that 'the nonhuman environment is present not merely as a framing device but as a presence that begins to suggest that human history is implicated in natural history' (Head 237; with reference to Buell 179), the four novels analysed here definitely foreground natural processes, using them as much more than just a backdrop for human affairs. Indeed, they often question explicitly any kind of anthropocentric perspective, as, for instance, in McEwan's novel, where the beach becomes the site of blurred identities, people 'flickering and dissolving at [their] outlines' (139), or as in Winterson's novel, whose protagonist sees life as a short 'stretch of sea and sand, [a brief] walk on the shore, before the tide covers everything we have done' (232). Thus these novels integrate the diachronic visions of both nineteenth-century evolutionary biology and geology, sharing both Darwin's and Lyell's *longue durée* perspectives which envisage life 'in a few centuries' as an integral part of their scientific conceptualisations (Lyell 534). But simultaneously the novels' depictions of the 'struggle for existence' remain 'Darwinisticist', in Peckham's sense of the term, by reducing these collective processes to the level of individual fates and characters; again, the images of the land-sea divide are also used, in quite a traditional way, as symbols of and catalysts for individual human development. Indeed, this is hardly avoidable, as the term 'nature' is always a discursive term and never 'simply' a material space and place. Thus in the realms of discourse, 'social relations [or] differentiations between subjects … are being proposed' through the depiction of 'natural' space (Ryle 12). As Head argues, 'the represented landscape becomes a text in which human interaction with the environment is indelibly recorded: it follows that a Green materialist reading of this inner text cannot divorce the social from the natural' (236). In order to be meaningful in representation, environmental deep time needs local time, and deep green readings seem to be impossible without the foil of anthropocentrism. Erosion zones, in other words, need the 'Homes Going over a Cliff', or the protruding skeletons.

Throughout, we have been concerned at least implicitly with recent ecocritical discussions of whether humans are part of a holistic natural system and thus 'naturally' subject to environmental change, and to what extent it is legitimate to figure such change as 'loss', or even more drastically as the 'havoc and ruin' that Lyell evokes (509). Yet what about changes induced by humans themselves? Rarely do the novels address that question; there is no conclusive differentiation between the 'natural' forces of currents and tides as described in the *Principles of Geology* and, for instance, the possibility of twentieth- and twenty-first-century human-induced phenomena such as climate change. Rather, the novels we have been looking at use the liminality of their seaside settings to provide, not for the first time in Western cultural history, 'a solid test of civilization, whose presence is hollow' (Corbin 224). They exploit the symbolic potential of coastal erosion to illustrate the futility of human endeavours; and, at the same time, as symbols of the human potential for perseverance, they emphasise the tenacious 'grip' on life of primitive coastal flora and fauna such as the 'stubborn' seaweed (Drabble 83; Winterson 6) or the barnacles that Darwin himself had studied so enthusiastically. In recent years, both crime and science-fiction writing have picked up on the metaphor of erosion in order to sensationalise the post-human or localise deep time: Elly Griffiths's crime novel *The House at Seas End* (2011) features a forensic archaeologist investigating the discovery, due to coastal erosion, of bodies dating from the Second World War (along with other buried secrets). While the bleak, eroding north Norfolk coast here becomes 'a metaphor for the decay of human sympathy' (Forshaw), Ian Creasey's science-fiction story 'Erosion' meditates about the 'scars' (8) of erosion on the Yorkshire coast, zooming in on derelict benches with paradoxical 'commemorative plaques' (10) that are ranged along a crumbling and disappearing cliff-top path. What we encounter in such cultural representations, in more or less strongly Darwinian, or Darwinisticist terms, are intimations of human extinction and the 'blurred boundaries between human and animal' that had begun to disquiet Victorians (Stott 178): potential extinction, staged through liminal life-and-death situations and post-human scenarios, set against a backdrop of coastal erosion.

Works Cited

'"Access All Areas" Plan for English Coast'. *UK Directgov* 19 June 2007. Web. 5 Aug. 2014. <http://webarchive.nationalarchives.gov.uk/+/www.direct.gov.uk/en/Nl1/Newsroom/DG_068655>.

Akwagyiram, Alexis. 'Villagers Living on the Edge'. *BBC News* 20 Oct. 2004. Web. 10 Aug. 2009. <http://news.bbc.co.uk/2/hi/uk_news/3755624.stm>.

Andermahr, Sonya. 'Jeanette Winterson's *Lighthousekeeping*'. *British Fiction Today*. Ed. Philip Tew and Rod Mengham. London: Continuum, 2006. 139–50.

Banville, John. *The Sea*. London: Picador, 2005.

Buell, Lawrence. *The Environmental Imagination: Thoreau, Nature Writing, and the Formation of American Culture*. Cambridge, MA: Harvard UP, 1995.

'Coastal Erosion'. *BBC Learning*. Web. 5 Aug. 2014. <http://www.bbc.co.uk/schools/ gcsebitesize/geography/coasts/coastal_processes_rev3.shtml>.

'Coastal Erosion Maps'. *Environment Agency*. Web. 25 May 2014. <http://apps.environment-agency.gov.uk/wiyby/134808.aspx>.

'Coastal Erosion: The First UK Map'. *BBC News* 6 Aug. 2001. Web. 10 Aug. 2009. <http://news.bbc.co.uk/2/hi/science/nature/1475905.stm>.

Coetzee, J. M. *The Lives of Animals*. Ed. Amy Gutmann. Princeton: Princeton UP, 1999.

Corbin, Alain. *The Lure of the Sea: The Discovery of the Seaside in the Western World 1750–1840*. Trans. Jocelyn Phelps. London: Penguin, 1988.

Creasey, Ian. 'Erosion'. *Maps of the Edge*. Leipzig: Amazon Distribution, 2011. 7–22.

Darwin, Charles. *The Origin of Species*. Ed. Gillian Beer. Oxford: Oxford UP, 1996.

Drabble, Margaret. *The Witch of Exmoor*. London: Penguin, 1996.

'Effects of Climate Change'. *UK Directgov*. Web. 5 Aug. 2014. <http:// webarchive. nationalarchives.gov.uk/20121015000000/http://www.direct.gov. uk/en/Environmentandgreenerliving/Thewiderenvironment/Climatechange/ DG_072929>.

Eliot, George. 'Journal, Ilfracombe, 8 May–26 June 1856'. *The George Eliot Letters*. Ed. Gordon S. Haight. Vol. 2. New Haven: Yale UP, 1956. 250.

Enright, Anne. *The Gathering*. New York: Black Cat, 2007.

Forshaw, Barry. '*The House at Sea's End*, by Elly Griffiths: Digging up some Well-Worn Thrills'. *The Independent* 19 Jan. 2011. Web. 25 May 2014. <http:// www.independent.co.uk/arts-entertainment/books/reviews/the-house-at-seas-end-by-elly-griffiths-2187779.html>.

Fryer, Jane. 'Living on the Edge: The Owners Whose Homes Are Going over a Cliff'. *The Daily Mail* 11 July 2008. Web. 24 Nov. 2012. <http://www. dailymail.co.uk/ femail/article-1034456/Living-edge-The-owners-homes-going-cliff.html>.

Garrard, Greg. 'From Dover to Chesil Beach: Ian McEwan at the Seaside'. 2011. Web. 5 Aug. 2014. <http://www.academia.edu/1598886/From_Dover_to_ Chesil_Beach_Ian_ McEwan_at_the_Seaside>.

Gennep, Arnold, van. *The Rites of Passage*. Trans. Monika B. Vizedom and Gabrielle L. Caffee. Chicago: U of Chicago P, 1960.

Griffiths, Elly. *The House at Sea's End. Some Secrets Just Won't Stay Buried*. London: Quercus, 2011.

Hardy, Thomas. *A Pair of Blue Eyes*. Ed. Alan Manford. Oxford: Oxford UP, 1985.

Head, Dominic. 'Ecocriticism and the Novel'. *The Green Studies Reader: From Romanticism to Ecocriticism*. Ed. Laurence Coupe. London: Routledge, 2000. 235–41.

'Heritage Coast'. *Heritage Coast*. Web. 10 Aug. 2009. <http://www.heritagecoast. org/ Content/default.asp>.

Kerridge, Richard. 'Ecothrillers: Environmental Cliffhangers'. *The Green Studies Reader: From Romanticism to Ecocriticism*. Ed. Laurence Coupe. London: Routledge, 2000. 242–9.

Lorenz, Paul H. 'The Interplay of Past and Present in Margaret Drabble's *The Witch of Exmoor*'. *Publications of the Mississippi Philological Association*, 1999. 57–64.

Lyell, Charles. *Principles of Geology, or the Modern Changes of the Earth and its Inhabitants Considered as Illustrative of Geology*. Vol. 1. London: John Murray, 1872.

McEwan, Ian. *On Chesil Beach*. 2007. London: Vintage, 2008.

Murdoch, Iris. *The Sea, The Sea*. 1978. London: Vintage, 1999.

Nicolson, Adam. 'Living on the Edge'. *The Guardian* 9 Oct. 2006. Web. 10 Aug. 2009. <http://www.guardian.co.uk/environment/2006/oct/09/ethicalliving.life andhealth>.

Onega, Susana. *Jeanette Winterson*. Manchester: Manchester UP, 2006.

Padel, Ruth. 'Interview with Colm Tóibín'. *The Independent* Sept. 1999. Web. 5 Aug. 2014. <http://www.ruthpadel.com/talking-to-colm-toibin>.

Parham, John. 'Was there a Victorian Ecology?' *The Environmental Tradition in English Literature*. Ed. John Parham. Aldershot: Ashgate, 2002. 156–71.

Peckham, Morse. 'Darwinism and Darwinisticism'. *Victorian Studies* 3 (1959): 3–40.

Persson, Åke. '"Do your folks know you're gay?" Memory and Oral History as Education and Resistance in Colm Tóibín's *The Blackwater Lightship*'. *Recovering Memory: Irish Representations of Past and Present*. Ed. Hedda Friberg, Irene Gilsenan Nordin and Lene Yding Pedersen. Cambridge: Cambridge Scholars, 2007. 150–166.

Pointon, Marcia. *William Dyce, 1806–64: A Critical Biography*. Oxford: Oxford UP, 1979.

Preston-Whyte, Robert. 'The Beach as a Liminal Space'. *A Companion to Tourism*. Ed. Alan A. Lew, C. Michael Hall, and Allan M. Williams. Oxford: Blackwell, 2004. 349–59.

Rudwick, Martin J.S. *Worlds before Adam: The Reconstruction of Geohistory in the Age of Reform*. Chicago: U of Chicago P, 2008.

Ryle, Martin. 'After "Organic Community": Ecocriticism, Nature, and Human Nature'. *The Environmental Tradition in English Literature*. Ed. John Parham. Aldershot: Ashgate, 2002. 11–23.

'Seaside Town "Top" for Retirement'. *BBC News* 29 March 2006. Web. 10 Aug. 2009. <http://news.bbc.co.uk/2/hi/uk_news/england/4853318.stm>.

Sellers, Frances Stead. 'A Cauldron of Troubles'. *The Washington Post* 5 Oct. 1997. Web. 5 Aug. 2014. <http://www.washingtonpost.com/wp-srv/style/longterm/books/reviews/ witchofexmoor.htm>.

'Shoreline Management Plan Policies – What Do They Mean?' *Environment Agency*. Web. 25 May 2014. <http://apps.environment-agency.gov.uk/wiyby/134834.aspx>.

Smith, Jonathan. *Charles Darwin and Victorian Visual Culture*. Cambridge: Cambridge UP, 2006.

Stott, Rebecca. 'Darwin's Barnacles: Mid-Century Victorian Natural History and the Marine Grotesque'. *Transactions and Encounters: Science and Culture in the Nineteenth Century*. Ed. Roger Luckhurst and Josephine McDonagh. Manchester: Manchester UP, 2002. 151–81.

Swift, Graham. *Last Orders*. London: Picador, 1996.

———. *Tomorrow*. London: Picador, 2007.

Tóibín, Colm. *The Blackwater Lightship*. London: Picador, 1999.

Tönnies, Merle. 'Foregrounding Boundary Zones: Martin Parr's Photographic (De-)Construction of Englishness'. *Landscape and Englishness*. Ed. Robert Burden and Stephan Kohl. Amsterdam: Rodopi, 2006. 225–41.

Turner, Victor. *The Ritual Process: Structure and Antistructure*. New York: PAJ Publications, 1969.

Winterson, Jeanette. *Lighthousekeeping: A Novel*. London: Harvest, 2004.

Worster, Donald. *Nature's Economy: A History of Ecological Ideas*. Cambridge: Cambridge UP, 1985.

Zsamboky, Mary, et al. 'Impact of Climate Change on Disadvantaged UK Coastal Communities'. *Joseph Rowntree Foundation* 2011. Web. 25 May 2014. <http://www.jrf.org.uk/sites/files/jrf/impacts-climate-change-disadvantages-communities-EBOOK.pdf>.

Chapter 4
Shorelines:
Littoral Landscapes in the Poetry of Michael Longley and Robert Minhinnick

Neal Alexander

Between land and sea is the beach, an ambiguous littoral zone in which elemental forces – rocks, water, air, sun – are in constant interanimation. According to the physical geographer Cuchlaine King, '[a] beach is one of the most variable of land forms. It can be there one day and gone the next' (3). To write about the beach, and other kinds of littoral landscapes, then, is to be attuned to the temporalities of such places and their characteristic changeability. It is also to recognise their at-least-dual status as material environments and cultural images. Noting the sensory richness of our encounters with the beach, Yvonne Rydin comments on its function as a conceptual border or boundary: 'A boundary between water and land, but also between the everyday and the holiday, the domestic and the natural, the stable and the shifting, the safe and the dangerous' (153). It is this manifestation of littoral landscapes, their role as physical and metaphorical boundaries, that I propose to explore in this essay. In particular, I want to try to read the multiple significations of the shoreline between land and sea as they are articulated in the poetry of Michael Longley and Robert Minhinnick.

Shorelines

As a place, the shoreline has an irreducibly ambivalent character, for it is perpetually in a state of *dis*placement, moving its position and altering its shape in response to the unceasing motions of the tide. In fact, it is precisely this mobile, fluid character that, paradoxically, defines the shore as the particular kind of place that it is. In ecological terms, the rapidly and constantly changing conditions of the seashore help to make it a site of particularly rich biological and environmental diversity.[1] In cultural terms, it is a meeting place for diverse and often divergent significations. Walking alone on Sandymount Strand in the third chapter of James Joyce's *Ulysses*, Stephen Dedalus reads the littoral landscape in terms of its historical and linguistic accretions, as a text composed in shifting and

---

[1]   See for example Hayward's *A Natural History of the Seashore* or Yonge's *The Sea Shore*. However, under extreme circumstances, this fluidity of the shore can lead to its eventual destruction; see Weik von Mossner in this volume.

unstable layers. 'These heavy sands are language tide and wind have silted here', he thinks to himself (37). The shoreline is, for Stephen, a place of 'ineluctable modality' (Joyce 31), of a contingency that is nonetheless given and inescapable: in this protean landscape, 'what does not change / is the will to change' (Olson line 1). It is also a space of multiple, overlapping inscriptions: 'Signatures of all things I am here to read, seaspawn and seawrack, the nearing tide, that rusty boot. Snotgreen, bluesilver, rust: coloured signs' (Joyce 31). In the course of the chapter, Stephen's thoughts shuttle from meditations on sensory perception and the vagaries of space-time to memories of his dead mother and an imaginative reconstruction of Ireland's successive waves of invasion, conquest and resistance. In all cases, his location on the beach is symbolically crucial, for in this liminal zone, land and sea meet in an ongoing process of accumulation and erosion that provides a model for the contrary movements of thought and history. Appropriately, Joyce's symbolic representative for this landscape of continual change is the mythical shape-shifter Proteus, who embodies a condition of flux that Stephen discovers at the heart of the apparently solid material world (see Budgen 48–50).

Joyce's representation of the shoreline as a place of dynamic equilibrium finds its echo in the words of the naturalist Rachel Carson. In *The Edge of the Sea* (1955), she writes of 'the interchangeability of land and sea in this marginal world of the shore', which prompts 'an awareness of the past and of the continuing flow of time' (6). As Carson acknowledges, the shoreline is a definite and yet inconstant boundary, varying between tides, and the beach itself is an unstable, shifting zone that is neither land nor sea. It is a space that is full of time, characterised by movement and transience, exemplifying Massey's point that the 'event' of place should be conceived as 'a constellation of processes rather than a thing' (141). In what follows, I will show how poems by Longley and Minhinnick depict the shoreline as an eventful place of flux and rhythmic continuities. In doing so, I hope also to reveal the possibilities and limitations of an ecocritical reading of their work, for both poets are centrally concerned with the relations between nature and culture, humans and the non-human world. The border zone of the shoreline functions as a particularly significant symbolic space in their texts; but it is also the shifting ground upon which Longley and Minhinnick often explore their respective ideas of 'home'. I argue that, in their different ways, poems by Longley and Minhinnick problematise the Heideggerian discourse of 'dwelling' that is current in much contemporary environmental criticism.

Dwelling and Displacement

The idea of dwelling does not only entail a particular conception of the relationship between self and place, human agents and the natural environment; it encapsulates an ideal and authentic mode of being. '"Dwelling" is not a transient state', writes Garrard, 'rather, it implies the long-term imbrication of humans in a landscape of memory, ancestry and death, of ritual, life and work' (*Ecocriticism* 108). Dwelling bespeaks permanence and continuity, grounding identity in the community's customary ties to place. Moreover, place is conceived as stable, familiar and intimately knowable, permitting an ideally unmediated encounter between people and their native landscapes. The origins of these influential ideas can be traced to the work of Heidegger, for whom dwelling manifests itself as essential to 'the basic character of human existence' ('Poetically' 213).[2] The earliest formulation of this principle occurs in Heidegger's *Sein und Zeit* in 1927, where dwelling describes the situated character of human existence, understood as Being-in-the-world. 'The expression "*bin*"', Heidegger argues, 'is connected with "*bei*, and so "*ich bin*" [I am] means in its turn "I reside" or "dwell alongside" the world, as that which is familiar to me in such and such a way' (*Being* 80). Much later in the same text, Heidegger offers a characterization of inauthentic 'curiosity' as 'never dwelling anywhere': 'In never dwelling anywhere, Being-there is everywhere and nowhere' (398). Without any firm grounding in place, Being cannot assume its authentic character for identity is both estranged and displaced.

The intrinsic connection between Being and being-in-place, and between 'dwelling' and 'authenticity', that is posited in *Being and Time* is developed in much greater detail in several late essays, where the concept of dwelling is also given greater prominence. In 'Building, Dwelling, Thinking', Heidegger further cements the etymological correspondences between Being and dwelling and espouses an essentially sedentary ideal for human relations to place. To dwell, he affirms, is 'to remain, to stay in place' (144): 'To say that mortals *are* is to say that *in dwelling* they persist through spaces by virtue of their stay among things and locations' (155; emphases in original). It is in this way that what Heidegger calls '*the fourfold*' (148; emphasis in original) of earth and sky, divinities and mortals may be brought together in '*primal* oneness' (147; emphasis in original). Dwelling thus concerns the kind of rooted being that may overcome difference and disparity, promoting a mode of mutual coexistence founded upon simple unity. Yet the emphasis placed upon continuity, authenticity and oneness in Heidegger's conception of dwelling should give us pause, for, as Garrard notes, it is precisely in these aspects that it shares some resemblance with 'the 'blood and soil' (*Blut und Boden*) ideology of National Socialism' ('Heidegger' 168; see also Bambach). There are, then, obvious political dangers attendant upon such naturalizations of identity in community and place, as well as evident critical attractions.

The appeal of Heidegger's work for many ecocritics derives in part from his claim that to dwell is 'to save the earth' ('Building' 148), but it is also strengthened by the prominent role he assigns to poetry in disclosing 'the very nature of dwelling' ('Poetically' 225). Indeed, for Heidegger, poetry is not really concerned with transcendence or personal expression; rather, it is concerned with grounding human existence in sensuous and responsible engagements in material reality: 'Poetry is what first brings man onto the earth, making him belong to it, and thus brings him into dwelling' ('Poetically' 216). Jonathan Bate presents the most fully developed version of this Heideggerian strand of ecocriticism in his book,

---

2   For a helpful discussion of 'dwelling' in Heidegger's philosophy, see Malpas, *Heidegger's* 74–83.

The Song of the Earth, which sets out an account of what he calls 'ecopoetics'. His definition of ecopoetics follows Heidegger closely in equating the proper relationship of people and place with dwelling, and dwelling with authenticity. 'Ecopoetics asks in what respects a poem may be a making (Greek *poiesis*) of the dwelling-place', he explains, going on to note that 'the prefix eco- is derived from Greek *oikos*, "the home or place of dwelling"' (75; emphases in original). Moreover, because building and dwelling are essentially synonymous, poetry is itself a mode of dwelling, of remaining in place.

Bate is canny enough, however, to recognise that the very medium of poetry, language, poses a problem for this formulation, because the signifying function of language distances and differentiates, opening a gap between the signifier and the signified, sign and referent. As a result of this divide created by language, '[t]he poet is often more vagrant than dweller, for he finds his home in the *logos* and not in the *oikos*' (149; emphases in original). The cultural function of language thus effects a kind of alienation of humankind from the natural world which is its (natural) home, and some of the most interesting passages of Bate's book are devoted to the problem of speaking for or on behalf of the environment. However, his conviction that this rift must be bridged leads Bate to reaffirm the intrinsically referential function of language and to argue that, as poetry, language can make the world present in all its phenomenological immediacy. Thus, through the literary image, 'oneness with the world can be experienced directly' (154), and this is possible because poetry is conceived as 'an experiencing of the world, not a description of it' (167). And the experience that really matters here is 'dwelling', which serves Bate as a kind of transcendental signified guaranteeing absolute presence, capable of ordering and balancing the relations of earth and world, nature and culture, human and non-human. Crucially, it is only through such a conception of authentic, non-alienated dwelling that he can conclude by claiming that poetry is 'the place where we save the earth' (283). In what follows, I want to problematise the dual emphasis in Bate's account upon immediacy and authenticity as they inhere in the condition of dwelling by describing other modes of being-in-place, and alternative conceptions of place itself.

Although they are in many ways very different poets, Longley and Minhinnick both display some affinities with the version of ecopoetics outlined by Bate. They share a fascination with the natural world and the place of human beings – both individually and collectively – in nature, which strongly indicates the presence of an environmental politics in their poetry. Longley's profound engagements with classical exemplars such as Virgil and Horace suggest that his work might be placed in a long pastoral tradition, but he has also recently taken to describing himself as 'an ecological poet' (Randolph 26), saying: 'The most urgent political problems are ecological: how we share the planet with the plants and the other animals' (Randolph 26). Minhinnick's links to the environmental movement are even more direct, for he is a longstanding activist and co-founder of Friends of the Earth Cymru, although he has also been charier of the notion of 'nature poetry' than has Longley (see Aplin 23). In their acutely observant studies of plants, animals and ecosystems, Longley and Minhinnick can each be seen to illustrate Bate's claim that the role of 'ecopoeisis' is 'to engage *imaginatively* with the non-human' (Bate 199; emphasis in original). Both are also exemplary poets of place: Longley writes obsessively and with compressed lyric intensity about the townland of Carrigskeewaun in County Mayo, on the edge of the Atlantic Ocean; whilst Minhinnick's expansive, quicksilver narratives often explore the seacoast and beaches of south Wales around Porthcawl. As lyric poets, they each articulate the relationships between place and identity in terms of 'environmental entanglement', whereby the very categories of 'human' and 'non-human' are revealed to be mutually interdependent (Buell 23). At the same time, this sense of embeddedness in ecological networks is combined with an alert awareness of the extent to which natural environments are necessarily mediated through, and shaped by, cultural practices and processes. Indeed, I argue that the entanglements of identity and place, nature and culture that their poetry explores contribute not to a sense of rootedness and consoling unity but, rather, to an awareness of the displacements that attend experiences of being-in-place, and that this is especially the case in those texts that take the beach as their characteristic locus. Through their representations of littoral landscapes, Longley and Minhinnick both, in their different ways, give expression to a view of places and identities as open and porous, rendering belonging necessarily precarious and provisional.

Michael Longley's Carrigskeewaun

This is not to deny the importance of questions of dwelling for these two poets. McDonald rightly notes the prominence and importance of ideas of 'home' in Longley's poetry, whether as a place of 'origin' or of 'intimacy', but his stress is appositely upon 'the whole complexity of "home" which Longley's poetry has always brought to bear' (113). The dual sense of home as both a place of profound affective resonance and an ambiguous site of conflicted identifications is one I want to pursue, because it productively complicates the reductive treatments of place that feature in some ecocritical readings of Longley's work. For instance, Alan Peacock reads Longley's relationship with Carrigskeewaun as expressing itself through an 'elemental identification' between self and place, his poetry turning to the landscapes, flora and fauna of the west of Ireland in order to present the reader with an essentially 'pre-political vision' (Peacock 272). According to this reading, the poet's situation on the remote western seaboard is to be understood in terms of oneness and primal belonging, and the place itself seems to offer respite from intractable social and political realities. In addition to implying a questionable separation of aesthetic and political concerns, Peacock sentimentalises Longley's conception of place and neglects the tensions that underlie his representations of his 'home from home' (Longley, 'The West' line 10), a place in which he typically presents himself as a visitor, someone who is as much a vagrant as a dweller (see Healy 559).

Such straightforward ecocritical readings not only oversimplify the relationships between identity and place in Longley's poetry but also overlook the extent to which Belfast and Carrigskeewaun are inextricably connected in his imagination, and the ways in which such juxtapositions underpin the poems' representations of home. For instance, in 'The West', Longley's poet-speaker is presented in the kitchen of his cottage at Carrigskeewaun, within earshot of the beach, tuning in to the multiple signals of place:

> I listen for news through the atmospherics,
> A crackle of sea-wrack, spinning driftwood,
> Waves like distant traffic, news from home. (lines 3–5)

In these lines, the sounds of the Atlantic seaboard intermesh with radio waves broadcasting news of the Northern Irish Troubles, their mutual interference serving to render the notion that Mayo represents an idyllic escape from history and politics implausible. Moreover, the scenario that is framed here – of listening for 'news from home' – implicitly situates the speaker in a space that is *not* home, at a distance from, but still connected to, what is familiar but also troubling. Indeed, in the poem's second stanza the speaker's own identity is revealed to be split, for he watches himself 'Materialising out of the heat shimmers' (line 7) on the coastal path, making his way back from the beach to the rented cottage that is a 'home from home' (line 10). 'The West' is therefore self-conscious about the possibilities and tensions that arise from being in two places at once – coast and city, west and north, land and sea – and begins to destabilise the equation of home with dwelling, remaining in place. Instead, being-in-place is experienced in terms of division and displacement; home comes into focus through the lens of elsewhere, but it is often difficult to be sure which is which.

A different kind of western landscape is depicted in 'The Hebrides', but again Longley's complex meditation on the meanings of home finds its articulation on a windswept and wave-beaten shoreline, a beach facing the Atlantic swells. Fran Brearton contends that this important early poem is chiefly concerned with 'a problematical – or rather paradoxical – relationship with "home" which is lost to be found, and *vice versa*' (27–8; emphasis in original). From the outset, the speaker's sense of a long-postponed encounter is balanced against a profound experience of uncertainty that is mirrored, and perhaps intensified, by the rapidly changing character of the seashore itself:

> The winds' enclosure, Atlantic's premises,
>   Last balconies
>   Above the waves, The Hebrides –
>   Too long did I postpone
> Presbyterian granite and the lack of trees,
>   This orphaned stone
>
> Day in, day out colliding with the sea.
>   Weather forecast,
>   Compass nor ordnance survey
>   Arranges my welcome
> For, on my own, I have lost my way at last,
>   So far from home. (lines 1–12)

For the traveller who has (deliberately or accidentally) lost his way, there is a dual sense of distance and violent collision, and the poem tells of an encounter with what is at once strange and familiar – as that 'Presbyterian granite' surely is. Indeed, like the narrator of 'The West', Longley's speaker is one in whom 'the city is continuing' (line 13) in spite of his Hebridean adventure, remembering home through his encounters with elsewhere and finding himself 'in two minds' (line 36) on the shore. Haunted by the ghosts of his past, he drifts between resolution and indecision, announcing his 'journey back from flux to poise' (line 59), only to be thrown back on confusion and dissolution:

> Here, at the edge of my experience,
>   Another tide
>   Along the broken shore extends
>   A lifetime's wrack and ruin –
> No flotsam I may beachcomb now can hide
>   That water line. (lines 61–6)

Like Joyce's Stephen Dedalus, Longley's speaker reads the vagaries of his own experience in the ceaseless motions of time and tide, whilst the poem matches the restless changeability of the shoreline with its manifold variations of tone and mood, from purposeful reflection to incomprehension and despair. Even the elaborate formal shape of the poem's stanzas, which is borrowed from George Herbert, seems to echo the incursions and withdrawals of the tide, its indentations and enjambments reflecting the fluctuating lineaments of 'the broken shore' (see Brearton 27). It is also telling that, although the speaker retreats from the beach in the poem's final sections, climbing to the cliff tops in search of a sense of perspective on his past, he still finds that he must 'fight all the way for balance' (line 105) and ends by accepting his condition of ontological instability: 'In the mountain's shadow / Losing foothold, covet the privilege / Of vertigo' (lines 106–8).

That vertigo should be deemed a 'privilege' worthy of coveting underlines the extent to which the very fundamentals of being are placed in question in Longley's poetry, and this has consequences for the relation of identity and place posited in dwelling. Elmer Kennedy-Andrews is therefore right to speak of 'the provisional nature of [Longley's] dwelling in the West' (139) but slips too easily into the discourse of authentic being when he foregrounds the poet's 'oneness with the natural environment' (144). Such a notion of 'oneness' is problematic because Longley's versions of place are always attuned to particularity and multiplicity, displaying a keen sense of their temporal unfolding. His richly sensuous apprehension of the material world, which is enacted through naming and remembering, contributes paradoxically to an awareness of the impermanence of things, and this means that both place and identity are regarded as fundamentally transient and unsettled in Longley's texts, but all the more precious for that. As Terence Brown observes, Longley's cottage in Carrigskeewaun has become 'a settled point of reference' in his oeuvre, yet that settled point is itself unsettled by the fact that Longley's accounts of Being-in-the-world are typically 'haunted by dissolutions, altered states, posthumous conditions' (145). The apparent stabilities of place and identity are at once extolled and deconstructed in Longley's poetry, which frequently regards littoral landscapes as paradigmatic of such fertile and unsettling provisionality.

The dialectic between a settled sense of place and experiences of radical displacement can be seen, for example, in a poem like 'Landscape', in which the initial metaphor of entanglement implies that the poet's imagination is *a part of*, rather than *apart from*, the natural landscape it translates into language. It is also important that this landscape is explicitly liminal and littoral, the 'machair' of grassy dunes that provides a buffer between beach and fields on some areas of the western coasts of Ireland and Scotland. In the poem's opening lines, the speaker's imagination manifests itself as 'skeins of sheep's wool' (line 3) or 'a bull's horn silting / With powdery seashells' (lines 4–5), natural objects that provide a point of contact between human and non-human fields of experience. Yet the rapid slide from one metaphor to another – fabric to receptacle – and the choice of 'silting' as a main verb introduces the idea of metamorphosis which the poem goes on to develop in the following stanzas, chiefly through images of unravelling and dissolution:

> I am clothed, unclothed
> By racing cloud shadows,
> Or else disintegrate
> Like a hillside neighbour
> Erased by sea mist.
>
> A place of dispersals
> Where the wind fractures
> Flight-feathers, insect wings
> And rips thought to tatters
> Like a fuchsia petal. (lines 6–15)

Mind and body, body and landscape, landscape and weather all begin to blur into one another in these lines, but this version of 'oneness' with the natural environment also entails fracture and dispersal, a radical process of dissemination plainly at odds with rooted dwelling. Walking on the beach, Longley's poet-speaker is engulfed in what Ingold calls 'the wider sphere of forces and relations comprising the weather-world' (132), and that experience of immersion in 'the currents of a world-in-formation' (129) is profoundly ambiguous. The poem's title invokes a whole tradition of literary and artistic representations of place only to collapse that tradition's conventional opposition between subject and object, observer and observed. In Longley's version of landscape, the human and non-human worlds interpenetrate one another freely, but the elision of boundaries that results is as disturbing and destructive as it is liberating. Tellingly, the landscape's 'inscriptions' (line 18) may only be read momentarily before 'Melting into water' (line 21), and the poet-speaker repeatedly gives expression to his own erasure in this ambiguous coastal zone: 'A mouth drawn to a mouth / Digests the glass between / Me and my reflection' (lines 23–5). Spatial planes, surfaces and boundaries are prone to disorienting reconfiguration throughout the poem, whilst the surety of the lyric self is not simply destabilised but also 'digested' in the very act of self-scrutiny.

'Landscape' provides an arresting example of Longley's dynamic conception of place, illustrating McDonald's point that Longley's 'West' 'offers a way of *undoing* the settled nature of an identity rooted in its own place of origin' (120; emphasis in original). As I have suggested, this mutual unsettling of identity and place extends to Longley's recurrent explorations of the idea of 'home', a word that is typically charged with both familiarity and strangeness in his texts. It is, moreover, most in evidence where littoral landscapes are the focus of attention. In 'Remembering Carrigskeewaun', he writes:

> Home is a hollow between the waves,
> A clump of nettles, feathery winds,
> And memory no longer than a day
> When the animals come back to me
> From the townland of Carrigskeewaun,
> From a page lit by the Milky Way. (lines 8–13)

In these lines, dwelling is precarious rather than permanent, and an image of home must be reconstructed at a distance through the fallible instruments of memory and writing. Note also that home is not exactly Carrigskeewaun in this poem but 'a hollow between the waves', a liminal space subject to the action of tides and winds. Similarly, in 'Architecture', the poet-speaker describes building a house from sand, shingle and seaweed, thereby making an 'echo-chamber' of his 'home' (line 3) that keeps him in tune with mutability, 'the sea's whisper and the seashore' (line 6). By locating his 'home' in such transient, in-between spaces, Longley complicates the notion that dwelling simply entails remaining in place, for places are themselves mutable, manifesting both settledness and flux simultaneously.

Robert Minhinnick's Porthcawl

Longley's Carrigskeewaun, which is located in a remote and picturesque area of south-west Mayo, makes something of a contrast with the post-industrial coastline of south Wales depicted in Minhinnick's poetry. Although, like Longley, he is keenly responsive to the flora and fauna of the natural environment, Minhinnick's poetry is centrally concerned with the ways in which places and landscapes are shaped by human activity and habitation. As Jeremy Hooker observes, Minhinnick is both 'a poet of worked historical place' (181) and 'a poet of borders or margins' (182), interested in the interfaces between past and present, self and other, nature and culture. Several of his early poems respond to the worked-out industries of the Glamorgan coast, tracing the effects of economic and social decline on both people and environment. In 'Old Ships' the dismembering of the Glamorgan fleet, a 'decrepit navy / Of coaster, frigate, submarine' (lines 13–14), serves as an allegory for the breakup of Empire and perhaps also the Union. Similarly, 'Salvage' dwells on the aftermath of industry by figuring the beach at Tremorfa as 'a landscape of exhaustion' (line 19) and has its disaffected narrator observe sourly 'a coast poisoned / By people, crossboned with shipwreck' (lines 23–4). The occasional note of misanthropy in these early poems is tempered in Minhinnick's more mature work by an empathetic social conscience informed by socialist as well as environmental politics. So, in 'Rhigos' he anatomises the marginalization of an unemployed underclass, marooned in 'stacked flats' (line 8) where their frustration has 'burnt out' (line 20). And in 'The Saltings' the middle-class narrator draws the reader's attention to the unvoiced and disregarded inhabitants of a coastal housing estate, implying their shared complicity in the silencing described: 'This is the life that persists beyond our thought / And has no one to speak for it' (lines 17–18).

Minhinnick's interest in probing the limits of thought and language frequently finds expression through his concerns with place and geography. To this end, Peach remarks upon his 'recurring concern with the space that people occupy, which is often a restrictive space' (388). Yet Minhinnick's poetry also recurrently emphasises the material and imaginative connectivity of particular places as sites of exchange, overlap and confluence. His characteristic landscapes are liminal or littoral, the long beaches and extensive dune systems around the coastal resort of Porthcawl serving as a focal point for an aesthetic that conjoins the local and the global. As Ian Gregson observes, the ecological cast of Minhinnick's imagination, which identifies connections and interdependencies between species and habitats, gives rise to a dialogic spatial poetics that is characterised by 'an increasing tendency … to allow places to overlap' (49). For instance, in a recent poem, 'The Cormorant', the narrator's figurative transformation of a common seabird into a 'cruise missile / on its flyby of El Rashid Street' (lines 5–6) and a 'stealth-bomber' (line 45) trailing 'death / across the sky' (lines 46–7) serves to conflate the Porthcawl shoreline with the bomb-damaged cityscape of contemporary Baghdad. Such uses of juxtaposition and double focus in Minhinnick's texts imply that the meanings of any given place are often dependent upon the relations that it has with other places, and that idea is here given a pronounced geopolitical emphasis.

A similar grasp of spatial interconnections informs 'Songs for the Lugmen', in which a weather system making landfall as men dig for fishing bait links a stretch of the south Wales coast with 'A swell off the Azores' (line 7) and 'Africa's red rains' (line 88). But this intuition of geographical and meteorological contiguities is further complicated by the shifting metaphors through which Minhinnick describes the beach and dunes: as a 'desert' (line 21) and a 'golden tarp' (line 21); a 'pampas / Of viper and thorn' (lines 24–5); and 'this savannah / Where the coming and the going meet / And transform one another' (lines 64–6). Through the playful substitutions of Minhinnick's language, diverse ecological habitats are brought into imaginative conjunction, and the beach itself figures as a protean space of intersection. The images of confluence and mutual transformation that are foregrounded in the poem are crucial, for his representations of the shoreline derive much of their energy from the flux and indeterminacies that he observes there. Indeed, there is a visceral sense that the inhabitants of Minhinnick's coastal landscapes share in such shiftiness and mutability themselves and that distinctions between inside and outside, people and place are thoroughly permeable: 'The sea's within' (Minhinnick, 'The Porthcawl' line 102).

These slippages and confusions between apparent oppositions also extend to the very act of representing place itself, for in several poems Minhinnick follows the lead of Joyce's Stephen Dedalus by reading the Welsh coastal landscape as if it were a text. In a recurrent trope, the sea and shoreline become places of cryptic inscription that both invite and resist interpretation simultaneously. What is interesting here is the way in which the natural environment is textualised in order to raise the problem of how we ought to 'read' landscapes. For instance, 'Questions of the Woman Who Fell' meditates on the mysterious death of a cliff-walker and apostrophises the dead woman: 'Your name's rubbed smooth / Within the book of tides' (lines 144–5). Tidal erosion and textual erasure coalesce in this image of death's diminution, as natural processes and cultural practices are run together. Yet, in the same poem, Minhinnick also reverses the direction of this guiding metaphor, having language figure as a liminal place in which contraries meet:

> We live in language,
>   That limestone fault
> Between sweetwater
>   And mortifying salt. (lines 63–6)

To live in language is to acknowledge the extent to which our dwelling in the natural world is inevitably culturally mediated, for the very ideas of nature upon which our engagements with real landscapes are premised are themselves cultural constructions. Equally, though, Minhinnick's 'limestone fault' implies separations and necessary distinctions, not just between life-giving 'sweetwater' and 'mortifying salt' but also between ideas of nature on the one hand, and nature's non-human reality on the other. As Soper affirms:

> It is one thing to recognize that much that is referred to as 'nature' takes the form it does only in virtue of human activity, another to suppose that it has no extra-discursive reality, or that there are no discriminations to be drawn between that which is and that which is not an effect of culture. (152)

The contemporary ecological poet therefore occupies an interstitial space in which the tension between a desire to engage with nature directly and an abiding commitment to the artifice of language and poetic form has always to be negotiated. Perhaps this is why Minhinnick's speaker, in a rather didactic flourish, proposes that the fluctuating frontier of the shoreline provides a 'lesson' in living ethically and imaginatively: 'We have to learn the tide's lesson: / Avoid the literal. / Live the littoral' ('Questions' lines 43–5). To juxtapose the 'literal' and 'littoral' in this manner, through the discordant rhyming of near-homophones, is to imply that the reality of the shoreline is at odds with that which prevails elsewhere in the terrestrial world, and so to conceive it as a space of aesthetic (and political) alternatives.

Another prominent feature of Minhinnick's littoral landscapes is the omnipresence of litter, especially plastics and the detritus of consumption, for it is on the beach that the residues and leftovers of a reckless consumer capitalist society accumulate. To that end, his poems often play upon the incongruous juxtaposition of fragile ecosystems and wildlife habitats with the dubious attractions of Porthcawl's pleasure beach and fairground. In the sequence 'Fairground Music' the speaker listens to 'the voices of children spinning / On a ferris wheel' (lines 176–7) whilst making his way towards the beach, a 'three thousand year-old road / Of plastics and corals and the compass points / Of gentians pricked out of chalk' (lines 178–80). Similarly, 'The Swimming Lesson' dwells upon 'lipsticked Marlboros that paint the beach / Like sea-rocket' (lines 16–17) and 'the international / Brand-names discarded by the tide' (lines 17–18). In both poems, Minhinnick voices environmental protest but also makes it difficult to distinguish clearly between the natural and the unnatural, the authentic and the artificial. The sandy foreshore of this stretch of coast is revealed to be both organic and inorganic, composed of the pulverised remains of dead coral reefs and man-made plastics alike. Cigarette butts can be mistaken for sea-rocket, and the anthropomorphised tide is implicated in humankind's heedless wastefulness. A further example of such commingling can be found in another sequence, 'Breaking Down', towards the end of which Minhinnick's speaker surveys a representative scene:

> And surf is booming at the mouths of caves,
> The moraines of coloured plastics on the shore
> And all the bleached hillocks of sea-litter. (lines 351–3)

In these lines, which preface a climactic drowning, there is a marked contrast between the picturesquely 'booming' surf and resonant cave-mouths upon which attention is initially directed, and the mounds of refuse to which it is subsequently turned. However, rubbish does not simply despoil the environment but is actually rendered part of the landscape, so that natural and artificial again blur together in the defamiliarised topography of the beach's 'moraines' and 'hillocks'. As Matthew Jarvis perceptively observes, Minhinnick's poetry discovers human traces and residues everywhere in the natural environment, exhibiting a tendency to 'imagine the denaturing of nature' (85) in its depictions of the south Wales coastline. His texts enact what Jarvis describes as 'a *thinking together* of the human and the non-human' (83; emphasis in original) through their subtle smudging of the conventional divisions between the worlds of nature and culture.

Minhinnick's poetry disrupts the dualism of nature and culture by implying that the natural world is, for better or worse, already thoroughly imbricated with human processes and values. Of course, this can hardly be construed either as the intimate 'oneness' promoted by Heideggerian dwelling or as the 'monistic, primal identification of humans with the ecosphere' (Garrard 21) advocated by deep ecologists. Rather, like Longley's, Minhinnick's depictions of the seashore foreground a conception of place that acknowledges transience and contingency, as borders shift and contexts change. Moreover, the unstable elements of sand and tide disorient all impulses for rooted dwelling on the coast. Consider the final lines of 'The Coast':

>   Our ground is blurring,
> Losing its angles, but the brand-names push
> Out of the sand their familiar epitaphs,
>
> And a shattered bottle reassures that our claim
> Was made. Here a tidy rank of caravans
> Floats axle-deep upon the creeping tide. (lines 16–21)

On the one hand, litter is here made to seem oddly 'familiar' and 'reassuring', traces of human habitation that mark the landscape ambiguously with cultural significations. On the other, human dwelling is rendered vulnerable and precarious by the forces of nature, as sands drift and a high tide sets caravans afloat. The final image of Minhinnick's poem recalls Longley's 'Spring Tide', in which the incoming sea 'has ferried jelly fish / To the end of the lane, pinks, purples, / Wet flowers beside the floating cow-pats' (lines 25–7). Both poems balance human threats to the environment against the natural world's capacity to undermine human habitations, and they are thereby doubly attuned to the ways in which a sense of place is always and necessarily *un*settled. As the philosopher Jeff Malpas warns, the longing for a secure dwelling-place can lead to an impoverished sense of the significance of place, for 'to seek an escape from the transience and fragility of place is to seek an escape from place itself' (*Place* 191). Change, agency and movement are at the heart of how place is both experienced and understood.

Conclusion

As I have tried to show, the insufficiency of dwelling as a concept is chiefly illustrated through the emphasis placed upon transience, mutability and alterity in Longley's and Minhinnick's representations of place, pre-eminently the shoreline between land and sea. Although their poetry is frequently preoccupied with the mutual entanglements of humans and non-humans, nature and culture, it ultimately confounds the alignments between place and identity that are posited in Bate's model of ecopoetics. Littoral landscapes recur in the work of both poets, and whilst there are notable contrasts between the wild remoteness of Longley's Carrigskeewaun and the post-industrial patchwork of Minhinnick's Porthcawl, these are typically places where flux and transience are regarded as creatively fertile. As a result, the beach and its shifting, inconstant shoreline emerge not as the ground of being but as a place of encounters with otherness, in which the values and meanings of 'home' are called into question and sometimes, provisionally, reaffirmed.

Works Cited

Aplin, Jackie. 'Interview with Robert Minhinnick'. *Poetry Wales* 25.2 (1989): 23–7.

Bambach, Charles. *Heidegger's Roots: Nietzsche, National Socialism, and the Greeks.* Ithaca: Cornell UP, 2003.

Bate, Jonathan. *The Song of the Earth.* London: Picador, 2000.

Brearton, Fran. *Reading Michael Longley.* Tarset: Bloodaxe, 2006.

Brown, Terence. 'Mahon and Longley: Place and Placelessness'. *The Cambridge Companion to Contemporary Irish Poetry.* Ed. Matthew Campbell. Cambridge: Cambridge UP, 2003. 133–48.

Budgen, Frank. *James Joyce and the Making of 'Ulysses' and Other Writings.* Oxford: Oxford UP, 1972.

Buell, Lawrence. *The Future of Environmental Criticism: Environmental Crisis and the Literary Imagination.* Oxford: Blackwell, 2005.

Carson, Rachel. *The Edge of the Sea.* London: Staple, 1955.

Garrard, Greg. *Ecocriticism.* London: Routledge, 2004.

———. 'Heidegger, Heaney and the Problem of Dwelling'. *Writing the Environment: Ecocriticism and Literature.* Ed. Richard Kerridge and Neil Sammels. London: Zed, 1998. 167–81.

Gregson, Ian. *The New Poetry in Wales.* Cardiff: U of Wales P, 2007.

Hayward, Peter J. *A Natural History of the Seashore.* London: Collins, 2004.

Healy, Dermot. 'An Interview with Michael Longley'. *The Southern Review* 31.3 (1995): 557–61.

Heidegger, Martin. *Being and Time.* Trans. John Macquarie and Edward Robinson. Oxford: Blackwell, 1962.

———. 'Building, Dwelling, Thinking'. *Poetry, Language, Thought.* Trans. Albert Hofstadter. New York: Harper, 2001. 141–60.

———. '…Poetically Man Dwells…'. *Poetry, Language, Thought.* Trans. Albert Hofstadter. New York: Harper, 2001. 209–27.

———. *Sein und Zeit.* 1927. 19th ed. Tübingen: Niemeyer, 2006.

Hooker, Jeremy. *The Presence of the Past: Essays on Modern British and American Poetry.* Bridgend: Poetry Wales, 1987.

Ingold, Tim. *Being Alive: Essays on Movement, Knowledge and Description.* Abingdon: Routledge, 2011.

Jarvis, Matthew. *Welsh Environments in Contemporary Poetry.* Cardiff: U of Wales P, 2008.

Joyce, James. *Ulysses: The Corrected Text.* Ed. Hans Walter Gabler. London: Bodley Head, 1986.

Kennedy-Andrews, Elmer. *Writing Home: Poetry and Place in Northern Ireland 1968–2008.* Cambridge: Brewer, 2008.

King, Cuchlaine A.M. *Beaches and Coasts.* 2nd ed. London: Arnold, 1972.

Longley, Michael. 'Architecture'. Longley, *Collected.* 122.

———. *Collected Poems.* London: Cape, 2006.

———. 'The Hebrides'. Longley, *Collected.* 22–5.

———. 'Landscape'. Longley, *Collected.* 91.

———. 'Remembering Carrigskeewaun'. Longley, *Collected.* 170.

———. 'Spring Tide'. Longley, *Collected.* 124–5.

————. 'The West'. Longley, *Collected*. 69.

Malpas, Jeff E. *Heidegger's Topology: Being, Place, World*. Cambridge: MIT, 2006.

————. *Place and Experience: A Philosophical Topography*. Cambridge: Cambridge UP, 1999.

Massey, Doreen. *For Space*. London: Sage, 2005.

McDonald, Peter. *Mistaken Identities: Poetry and Northern Ireland*. Oxford: Clarendon, 1997.

Minhinnick, Robert. *After the Hurricane*. Manchester: Carcanet, 2002.

————. 'Breaking Down'. Minhinnick, *The Dinosaur*. 41–60.

————. 'The Coast'. Minhinnick, *The Dinosaur*. 12.

————. 'The Cormorant'. *King Driftwood*. Manchester: Carcanet, 2008. 7–8.

————. *The Dinosaur Park*. Bridgend: Poetry Wales, 1985.

————. 'Fairground Music'. *The Looters*. Bridgend: Seren Books, 1989. 39–51.

————. 'Old Ships'. Minhinnick, *Selected*. 11–12.

————. 'The Porthcawl Preludes'. Minhinnick, *After*. 98–105.

————. 'Questions of the Woman Who Fell'. Minhinnick, *After*. 26–9.

————. 'Rhigos'. Minhinnick, *Selected*. 41–2.

————. 'The Saltings'. Minhinnick, *The Dinosaur*. 11.

————. 'Salvage'. Minhinnick, *Selected*. 12–13.

————. *Selected Poems*. Manchester: Carcanet, 1999.

————. 'Songs for the Lugmen'. Minhinnick, *After*. 32–5.

————. 'The Swimming Lesson'. Minhinnick, *Selected*. 114–9.

Olson, Charles. 'The Kingfishers'. *A Charles Olson Reader*. Ed. Ralph Maud. Manchester: Carcanet, 2005. 32–8.

Peach, Linden. 'Wales and the Cultural Politics of Identity: Gillian Clarke, Robert Minhinnick, and Jeremy Hooker'. *Contemporary British Poetry: Essays in Theory and Criticism*. Ed. James Acheson and Romana Huk. Albany: State U of New York P, 1996. 373–96.

Peacock, Alan J. 'Michael Longley: Poet Between Worlds'. *Poetry in Contemporary Irish Literature*. Ed. Michael Kenneally. Gerrard's Cross: Smythe, 1995. 263–79.

Randolph, Jody Allen. 'Michael Longley in Conversation'. *PN Review* 31.2 (2004): 21–7.

Rydin, Yvonne. 'Beaches'. Ed. Stephan Harrison, Steve Pile and Nigel Thrift. *Patterned Ground: Entanglements of Nature and Culture*. London: Reaktion, 2004. 151–3.

Soper, Kate. *What is Nature? Culture, Politics and the Non-Human*. Oxford: Blackwell, 1995.

Yonge, C.M. *The Sea Shore*. London: Fontana, 1963.

Chapter 5
John Burnside's Seascapes

Julika Griem

Conceptualising Literary Seascapes

In a recent attempt to decipher the 'marine imaginary' of Colm Tóibín's writing, Harte has characterised the Irish author's seaside settings as 'enabling metaphors for the transitional state of contemporary Irish society' (333). In his reconstruction of Tóibín's 'symbolic exploitation' (339) of coastal scenarios Harte construes their 'signifying potential' (346) according to a correlation between shifting shorelines and shifting semantics, between a geological erosion and an ideological deconstruction of received myths of Irishness: Tóibín's specific seasides are shown to foreground the 'malleable condition of contemporary Ireland' insofar as they 'gesture toward new, more pluralistic forms of cultural identity and more enlightened forms of self-knowledge and historical understanding that are postnationalist in their inflection' (339).

Harte's reading of Tóibín's imagined maritime geographies is driven by an instrumental approach towards literary space – instead of focussing on the aesthetic features of Tóibín's texts, he sees their verbal evocations of seascapes as predominantly symbolising certain social and ideological formations. To invoke the representational power of Tóibín's marine imaginary, Harte relies on what James identified as the 'compelling metaphoricity' (*Contemporary* 2) of spatial thinking as well as the 'temptation to recruit literary fiction as emblematic of sociogeographical issues and forces' (*Contemporary* 20). Accordingly, Harte's association-rich analogies between eroding shorelines and eroding concepts of national identity can be seen to be tapping into the metaphorical inventory of spatial theory's current master tropes as well as into a specific literary iconography. In a context offering, on the one hand, much-quoted configurations of thirdspace and heterotopia but also, on the other hand, iconic texts such as James Joyce's *Ulysses* and John Banville's *The Sea*, the Irish shoreline seems to suggest itself as a 'palimpsestic contact zone' (Harte 341), as 'a space of transgressive, potentially transfiguring interjacency' (338).

Following on from Harte's essay, it seems promising, for a start, to apply the concept of a marine imaginary to the writings of the Scottish author John Burnside, as his works demonstrate a similarly strong fascination with seaside settings. Like Banville's novel *The Sea*, however, Burnside's marine imaginary does not easily yield an ideological dimension. Having rather mixed feelings about notions of home and belonging, Burnside has rejected being enlisted for the tribal routines of a post-devolution Scottishness that invites and recruits literary texts to engage with the buzzwords of received identity politics such as 'class, sexuality and gender, globalisation and the new Europe, cosmopolitanism and postcoloniality, as well as questions of ethnicity, race and postnational multiculturalism' (Schoene 2).[1] Unlike Tóibín's work, then, Burnside's writing does not primarily turn to seascapes and littoral topographies to 'figure an alternative, more liberal and cosmopolitan future' (Harte 336). What this author rather dramatises, as we shall see, is a more existential kind of alternative: instead of employing the coast as a metaphor enabling postnational concepts of cultural identity, Burnside's littoral landscapes first of all function as an aesthetic configuration generating reflexion about being in and speaking about the world.

It would not do justice to this author's achievement if we were to read Burnside's rather existential and phenomenological take on the shifting and elusive topographies of the seaside as an apolitical project. Burnside has in fact been known to voice ecological anxieties in his journalistic work, in essays and in the polluted coastal setting of his novel *Glister* (2008). The many beaches and maritime scenarios in his lyrical and prose texts are explored as contested habitats in a very specific sense, however: Burnside's littoral landscapes entangle and interweave the physical and the metaphysical in often disturbing and conflictual ways; they challenge us to revise notions of entitlement and belonging, of beauty and enchantment. It is thus from a decidedly aesthetic and philosophical point of view that Burnside's coastal vistas invite us to reconsider the relationship between questions of literary form and of environmental conflict. Such a reconsideration will furthermore provide an opportunity to discuss different heuristic possibilities of conceptualising the oeuvre of a contemporary author whose impressive credentials so far have attracted surprisingly few critical responses: an analysis of the clearly recognisable but also subtly shifting functions of Burnside's seaside settings will cast light, I shall argue, on the generic and trans-generic dynamics of this author's rather specific 'explorations of the liminal' (Borthwick 77).[2]

Recurring Emplotments: From Land to Sea

Within the symbolical geography of John Burnside's writing, the seaside represents a characteristic site interacting with other settings, producing an ensemble of significant spatial relations. One of these recurring sites appears in the prose poem 'Suburbs' (1991), where Burnside refers to a richly semanticised topos: time and again, suburbia has been staged as a non-space on the periphery of the city, a dormitory town where middle-class aspirations are buried under the surface of commodified, standardised lives. The poem, accordingly, stages its suburban setting as a locale where '[p]lace is not important' (6), defined by an

---

[1]   On Burnside's resistance to being pinned down to categories such as 'nature poet' or 'Scottish poet' see his interview 'Strong Words' 259.

[2]   Also see Galbraith, who hints at the need to consider the development of Burnside's work not just along but also across generic lines (148).

'abstracted quality, like a sentence learned by heart and repeated till the words are finally magical' (3). In a similar vein, the suburbs are characterised as an 'invented place whose only purpose is avoidance' (2), representing the speaker's 'idea of order, which is nothing more than a notion of worthwhile and calculable risk' (6). Suburban order, in this poem, seems to be achieved at the expense of reducing the material and historical specificity of places. It is therefore not surprising that the speaker imagines the suburbs as a spatial constellation where 'everything is implied: city, warehouse district, night stop, woods emerging from mists' (5). However, despite the speaker's impression that the suburb, as it were, appropriates most other places, there remains a sense of beyond, suggested by a conspicuous absence in the list of implied places: what is not mentioned is the seaside, even though coastal settings are at the centre of so many of Burnside's poems.[3]

Why the seaside could be seen to be escaping the appropriating spatial logic of the suburb is hinted at in the poem 'Pisces', published three years after 'Suburbs'. In contrast to the speaker in the earlier poem, who imagines himself as 'already present somewhere else' ('Suburbs' 5), the female *persona* observed in 'Pisces' is granted an experience of intensified presence, focussing her attention entirely on the beach she is shown to be walking along:

> She loved the wet whisper of silt
> when tidewater seeped away
> and the estuary rose to the town
> through copper light,
>
> a tender of glass and scales
> and driftwood varnished with salt,
> a circle she walked for miles
> in search of shells … (lines 1–8)

At first glance, the characters in both poems seem to be exploring their respective locations in terms of a circular movement: the woman is tracing 'a circle she walked for miles', whereas the speaker in 'Suburbs' notes 'a tendency towards the circular, a neatness I have known about for years, expressed in a strange algebra of place names and symbols on road maps' (4). Despite these similarly circular movements, however, the two poems' representations of suburb and beach differ considerably. The man's 'reading' of the suburb is presented as a fairly abstract and abstracting activity, transforming local specificity into symbols, patterns, ideas of order and a 'strange algebra'. The woman's perception of the beach is characterised by an attitude foregrounding the physical and bodily details of her surroundings – conspicuously circumventing the abstracting and conventionalising arbitrariness of semiotic mediation:

---

[3]   Many of the poems published in the collections *The Asylum Dance* and *Selected Poems* contain maritime settings, while Burnside's 'Four Quartets', published in *Gift Songs*, are explicitly dedicated to the seaside locations of Saint-Nazaire, Pittenweem, Le Croisic and Ny-Hellesund.

> picking starfish from a sheet
> of silver tension, puzzled by the trails
> of viscera, the threads of bloodless meat
> and resurrected forms that had no names
>
> but offered kinship, memory, regret,
> a pulse between the water and her hand,
> the feel of something old and buried deep,
> heartbeat and vision quickening the sand. (lines 9–16)

The vision of a sensuous bodily (re)connection between human beings and their natural environment is part of the attraction of many of Burnside's littoral spaces and maritime scenarios. A closer inspection of this vision in the context of his oeuvre reveals that it does not merely figure as an isolated *topos* but keeps recurring as an element of an emplotment driving many of Burnside's texts. Within this characteristic emplotment, some of the author's revisited locations are endowed with a transitory quality. Thus, in texts such as the second memoir entitled *Waking Up in Toytown* (2010), even suburbia gains a regenerative potential, as it is into the petty monotony of suburban ordinariness that the autobiographical first-person narrator vanishes in order to start rebuilding his life (25–8). In the emplotments organising the quests of Burnside's predominantly male focalisers, narrators and speakers, the seaside still exerts a different narrative pull, however: time and again, his characters are sent on journeys leading them from the suburb to the beach, from the country to the sea. An early example of this type of narrative trajectory can be found in the short story 'Decency' (2000). The story accompanies two British suburbanites to a vacation spot on the Spanish Mediterranean coast. Having arrived, the middle-aged couple's crumbling marriage quickly deteriorates: while the wife shuts herself off reading romances in the hotel room, the husband recklessly roams the town's environments where he eventually meets an uncanny compatriot whose enigmatic comments introduce him as the possible serial killer of a number of young local females. Before this acquaintance completely changes the protagonist's life, his transformation is anticipated and triggered by a 'sanctuary' above the sea, allowing him 'to lose himself in the noise the waves made crashing against the cliff face below', making him listen 'intently to the sound, as if hearing it for the first time' (85).

As it induces a state of acute perceptivity in him, the coastal lookout soon grants the protagonist a degree of lucidity reminiscent of the 'pulse' connecting the woman and the water in 'Pisces':

> he became aware of a new sensation: an odd, near-palpable pressure on the surface of his skin, a tight warmth in his face and scalp that brought to the surface something old and residual, a sluggish, reptilian element deep in his flesh, slowly coming to life. He had noticed it before, though it had never been so acute: it was something detached from any human concern, something neutral, or even alien: the more it awoke, the more he felt himself altered, receiving signals and stimuli he normally missed – a gust of scent on the air, a flicker of

movement among the hibiscus shrubs at the square's edge; a new resonance, or some bright splash of noise in a side street, that sent tremors through some fine cord in his spine that he had never been aware of until that moment. (86)

In this passage, Burnside seems to be drawing on the invigorating, vitalising and regenerative qualities cultural historians such as Alain Corbin have identified as a source of early tourist interest in seaside holidays.[4] At the same time, the tourist in the short story is introduced to a littoral ecotone endowed with a temporal depth and evolutionary echo Burnside often ascribes to his seaside settings. Quite frequently, the spatial emplotment taking this author's characters from the country or from the suburbs to the sea seems to be directed towards reconnecting them with 'something old and buried deep' ('Pisces' 15), with bodily memories transcending the limits of conscious reflexion. As can be observed in the passage quoted above, the prose texts frequently use the beach as a site of reversed evolution that depicts some characters' liberating transformation as a potentially destructive process: in these examples, mainly found in the novels and stories, regeneration tips over into forms of regression not necessarily compatible with social rules and conventions. In some of Burnside's longer poems, such as 'Hay Devil', published in the same year as the short story 'Decency' (2000), the narrative pull towards the coast results in situations chronicling the minutiae of beach life as indicators and triggers of a state prioritising the intensifying of sensory perceptions over moral regression. At the beginning of 'Hay Devil', the speaker's journey is merely motivated by his longing for a 'home and a sense of direction' (46). Soon after, this longing manifests itself as a 'warmed magnetic force that bled into my fingers like a pulse' (48), resonating with the woman's pulse in 'Pisces'. Still later, in the fourth section, the speaker seems to have arrived at a home that is 'a different country', the 'pulse in my spine' reconnected to 'shoreline' and 'firth', to 'the taste of salt' and 'tidewashed sand', creating an experience of 'becoming re-attuned to some pure rhythm written on the air' (22). In the last section of the poem the speaker stays by the sea to revel further in a state of heightened awareness nourished by 'dock-lights spotting the further shore' by 'counting out a lifetime's worth of sails' (52): here, the frequently mentioned clear patterns and rhythms of Burnside's tidal beaches assist the lyrical speakers in arresting those permanently changing and vanishing details by 'imagining a world' (52), a world as precise as the unreceived letters the speaker of Burnside's poem 'Arrival of the Mail Boat, after Edvard Munch' envisions in the hold of the approaching vessel (30).

Still another example demonstrating the productivity of the emplotment reaching out towards the seaside can be found in the novel *Living Nowhere* (2003). In his fourth and most openly autobiographical novel, Burnside interweaves the lives of several young people growing up in Corby, the steel town the author's family moved to when Burnside was still a boy. Compared to 'Hay Devil', *Living Nowhere* engages in a much more sustained and painful meditation on ideas of home and belonging. In the first chapters, Burnside embarks on an excruciating

---

[4]   See also Richter and Kluwick's introduction to this volume.

dismantling of received myths of Scottishness, involving various sons refusing to follow their fathers' masculine code of the working-class hard man. In its autobiographical context, the novel can be seen as an attempt to exorcise Burnside's own traumatic memories of Corby, which in the diegetic world of the narrative, following the spatial emplotment characterising so many of Burnside's texts, is left in favour of a place at the seaside. After the protagonist named Francis has left Corby because of the violent death of his friend Jan, he chronicles an odyssey leading from California back to the eastern Scottish coast in letters written to his dead companion. Finally, the novel's year, 1993, finds Francis in the little coastal town of Fasthaven near Fife, where he seems to have found a provisional 'dwelling place' (312), 'a life that had been stripped down to its essentials: a clean, well-lighted house by the sea, a basic, almost invariable pattern to the days, the space and the quiet to work' (318).

Considering these examples, it seems hard to deny that Burnside's writing ascribes a positive narrative *telos* to its maritime and littoral locations. This impression is further underscored by two texts, both published in 2006, programmatically foregrounding a seaside scenario invested with emphatic significance. The scene is, again, a small fishing town on the east coast of Scotland, and the wording is near to identical: whereas Burnside's first memoir, *A Lie About My Father*, rounds off its moving examination of the author's highly dysfunctional relationship to his own father with a reconciliatory scene showing Burnside and his two-year old son on a peaceful excursion to the harbour, the essay 'A Science of Belonging: Poetry as Ecology' sets out from exactly this scene to develop a poetics of the 'enduring mystery' (91), an ecologically aware 'discipline of poetry as a slow, lyrical, and fairly tentative attempt to understand and describe a meaningful way of dwelling in this extraordinary world' (95).[5]

Burnside's use of the term 'dwelling' in this essay and many other fictional texts explicitly refers to Heidegger's notion of dwelling, which already provided Jonathan Bate with one of the key terms of the ecocritical programme set out in his seminal study *The Song of the Earth*.[6] Encouraged by such authorial gestures of ecocritical engagement, Borthwick has identified a storyline running through Burnside's oeuvre which resonates with the emplotment described above. In his

---

[5] For a further attempt to develop an ecological aesthetics inspired by phenomenological philosophy, see Burnside and O'Riordan 21.

[6] Burnside explicitly refers to Heidegger's 'Building, Dwelling, Thinking' in the first epigraph to his collection *The Asylum Dance*: 'The proper dwelling plight lies in this, that mortals ever search anew for the essence of dwelling, that they *must ever learn to dwell.* What if man's homelessness consisted in this, that man still does not even think of the *proper* plight of dwelling as *the* plight? Yet as soon as man *gives thought* to his homelessness, it is a misery no longer. Rightly considered and kept well in mind, it is the sole summons that *calls* mortals into their dwelling' (emphases in original). See also Bate 261–2; for Burnside's references to Heidegger in an eco-critical context, see Gairn 159, 166–7. For a sustained discussion of dwelling and of ecocritical investment in this notion, see Alexander's contribution to this volume.

essay, Borthwick traces two strands in Burnside's poetry: on the one hand, he sees poems of a 'malignant masculinity' (73) dominated by the 'defiant, problematic figure' (71) of the working-class hard man, populating the northern steel towns of Burnside's own youth as a 'thwarted, emotionally stunted' creature 'disconnected from a wider social sphere' (70). On the other hand, this type of violent, silently brooding hard man is contrasted with representatives of a 'sustainable masculinity': in what Borthwick calls Burnside's 'poems of regeneration' (72), the male personae seem to be able to rediscover repressed emotional and spiritual sides of their personalities and reintegrate themselves by 'immersion into the natural world' (74).

At first glance, it is quite tempting to turn these two positions into a narrative delineating the development of Burnside's life and writing. Taking into account the spatial emplotment of many of Burnside's narrative journeys it is equally tempting to locate the *telos* of such a storyline in the evocative contact zones between land and sea: in the poem titled 'The Men's Harbour' (2000), the speaker, for instance, reflects on 'the grace that distinguishes strength from power' (60), whereas the autobiographical narrators of the memoirs also choose the eastern Scottish coast when they wish to settle down finally after years of dazed and disconnected wandering. More importantly, many of Burnside's texts do indeed suggest seaside 'dwellings' to explore – in the words of Garrard – 'the long-term imbrication of humans in a landscape of memory, ancestry and death, or ritual, life and work' (Garrard 109; as quoted in Borthwick 66).

The conceptual emplotment of Burnside's life and work as a process of healing brought about by reintegrating oneself into a coastal landscape no longer dominated by exclusively human needs and standards is fraught with a number of problems, however. First of all, as a therapeutic project, the above-mentioned reform of a so-called 'malignant masculinity' is questioned by many of the most interesting male protagonists of Burnside's texts. It is certainly true that many of them struggle to cope with relations steeped in denial, violence and fear. It is also made very clear, though, that these men – and especially the artist figures among them – do not aim at reconnection and reintegration through 'talking it over'. On the contrary, the kind of healing many of Burnside's men are yearning for implies a defence of silence and solitude that runs through this author's oeuvre. What his protagonists are interested in is neither the routine, therapeutical conversation presented at the beginning of *Waking Up in Toytown* nor the girlfriend's mantra of 'healthy relations thriving on shared stories, shared emotions, shared everything' in *Living Nowhere* (324). It is, rather, 'the quiet to work' (318), the freedom 'to be alone when one chooses' (324). In many of Burnside's texts, such liberating isolation is indeed often found in seaside scenarios; yet there again, in many of them, the maritime settings do not grant a final and unequivocal sense of belonging. Thus the opening section of the poem 'Settlements' (2000), entitled 'A Place by the Sea', begins with the programmatic disclaimer 'Because what we think of as home / is a hazard to others' (lines 1–2). In *Living Nowhere*, Francis finally returns to Corby as Fasthaven only grants a temporal dwelling place, while the narrative's spatial trajectory towards the sea is undermined by a sequence of subtitles arranging the four elements in inverse order: on this level of textual organisation, the novel is moving from 'The Perfection of Water' to 'Keeping Fire', 'The Air of the Door' and, finally, to 'Earth Light'.

Like many other authors and observers drawn to the shape-shifting qualities of shorelines, Burnside invests his seaside settings with a *telos* that is transient at most. If we consider his work in its entirety, such an effect of transience is achieved by constantly revisiting and rewriting paradigmatic maritime scenarios. This rewriting easily travels across generic boundaries without ignoring them. Looking for a possible division of generic labour in Burnside's imagined seascapes will therefore reveal that, on the one hand, the tendency to stage the seaside as a regenerative site of reimmersion and reconnection is more dominant in this author's poetry than in his prose works. At the same time, however, the frequently recurring and subtly shifting coastal settings evince a degree of intratextual density and complexity which prevents any harmonising application of the label 'nature poetry' in the name of a facile regeneration and closure. What these polyvalent littoral ecotones are rather endowed with, then, is a potential for aesthetic unrest and metamorphic inspiration that nourishes both the prose and the poetry of Burnside's work.

Trans-generic Differentiation: The Coast as a Site of Erasure and Inscription

As argued above, Burnside's constantly questioned and rewritten seaside settings cannot provide an unconditional narrative *telos*. In many of this author's texts, the questioning is performed along the lines of generic differentiation. A brief look at two exemplary maritime scenarios may illustrate some of the different means and effects of Burnside's prose and poetic evocations of the coast. In the short story 'Decency' mentioned earlier, the protagonist finally decides to leave his wife and his former life before he undergoes the following dispiriting and deeply disturbing epiphany:

> he must have slept, for he found himself lying in a pool of warm water, the sunlight streaming through his closed eyes. He was swaying slightly with the motion of the tide as a school of tiny fishes – he could feel them, but he couldn't see – rose from the depths of the pool and began biting softly into his flesh, eating him away slowly, quietly, without pain. As they worked, gnawing him away, eating in towards the bone, Robert felt happy. It was good, he knew, that he would be gone soon; but when he woke, he was crying, noiselessly, the tears running into his hair and along his temples, crying for everyone – for the dead girls, for the woman with the ice-cream, for the hashish seller, for Marion, for Sandra, even for Gold. But most of all he was crying for himself, and for the notion he had taken for granted that, no matter how cold it might be, there was a harbour somewhere, a place where he could rest, and think of himself as happy and free, and intrinsically, incontrovertibly, decent. (116–7)

In this prose text, Burnside uses the iconographic inventory of a seaside scene – a pool of water, the motion of the tide, a school of fishes and a harbour – to subject his protagonist to a violent self-annihilation that leaves open the possibility of a cathartic and healing transformation. In the poem 'Varieties of Religious Experience', the final passage culminates in a vision assembling very similar maritime motifs, yet yielding a much more positive, regenerative mood:

> that inlet on the far side
> of the island, where we swam
>
> alone, among the fishes,
> in a sea
>
> so clear
> we could imagine ourselves healed
>
> and true again
> to what we used to know:
>
> the open sky,
> the part-song of cicadas. (lines 86–95)

These two exemplary scenes illustrate some of the main differences between Burnside's prose and poetic seaside settings. For a start, there is a clearly recognisable difference in terms of voice: whereas most of the coastal episodes in the prose texts are coloured by the perspective of individualised and often solipsistically isolated male first-person narrators and focalisers, many of the poems approach their seaside settings through the perspective of an unidentified first-person plural point of view. The 'we' dominating many of Burnside's seaside poems refers to different kinds of communal experience – it sometimes reaches out to the closely knit communities of little harbour towns, sometimes includes a beloved person, sometimes even the author's family, as in the openly autobiographical poem 'History' (2002), depicting the parents and their little son flying kites on an eastern Scottish beach right after the 9/11 terrorist attacks.

As a result of these different perspectives, the coastal locations of Burnside's prose and poetry are given distinctly different qualities. Many of the stories and novels tend to be driven by a violent sense of departure, with the seaside construed as a temporary destination that exerts a compelling and sometimes devastating narrative pull. In contrast, many of the poems follow a different rhythm and movement. Here Burnside allows his speakers and personae to linger and dwell, to explore tentatively and to enjoy a sense of arrival (see Burnside, 'The Arrival'). If we want to summarise these different means, modes and moods, two key scenes from the novel *The Devil's Footprints* (2007) and the poem 'Ports' (2000) can be taken to offer a shorthand version of the prose and the poetic version of Burnside's marine imaginary. In the novel, the first-person narrator finally finds peace in a house by the sea, having retraced a coastal legend portraying the devil stepping out of the sea, carrying with him 'hints of a terrible beauty' (203). In the poem, one of Burnside's most extensive meditations on recovering a sense of home by the sea, the speaker again sets out to find 'our dwelling place' (line 1) by sifting through 'the beauty of wreckage' (line 29) before he settles on the name of a pleasure boat described as 'no more or less correct than anything / we use to make a dwelling in the world' (lines 231–2): 'SERENITY' (line 216).

Due to the trans-generic density of Burnside's writing, the seaside's terrible and serene beauty represents not opposite but complementary aspects of this author's marine imaginary. This becomes particularly obvious if one traces the development of Burnside's artist figures, so often perched in some liminal coastal location, investing the territory between land and sea with a power to trigger aesthetic production and reflexion. Not surprisingly, then, some of the novels use the eastern Scottish coast as a scene of artistic initiation. In the earlier novel *Living Nowhere*, this initiation follows a deconstructive impetus, staging the protagonist's trajectory towards the sea as determined by a double logic of obliteration. While Francis's odyssey is initially driven by his will to exorcise the legacy of Corby, his polluted industrial hometown in the northern Midlands, he eventually finds a temporary home on the Scottish coast where he engages in a painting project whose haunting quality is explained as a 'process of erasure': 'It was a necessary ritual ...: I had to become myself again, a non-person, someone with no defined identity, without family or friends or fixed abode' (317). Francis's project of self-annihilation aims at making himself invisible, allowing him to vanish and obliterate all traces of the past in order to reinvent himself as an artist. In a corresponding way, the novel's maritime scenario is staged as a *tabula rasa* situation, preventing the protagonist from fixating any artistic image in a poetological scenario foregrounded by the elements of water, snow and a cold white mist called 'haar': 'I couldn't get what I wanted from the haar, though. The image I had in mind – something I would only know when I saw it – kept eluding me' (311).

In various poems, Burnside returns to the poetological scene of a visual artist trying to translate the seaside's physical and sensory details, 'the beauty of wreckage', into an image. In these texts, several variations of the ekphrastic motif occur. In the seminal poem 'Ports', the speaker mentions a neighbour called John, 'who spends his free time diving / plumbing the sea for evidence and spilt cargoes / who has burrowed in the mud / to touch the mystery of something absolute' (lines 72–6). Having found a mysterious skeleton that promises to set free 'ancient voices' (line 116), John cannot turn this maritime soundscape into a visual representation, though:

> He had his camera
> but couldn't take
> the picture he wanted
> the one he thinks of now
> as perfect
> – he couldn't betray
> that animal silence

the threadwork of grass through the hide
the dwelling place
inherent in the spine. (lines 118–27)

The later poem 'Haar', again referring to the cold white mist that occasionally whitens out all contours of the coastal landscape, grants the speaker a similarly elusive experience evoking absence, not presence, again culminating in a paradoxical vision of erasure:

and as I walk back from town with the milk and a paper,
the haar whites out the main streets, one by one:
James Street, John Street, Burnside, Tollbooth Wynd,
one step ahead all the time, as I make my way home,

tracing a path of erasure back to the house
where all I possess is laid up, like a storm:
my furniture, my books, my ornaments,
my lost love in the kitchen, brewing tea. (lines 61–8)

Despite its erasing impetus, the poem's poetological reflexion of its coastal setting also presents a gesture of reclaiming authorship. Just as in 'Ports', the names and toponyms referring to the author's name ('neighbour John', 'John Street', 'Burnside') introduce a self-reflexive shift from erasure into inscription: here the seaside is not only staged as a *tabula rasa* foregrounding the gesture of obliterating traces but becomes equally important as a space revealing a possibly meaningful interplay of natural and cultural, elementary and authorial traces.

This more constructive ekphrastic project is also revisited in the novel *The Devil's Footprints*. In this text, Burnside again repeats and rearranges a number of recurring maritime motives. Regarding the legend hinted at in the title – the story of the devil emerging from the sea and leaving his footprints in the snowy landscape on the eastern Scottish coast – the novel once more unfolds an imagery of tracing and retracing. In contrast to *Living Nowhere*, however, the story of the first-person narrator following the devil's prints in a vaguely amorous search for a young woman who might turn out to be his daughter follows a different spatial *mise-en-scène*. Unlike Francis, whose trajectory leads him from Corby to Fasthaven and back to Corby, Michael Gardiner begins his strenuous walk on the coast, eventually moves inland and finally back to his house by the seaside. The modified trajectory of the later novel stages Michael's house as a more permanent dwelling place, granting him a sense of arrival and belonging in a home that, thanks to its situation right on the coast, provides a privileged aesthetic position: 'a house that was, in itself, a sensitive membrane, a register, where every shift in the atmosphere – weather and gossip and the most subtle demographics – was brought to my awareness in real time, as it happened' (109).

Burnside also uses the inverted spatial emplotment of the later novel to recast its father-son relationship. Here again, the earlier novel's constellation is not just repeated but significantly modified: whereas Francis's much more autobiographically grounded story still seems to be fixated on erasing all traces of a past binding him to the polluted masculine codes and industrial infrastructures of Corby, Michael is set free to explore the aesthetic potential of his father's photographic projects. *Living Nowhere* is dedicated to delineating the symbolic geography of Burnside's youth whereas *The Devil's Footprints* resonates with the geographical symbolism of the more mature author, locating some of the father's photographs in La Brière, a marshy region on the coast of Brittany to which one of Burnside's four maritime *Quartets* is dedicated.[7] The later novel's more reconciliatory storyline and tone finally foreground a perspective casting the poetological territory between land and sea as a space not so much of obliteration but of emergence. Accordingly, both Michael and his father are not just occupied with erasing their traces but are able to see new patterns. As a photographer attracted by the marine light of the family's house, exposed to sea and sky, the father was looking 'to withdraw from the lesser, more local patterns, in order to work through to something wider' (209). In a similar vein, re-enacting his father's aesthetic initiation, Michael finally returns to the house on the coast, having learnt

> that [he] also belonged to those wider eternal patterns, those laws that guided the birds and the tides and the weather that had brought [him] home; the pattern, the law, that kept everything in motion and the pattern that allowed it all to open a little, every hundred years or so, to let the devil in. (199)

In *The Devil's Footprints* John Burnside spells out the productive liminality of his recurring maritime settings on different levels. As a coastal wanderer whose footprints are retraced by the novel's protagonist, the legend's devil allows Burnside to retrace the minute details of the coastal flora and fauna, registering the littoral ecotone as a dense cumulative texture interweaving human and non-human, cultural and natural patterns. As a creature 'somewhere between angel and beast, between Ariel and Caliban' (4), the sea-born devil furthermore epitomises Burnside's tendency to defamiliarise any realistic representation of Scotland and Scottishness by metamorphic creatures linking the Scottish tradition of doubles and doppelgangers to a larger literary repertoire of liminal actants (see Galbraith 154; or Gairn 174–5). Such a defamiliarisation of Scottish local colour in most of Burnside's texts goes along with an aesthetic revitalisation triggered by the 'perpetual movement, constant change, Heraclitean flux' (24) of his coastal scenarios. Finally, in its very last pages, the novel also clearly addresses Burnside's interest in the spiritual dimension of maritime contact zones, making the protagonist ponder 'some fault line where the land meets the sea, a gap between this world and another kingdom, another realm, a separate world like the separate world where God dwells, forever in the present tense' (201).

---

[7]   See Burnside 'Saint Nazaire', whose fifth part is entitled 'La Brière'.

Oceanic Temptations in *Glister* and *A Summer of Drowning*

Burnside's oeuvre abounds with such fault lines and gaps, with liminal spaces inviting both tentative and radical, tender and violent movements of transgression.[8] In his latest two novels, the author's penchant for maritime margins is carried into a dimension charged with intense metaphysical, political and artistic self-questioning. As James has argued, both *Glister* and *A Summer of Drowning* can be read as 'ecological thrillers' ('John' 605) employing their seaside settings as polyvalent liminal sites provoking a fundamental interrogation of critical routines:

> As he reanimates the regional novel for the twenty-first century while refusing
> to instrumentalize his settings by turning them into functional backdrops to
> ecopolitical interventions, Burnside's liminal landscapes admit no clear-cut
> answers to the question of what they are for, except to imply that we should think
> about what it means to entertain liminality itself as a critical posture, posed as
> one can often be between the reassurance of taking delight in literary descriptions
> and resisting their affective appeal in the interest of diligent critique. ('John' 614)

Even though the most recent novels are set in different maritime locations in Scotland and Norway, they still revisit a number of Burnside's recurring motifs. While the protagonists are involved in processes of recultivating and defending a sense of dwelling, their painstaking attempts to reimmerse themselves in highly specific environments are challenged by uncannily tempting representatives of liminality – the mysterious Moth Man in *Glister*, luring the narrator and further boys into violent and disturbing acts of initiation; and a young girl in *A Summer of Drowning*, appearing as a reincarnation of the Scandinavian folk spirit of the 'huldra', who in this novel is no longer associated with the woods but, like a classical siren, seems to be luring various boys and men into the depths of the sea.

In spite of their similar engagement with Burnside's philosophy of vanishing, the two novels also differ significantly, however. In *Glister*, Burnside again stages a search for a gap in the fabric of life, to reach out into the explicitly metaphysical realm of what in the text is paraphrased as, variably, 'Heaven, Hell, Tir Na Nog, the Dreamtime' (2) or, as in *Waking up in Toytown*, 'the afterlife' (2). Compared to earlier works, *Glister* presents Burnside's most unsettling version of an afterlife offering both dissolution and reintegration. In the novel's disturbing apotheosis, the first-person narrator Leonard, a thirteen-year-old boy who had been following his vanished friends through the wasteland of a town contaminated by a derelict chemical plant, finds himself in the hands of his possible abductor. The final kidnapping – and, we suspect, murder of the narrator – is staged as a ritual of destructive, 'terrible' beauty (212), promising the tortured protagonist an escape into a different kind of existence, evoked by an unstable first-person voice hovering on a threshold between here and there, between a specified fictional world and its

---

[8]   The leitmotif of the gap can be found, for instance, in *Living Nowhere* (where the gap is already characterised as a 'portal' (234)) as well as in the poem 'Ports'. For Burnside's fascination with liminal configurations, see Gairn 174.

vague beyond, denying a dénouement of the mystery of the vanishing boys the novel plays with in the manner of a detective story.

In terms of setting, *Glister* affords a further 'exploration of the liminal' (Borthwick 77) that departs from a coastal geography and its aesthetic repercussions. The diegetic world of the novel is centred around Leonard's hometown, divided into a posh 'Outertown' and an 'Innertown' populated by the laid-off and dying families of the workers whose lives have been ruined by the chemical company's criminal deals. The Innertown and its contaminated industrial sites are located on a peninsula, and one of Leonard's favourite spots is a ruined crane above the docks, from where he looks

> out over the water, to a point on the horizon that seems to belong, not just to another place, but also to a different time, the past maybe, or maybe the future, when the derelict buildings rot away and the poison in the ground, the poison nobody can see, loses its deadly power. (60)

Perched on the crane in the midst of an industrial wilderness, Leonard carefully maps out the possible ways in which he can transcend the polluted seaside of his hometown. 'Maybe there are more obviously beautiful places in Canada or California' (60), yet 'this apparent wasteland is all the church we have' (66), which is why the narrator sets out to wrest a 'beauty of wreckage' (Burnside, 'Ports' line 29) from the rotting carcasses of crippled boats and contaminated storerooms. The aesthetic value Leonard ascribes to the industrial ruins is laden with political implications. The boy's 'attempt at re-illuminating what appears to be a place of ruin' (James, 'John' 603) performs a conscious act of reclaiming an industrial heritage, not just for himself but also for a fragmented working-class community which has been disempowered and deprived of its sense of home. This gesture of reclaiming is strongly reminiscent of Francis's return to Corby in the earlier novel *Living Nowhere*. Just like the earlier protagonist, Leonard also enlists the element of snow to redefine the wasteland;[9] just like his predecessors in a number of Burnside's texts, he also reflects on the poetological potential of such a cleansing transformation, envisioning a catharsis which would translate the ruins 'into a music that sounds repetitious when you first hear it but soon begins to reveal itself as an infinitely complex fabric of faint overtones and distant harmonies that is never quite the same from one moment to the next' (65).

---

[9]   'Sometimes I [Leonard] think the headland is at its most beautiful in winter, when everything you take for granted, everything you don't bother to look at during the rest of the year, all the hidden angles and recesses, the unseen pipework and fields of rubble, come back new, redefined by the snow and, at the same time, perfected, made abstract, like the world in a blueprint. ... Under the snow, it all looks pure, even when a wet rust mark bleeds through, or some trace of cobalt blue or verdigris rises up through an inch of white, it's beautiful' (Burnside, *Glister* 64). Needless to say, Burnside's exploration of the industrial wasteland of the Innertown is also reminiscent of T.S. Eliot, to whom the author pays homage not only in his 'Four Quartets' but also in the novel's second part, titled 'The Fire Sermon' (173).

In *Glister*, Burnside's exploration of the liminal beauty of seaside wreckage also gains a different quality, however. This is not due simply to the intensely apocalyptic tone of the novel but also results from a different use of maritime settings and motives. In comparison with what we find in Burnside's earlier prose works, the spell cast by the seaside no longer predominantly manifests itself as a storyline plotting the protagonist's movements as organised by the *telos* of the coast. In contrast to the restlessly wandering protagonists of *Living Nowhere* and *The Devil's Footprints*, Leonard remains locked in the Innertown. Caring for his dying father, he has given up all hope of ever leaving his doomed surroundings, and hence allows only his mind to travel and roam freely. Accordingly, the fascination still ascribed to seaside settings in *Glister* operates rather on the level of discourse than on the level of the story. It is, for instance, in the richly layered intertextual structure of the novel where Leonard's disturbing journey into an afterlife is substantiated by his avid reading of Melville and his discovery of a Proust edition 'blue on the cover, like some French song about *la mer*' (85; emphasis in original). More obviously, Leonard's narrative voice is explicitly grounded in a littoral scenario. Confronting us with a highly unnatural, unsettlingly displaced narrative originating from a realm beyond the grave, Burnside nonetheless clearly associates Leonard's voice with the seaside: at the beginning of the novel, the narrator 'can still hear the gulls' and 'a last faint trace of tidewater and shingle', of 'cold, grey water turning on the shore' (1). In its final pages, Leonard's narrative, having taken a characteristically circular turn, returns to the novel's initial maritime location: 'all that remains is the calling of the gulls, above and around me the calling of the gulls and the slow, insistent motion of the waters, slow and far away and barely audible, turning on the shore and in my mind' (255).

Glister illuminates a darker side of Burnside's eco-philosophical project, as it confronts the Heideggerian plea for a situated, grounded dwelling with the potential of a Deleuzian kind of becoming. As the author's most radically formal meditation on the possibilities of an aesthetics of maritime liminality so far, the prose of *Glister* is imbued with lyrical density, translating a recurring site into a characteristic sound. Even though the novel, like many of Burnside's previous prose works, again singles out a male protagonist whose searching is orchestrated by the rhythms of the seaside, the text's multi-perspectival narrative nevertheless reaches out towards the more collective and communal littoral landscapes of Burnside's poetry. In sending his young protagonist through the ambiguous portal of the 'Glister', Burnside seems to be sacrificing Leonard in the name of a daring narrative and spiritual project. As it reimmerses Leonard's disembodied voice into the soothingly repetitive sounds of the seaside, the novel most impressively demonstrates what is at stake in John Burnside's paradoxical poetological programme dedicated to 'the pattern that kept everything in motion' (*Devil's* 199).

While *Glister* invites its readers to imagine the end of the world along apocalyptic lines, the most recent novel, *A Summer of Drowning*, evokes a different sense of an ending. This difference is accentuated by the fact that Burnside focuses for the first time on two female protagonists: the novel takes us to a remote Norwegian island where an artist and her daughter have settled in a house on the beach, engaging in increasingly ambivalent acts of observing their environment, their neighbours and visitors, their paintings and maps and, most importantly, each other. It is the daughter, named Liv, who acts as the single first-person narrator of this novel; and the events she ponders without clarifying them date back to the summer during which not only two boys, who are twins, but also a Scottish tourist and an elderly neighbour vanished under mysterious circumstances. In her retrospective narration Liv tries to make sense of those disappearances by enlisting the evil powers of an enigmatic girl reminiscent of the forest spirits populating the fairy tales of her childhood.

The story also follows Liv to England, where she arrives too late to meet her father, whose identity was never disclosed to her, before he dies. Haunted by the unresolved conflicts lurking under the surface of the symbiotic mother-daughter relationship, Liv abruptly terminates her attempt to find out more about her origins. Before she returns to the island and her mother's splendid isolation, the claustrophobic relationship between the two female protagonists is expressed by one of those ekphrastic scenes we often find at the centre of Burnside's poetological self-questioning. In an exhibition mounted in the English town where her father has just died, Liv comes across one of the paintings that have shaped her mother's artistic development. For this seminal scene Burnside has chosen Harald Sohlberg's *Et Hus Ved Kysten* (1906), which was also used for the cover illustration of the novel. The depiction of a tiny white fisherman's cottage surrounded by dark trees before a mysteriously illuminated coastline distils the novel's atmosphere of brooding intensity and isolation. It also delivers an epiphany, providing Liv with a solipsistic moment of dwelling:

> I sat there for fifteen minutes, or longer even, but I wasn't in that gallery, in that English market town any more, I was *home*. Not just home, on Kvalöya, but home in my own head, in the place where dreams happened. I was in a place that nobody else could ever see, and I was completely alone there. (207; emphasis in original)

Liv's precarious notion of home is associated with the metamorphic qualities of the novel's seaside settings which throw light on the complex relationship between the narrator and her mother. For a start, it seems as though the crucially liminal grounds of her mother's property are organised according to a principle of two directions reminiscent of the famous 'deux cotés' in Marcel Proust's *A la Recherche du Temps Perdu*. Thus a situation 'where meadow met shingle', 'where the land can't decide whether it's in colour or black and white and so settles for something that is neither one nor the other' (236), is temporarily sorted into the mother's and the daughter's point of view. While the former cultivates an exotic garden facing the land, the latter is clearly oriented towards the sea:

> It's just that I prefer being out in the open, out on the meadows with the salt wind blowing up from the shore, out with the birds and the clouds and the line of the horizon. For me, Mother's garden is too sheltered. Too sheltered, and too enclosed, hemmed in by the birch woods and the carved rocks that rise on the north and west side. You can't really see into the distance – or rather, in those

places where you can see, it feels like a calculated illusion. A vista. Out in the open, I can turn and see the whole world stretching away to the horizon and, at the same time, I feel myself in heaven's eye. (237–8)

As in Proust's *Recherche*, however, the illusion of dividing the world into neatly separated perspectives cannot be maintained. In a scene again connecting the present of Liv's narration to the past of the narrated events, we see mother and daughter driving to a beach the girl had labelled 'the end of the world', 'thinking partly of a real place and partly of the true remoteness in some old fairy story, where ships sailed off the edge of the sea and strangers appeared, washed up on the shore, from the next world but one' (241–2). It is on this remote beach that Liv's mother seems to have found 'refuge, or solace' (242), but, as James has pointed out, Burnside's writing does not easily offer consolation by reconnecting his characters through Romantic experiences of nature ('John' 613).[10] Not surprisingly, then, the episode does not establish the beach at 'the end of the world' as a site of communal regeneration but ends on a note of solitary reflexion: 'Now, though, the stories we tell – or, at least, the story that *I* have to tell – seems merely curious, a grotesque and utterly unconvincing account of a series of tragic coincidences, told by a solitary woman who, by her own admission, has a history of *seeing things*' (243; emphases in original).

Even though *A Summer of Drowning* does not explore the ends of its characters' worlds in an apocalyptic mode, Burnside still endows his first female protagonist with similarly eerie visions to those of the narrator of the preceding novel *Glister*. Accordingly, Liv's way of 'seeing things' does not simply – or finally – set Burnside's allegedly flawed gender record straight. Due to the novel's many references to an iconography of sirens and mermaids, it might, at first glance, be tempting to read Liv's chronicle of drowning men as an invocation of a feminist tradition of oceanic liberation. In contrast to canonical works such as Kate Chopin's *The Awakening*, Adrienne Rich's 'Diving into the Wreck' or *The Piano* (directed by Jane Campion), however, Burnside's most recent novel cannot be considered as a case of revisionist writing back. Nor does it cure its male characters' 'malignant masculinity' through female focalisation. Instead, Liv's speculations on the Scottish tourist and the mysterious 'huldra' are linked to a context of paedophilic abduction: *A Summer of Drowning* revisits the constellation of travelling foreigners encountering young women as we find it, for instance, in the short story 'Decency' and in *The Devil's Footprints*, and it concretises these unsettling reverberations through several references to Lewis Carroll's *Alice in Wonderland* (108, 160). Furthermore, in an episode concerned with her mother's painting, Liv learns to appreciate the distant intensity of her mother's art through a decidedly unfeminist mythical conjecture. According to a sympathetic friend's explanation, it is not by putting the nymph Echo back into the picture but by

---

[10]   '[T]he issue Burnside leaves noticeably unresolved is whether the practices of landscape phenomenology that he not only dramatizes but also appears to endorse operate for disruptive or reparative ends'.

respecting Narcissus's fascination with his reflection in the pond that painting can be understood as an existential form of immersion:

> it's only when he [Narcissus] discovers the truth, and sees that his self is an object in a world, like all the other objects, that he becomes a painter. Because, for the first time, he is part of the world, and art is his way of confirming that. A way of saying that he is in the world, in the world and of it. Echo mouthing back to his own speech – that was a sad joke, a parody. Now, though, he's surrounded by the unexpected and the unpredictable. (143)

In a novel whose most dramatic and disturbing scenes are staged on the beach, Narcissus can be considered a key figure of artistic reflexion as he is himself poised in a liminal situation close to the water. Such a reading of the myth performs an abstraction which is also a vital element of Burnside's treatment of coastal and littoral landscapes. It is true that this author, on the one hand, engages in meticulously detailed descriptions demonstrating a phenomenological exploration of the transformative power of what he in a programmatic essay has characterised as 'region(s) of potential' (Burnside, 'Poetry'). The lyrical evocation of a world rich in suggestive natural details never aims at a facile regeneration, however. As a 'double-edged' project combining 'ineffability and actuality' (James, 'John' 602), 'bewilderment' and 'enchantment' (James, 'John' 614), Burnside's writing rather departs from geographically specific 'regions of potential' into more abstract realms of possibility and risk. Here the ecopolitical mantra of connectivity cannot be taken for granted.

In a further scene which finds Liv on the island's shore, it becomes obvious that Burnside's most recent novel, instead of exploring female alternatives to the 'malignant masculinities' of earlier prose texts, rather expands his defence of solitude and silence to include his first fully fledged female protagonists. In the aforementioned scene, Liv, just like many of Burnside's preceding male narrators and focalisers, appreciates the liminality of the beach she visits to be alone as an 'unnamed and indefinable borderline, a line that nobody could see on maps or ships' charts' where she finds 'constant traffic between one side and the other' (*Summer* 98). In the same way as Leonard invokes '*mon semblable, mon frère*' (*Glister* 258; italics in original)[11], Liv also dreams of doubles and phantoms trafficking the 'perilous edgeline' (*Summer* 242), a phenomenological threshold where her world becomes as 'shifting' and 'endlessly reshaping itself' (98) like Leonard's oceanic narrative rhythm at the beginning and end of *Glister*.

Whereas *Glister* is dedicated to Leonard's art of reilluminating polluted ruins, *A Summer of Drowning* offers a double portrait of creativity. Continuing and modifying an ekphrastic subtext running through his whole oeuvre,[12] Burnside

---

[11]   In this passage, Leonard's violent transformation is interwoven with allusions to Baudelaire and T.S. Eliot.

[12]   Examples of this subtext can be found in the meditations on photography in the novels *The Locust Room* and *The Devil's Footprints*, in the painting protagonist in *Living Nowhere* and also in poems such as 'The Arrival of the Mailboat', which is based on a painting by Edvard Munch.

here contrasts two modes of visual representation: gradually, the dominance of the mother's painting gives way to the daughter's art of making maps. It is the latter which provides the most powerful poetological metaphor of Burnside's ecological art as an enterprise dedicated to measuring liminality without routinely celebrating its promises of transgression:

> I don't like intertwined. I like intact. There is too much contact in the world. Too much *intertwined*. Maybe it *is* true that we all depend on one another, that everything in the world depends on everything else – but we also depend on the spaces in between. We need the spaces, because the spaces are where the order lies. That's why I like maps, because they recognise the gaps between one thing and another. They stand in mute opposition to those who think that the connections are all that matter. (62–3)

The programmatic rhyme of 'map' and 'gap' reveals one of the conceptual powerhouses of Burnside's writing (see Burnside, 'Mind the Gap'). In an almost identical passage connecting the beginning and the end of *A Summer of Drowning*, Liv characterises the gaps she tries to map as 'infinitesimal loopholes of havoc in the fabric of the given world that could spill loose and catch me out wherever I am' (328). The many beaches, shorelines and coastal regions orchestrating John Burnside's oeuvre provide both figures and grounds for the productive gaps this writer opens within the emerging orthodoxies of ecologically aware art.

Works Cited

Banville, John. *The Sea*. London: Picador, 2005.

Bate, Jonathan. *The Song of the Earth*. London: Picador, 2000.

Borthwick, David. 'The Sustainable Male: Masculine Ecology in the Poetry of John Burnside'. *Masculinity and the Other: Historical Perspectives*. Ed. Heather Ellis and Jessica Meyer. Cambridge: Cambridge Scholars Publishing, 2009. 63–83.

Burnside, John. 'Arrival of the Mail Boat, after Edvard Munch'. Burnside, *Asylum Dance*. 30.

———. *The Asylum Dance*. London: Jonathan Cape, 2000.

———. 'Decency'. *Burning Elvis*. London: Jonathan Cape, 2000. 81–118.

———. *The Devil's Footprints*. London: Vintage, 2008.

———. 'Four Quartets'. Burnside, *Gift Songs*. 49–78.

———. *Gift Songs*. London: Jonathan Cape, 2005.

———. *Glister*. London: Jonathan Cape, 2008.

———. 'Haar'. Burnside, *Selected Poems*. 101–3.

———. 'Hay Devil'. Burnside, *Asylum Dance*. 31–3.

———. 'History'. Burnside, *Selected Poems*. 89–91.

———. *A Lie About My Father*. London: Jonathan Cape, 2006.

———. *Living Nowhere*. London: Vintage, 2003.

———. *The Locust Room*. London: Vintage, 2002.

———. 'The Men's Harbour'. Burnside, *Asylum Dance*. 60–61.

———. 'Mind the Gap: On Reading American Poetry'. *Poetry Review* 96.3 (2006): 56–67.

———. 'Pisces'. Burnside, *Selected Poems*. 12.

———. 'Poetry and a Sense of Place'. *Nordlit* 1 (1996). Web. 1 May 2013. <http://www.hum.uit.no/nordlit/1/burnside.html>.

———. 'Ports'. Burnside, *Selected Poems*. 41–8.

———. 'Saint Nazaire'. Burnside, *Gift Songs*. 49–55.

———. 'A Science of Belonging: Poetry as Ecology'. Contemporary Poetry and Contemporary Science. Ed. Robert Crawford. Oxford: Oxford UP, 2006. 91–106.

———. *Selected Poems*. London: Jonathan Cape, 2006.

———. 'Settlements'. Burnside, *Asylum Dance*. 23–9.

———. 'Strong Words'. *Strong Words: Modern Poets on Modern Poetry*. Ed. W.N. Herbert and Matthew Hollis. Northumberland: Bloodaxe, 2000. 259–61.

———. 'Suburbs'. Burnside, *Selected Poems*. 2–6.

———. *A Summer of Drowning*. London: Jonathan Cape, 2011.

———. 'Varieties of Religious Experience'. Burnside, *Gift Songs*. 23–35.

———. *Waking Up in Toytown*. London: Jonathan Cape, 2010.

Burnside, John, and Maurice O'Riordan, eds. *Wild Reckoning: An Anthology Provoked by Rachel Carson's 'Silent Spring'*. London: Calouste Gulbenkian Foundation, 2004.

Carroll, Lewis. *Alice in Wonderland*. London: W.W. Norton & Company, 1992.

Chopin, Kate. *The Awakening*. Oxford: Oxford World's Classics, 2000.

Galbraith, Iain. 'Eclipsing Binaries: Self and Other in John Burnside's Fiction'. *Etudes Ecossaises* 8 (2002): 147–64.

Gairn, Louisa. *Ecology and Modern Scottish Literature*. Edinburgh: Edinburgh UP, 2008.

Garrard, Greg. *Ecocriticism*. London: Routledge, 2004.

Harte, Liam. "The Endless Mutation of the Shore': Colm Tóibín's Marine Imaginary'. *Critique* 51 (2010): 333–49.

Heidegger, Martin. 'Building, Dwelling, Thinking'. Trans. David Farrell. *Basic Writings*. Ed. David Farrell. New York: Harper & Row, 1977. 319–39.

James, David. *Contemporary British Fiction and the Artistry of Space*: Style, Landscape, Perception. London: Continuum, 2008.

———. 'John Burnside's Ecologies of Solace: Regional Environmentalism and the Consolations of Description'. *Modern Fiction Studies* 58.3 (2012): 600–615.

The Piano. Dir. Jane Campion. Perf. Holly Hunter and Harvey Keitel. Jan Chapman Productions. 1993. Film.

Proust, Marcel. *A la Recherche du Temps Perdu*. Paris: Gallimard, 2003.

Rich, Adrienne. 'Diving into the Wreck'. *The Columbia Anthology of American Poetry*. Ed. Jay Parini. New York: Columbia UP, 1995. 667.

Schoene, Berthold. *The Edinburgh Companion to Contemporary Scottish Literature*. Edinburgh: Edinburgh UP, 2007.

Chapter 6
Caribbean Beachcombers

Tobias Döring

There are few other places in the world that are as closely associated with the beach as the Caribbean islands. Both in their long history of colonial encounter, cultural trade and naval conquest and in their more recent marketing as paradise resorts of pleasure, these islands figure most prominently in our cultural imaginary as one long, though discontinuous, stretch of beaches – constantly exposing themselves to outside influences while, at the same time, promising protection or intimacy in the natural semicircles of their bays. While the tourist industry's invention of Caribbean beach life is a relatively new phenomenon, there may be more to such a notion than a simple PR ploy. As Caribbean writers such as Édouard Glissant have argued, the fragmented physiognomy of the archipelago and its coastlines offers a geographical basis for what he calls a 'poetics of relation' in which continuous exposure and exchange, rather than containment and absolute delimitation, determine the dynamics in the formation of local societies (see Glissant). In this sense, Caribbean beaches are important operators in the context of a culture of creolisation. At the same time, though, Caribbean beaches turn into sites of concrete work and cultural production – and it is this aspect which concerns me here. Not simply a space of leisure or carefree recreation, the beaches have for centuries exerted a powerful attraction on so-called beachcombers, that is to say, on local collectors and cultural labourers whose work I set out to discuss with reference to some pertinent examples from Caribbean literature. These beach workers offer the particularly localised version of a more general activity that is of special relevance, I shall argue, for the poetics of postcolonial writing and its contested engagements with tradition.

However, looking at Caribbean beaches as sites of labour and production, as I suggest, may well be regarded as a complex, even dangerous enterprise. Such a danger was, for instance, highlighted by Francis Bacon, the early modern English statesman who cautioned against seeing the seaside as a place for settlement and work in the New World. In spite of the obvious advantages of easy access, 'it hath been a great endangering', he writes in his essay 'Of Plantations', that such places of production have been 'built along the Sea, and Rivers, in Marish and unwholesome Grounds', not fit for human work and habitation (98). For my reading of some fragments from Caribbean-English literature, by contrast, it is just this marshland, situated between land and sea, this insecure and thoroughly unwholesome ground that may turn out to be the most productive territory. In the three parts of my discussion, I shall first establish the tropological particularity of beach writing, then offer a reading of a few Caribbean texts before trying, on this basis, to describe beachcombing as the central figure for a poetics of impure postcolonial beginnings.

Beach Tropes

In summer 1991, a new play opened at the National Theatre in London. Entitled *The Coup* and written by the Trinidadian and Black British playwright Mustapha Matura, it contains a scene of historical beginnings which is of particular interest for our topic. The stage directions read as follows:

> *A beach. Sunset. A boat arrives, on board are European men: the* **Captain** *of the ship,* **Christopher Columbus** *and a* **Monk**. *They disembark and the* **Captain** *plants the flag of Spain on top of a sandy hill.* (Matura 20; emphases in original)

The scene that opens here develops first along the lines suggested by this historically familiar constellation. Columbus, the Monk and the Captain claim possession of what they perceive as a virginal place; they name it 'Trinidad' (21) and, through a number of ritualised speech acts, subject it to Castilian rule. But then something quite unexpected happens, impinging on the highly predictable sequence of events. While the Captain and Columbus are going through the motions of their discoverers' routine, the Monk notices through a telescope a group of wondrous creatures approaching in the air: neither really human nor really inhuman, they contest the categories of perception because they fly like birds but look like men. When they arrive, they turn out to be Arawaks, 'dressed in feathers of gold', wearing 'golden jewellery' and 'carrying baskets of fruit' (22). Their encounter with the Europeans thus begins with offerings of food and the exchange of gifts but quickly leads to the inevitable question about Eldorado and the search for gold – in other words, to the economy of symbolic and of material value which served to justify the Columbian voyage in the first place.

The historical encounter enacted here has become fixed in the popular imagination and clearly fascinated many early modern minds as well: Columbus arriving in a marvellous place which he takes for the kingdom of the great Khan in the East; Europeans planting the royal standard on the sand so as to claim control over the new territory; Amerigo Vespucci facing the naked New World beauty who beckons to him with a smile, while the line of his enraptured gaze is crossed by tiny cannibal figures in the background having a barbecue party on the beach. Acts and images like these have long provided a foundational narrative of conquest and, for centuries, formed the substance of European fantasies of the New World. The same year that Matura's play came out, Stephen Greenblatt published *Marvelous Possessions*, his study of the 'wonder of the New World', in which he analysed this primal scene – in his words, 'the most famous of beginnings' – and discussed the various textualisations and cultural negotiations of what he called 'the great adventurer on the beach' (52). The founding function of this beach encounter, then, has been so well attested and thoroughly explored in literary and cultural studies that I need not go into detail here. What I would like to emphasise, however, is the constitutive partiality of all representations, textual or visual or otherwise, which try to reconstruct this moment. It is a simple point, though potentially rich in implications. For reasons easily appreciated, this adventure on the beach is only accessible and debatable from the particular perspective of the voyagers for whom the Caribbean beaches signified the place of landfall. The perspective of their counterparts, for whom these beaches signified the seaside, is, strictly speaking, not available.

In fact, Matura's theatrical stage version of the first encounter scene is most remarkable in that it tries to evade, perhaps even erase, such a discrepancy. It relies on the presence of an audience, watching the beach adventure between Europeans and Arawaks from the superior position of distanced spectators, that is to say, inhabiting an elevated point of view, literally a bird's-eye view, which cannot be historically postulated because it is impossible to take. And what is more, Matura's scene would seem to dramatise such an impossibility by letting the Arawaks appear as birds, much to the amazement of the Spaniards – flying figures who transcend the limitations of our familiar world. But when we analyse the New World beaches as a contact zone, a social space where, in the words of Pratt, 'disparate cultures meet, clash and grapple with each other, often in highly asymmetrical relations of domination and subordination' (4), we must acknowledge one of the most glaring asymmetries inherent in the basic fact that all available accounts and mappings of this space are entirely dominated by the side that designates this world as 'new'. The other side, for which the new has long been old, can only be imagined.

> Columbus from his after-
> deck watched stars, absorbed in water,
> melt in liquid amber drifting
>
> through my summer air.
> Now with morning, shadows lifting,
> beaches stretched before him cold and clear.
>
> Birds circled flapping flag and mizzen
> mast: birds harshly hawking, without fear.
> Discovery he sailed for was so near. (Brathwaite 52)

These lines, from the 1967 cycle *Rights of Passage* by the Barbadian poet Edward Brathwaite, immediately raise the question just discussed. What point of view is being hypothesised here? What is the deictic orientation of the space constructed? Who can see the 'beaches stretched before' Columbus and can, at the same time, say that 'discovery' is 'near'? And who would claim the 'summer air' as '*my* summer air' (emphasis added), when 'summer' clearly is a Eurocentric misnomer for the local seasons, which are very different in the tropics?

Such questions to the poem, I suggest, do not point to confusion on the poet's part; rather, they point to the consequences of the historical ruptures, cultural discontinuities and epistemic fallacies that constitute the Caribbean social space as a complex constellation of multiple contacts, dominations and subordinations. In fact, the prime concern of Greenblatt's *Marvelous Possessions*, in contrast to Tzvetan Todorov's earlier study of the conquest of America, is to explore the cultural poetics of this space for the disturbing traces of the local other which they involve and which may wield a greater influence on European travelogues and their discursive management of beach encounters than is usually acknowledged. It was Pratt who further focussed on this issue, with reference to the texts of later travel writers, when she identified the agency of so-called 'travelees' (7), that is to say, the people travelled to and represented in the Western record, as crucial for our present-day engagements with the perpetuated rhetoric of colonial exploration.

Against the background of such critical considerations, we may be able to address one of the fundamental questions underlying the entire project of the present volume: what can literature, what can literary studies offer to the study of beaches? No doubt, many fictional texts feature beaches as a setting. Caribbean literature is no exception, because writers from the region have, for obvious reasons, often chosen to locate some crucial moments of their stories at the seaside, the liminal space of promise, transformation and transgression where normal social regulations fall into abeyance, a place where, in the words of Robert Antoni's recent novel *Carnival*, it always somehow seems 'like carnival was still going on' (234). But the beach as setting is not all. We should go beyond such an approach and explore beaches not only as a site or place, that is, a *topos* in the literature; we should also explore beaches as a *trope*, that is to say, as a figure and operator of a specific rhetorical plot. I would suggest that the beach, in this sense, emplots the irreducible partiality of cultural encounter. Not simply a setting but a trope, it figures the two-sided nature and counter-discursive realities involved in the act while it, at the same time, refigures the one-sided perspective from which such acts are generally perceived. Without a bird's eye view, the two opposing sides of beach encounters cannot transcend historical divisions in favour of overarching visions. Seen from the land, that is, from the local, stable point of view, the beach is known as the seaside; seen from the ocean, that is from the foreign, displaced point of view, the beach is perceived as the place of landfall. Seaside as opposed to coastline: these two different views are not easily resolvable into some higher unity, which is why I suggest regarding their doubleness, duality or perhaps duplicity as a central trope of beach writing, the strategy by which familiar views are turned around and may return in defamiliarised perspectives.

With regard to the Caribbean islands, however, we must be clear about the basic fact that, historically speaking, no land-based inside views, no internal and indigenous perspectives have come down to us. After the early modern genocide following the Spanish conquest, few traces of the native presence can be found today, mainly in some linguistic legacies of naming, and certainly no cultural record of Columbus's travelees survives. Unlike African or Asian coasts or the Pacific islands, therefore, Caribbean beaches do not figure any longer as anybody's native seaside. Their indigenous land perspective has been lost. They are strictly places seen and entered from the sea. If the beach in general functions, as suggested, as a trope of doubleness, we must acknowledge that for Caribbean beaches, one part of this trope is absent – or, rather, that this part remains entirely imaginary.

And this is where the role of literary texts comes in. They could provide imaginative renderings of this absent side, the lost point of view, which may still be invoked in poetic reconstruction. Brathwaite's poem does indeed continue:

> Columbus from his after-
> deck watched heights he hoped for,
> rocks he dreamed, rise solid from my simple water.
>
> Parrots screamed. Soon he would touch
> our land, his charted mind's desire.
> The blue sky blessed the morning with its fire.
> …
> I watched him pause.
>
> Then he was splashing silence.
> Crabs snapped their claws
> and scattered as he walked towards our shore. (52–3)

Here an omniscient poetic persona is constructed who can both tell us what Columbus 'dreamed' and, at the same time, claim the beach he sails towards as 'our land' and 'our shore'. Where might such a speaker be located? What is the point of observation from which this persona can first watch Columbus on his ship watching the stars and then watch him walk on 'our' beach? The discoverer himself is being discovered here. In actual fact, such a double view comprising both perspectives of the first encounter is strictly impossible, just as the indigenous view from the island is historically lost. Columbus kept a journal of this voyage and wrote his famous letter to Lord Raphael Sanchez so as to relate to the most Invincible Majesties Ferdinand and Isabella all the details of his travels. For all we know, his travelees, by contrast, kept no such record – and if they did, it must have been erased. Brathwaite's poem, therefore, offers an imaginative substitute for it, a conjectural and second-best version of what this lost perspective might have been, a mimetic version which retrospectively attempts to imitate, to recreate, to represent and to perform the voice and view of others: a mimesis, in short, of alterity.

More generally speaking, then, the beach as trope turns out to be deeply implicated in the interplay of mimesis and alterity which Taussig has described: 'a space between', 'a space permeated by' colonial tension 'in which it is far from easy to say who is the imitator and who is the imitated, which is copy and which is original' (78), so that mimesis emerges not just as a reproductive but as a productive force. Precisely because no original for indigenous observers in the Caribbean is available or, at any rate, accessible to Caribbean writers, they can only copy it, as in Brathwaite's poem, by making it up and making do with whatever means and models for it they may find. The historical impossibility thus translates into the tropes of realistically impossible elements in Caribbean writing.

Beach Skills

In fact, such challenges to the economy of realism in Caribbean literature are nothing new or recent, as the following example from the early eighteenth century illustrates:

> It happen'd one day about noon going towards my boat, I was exceedingly surpris'd with the print of a man's naked foot on the shore, which was very plain to be seen in the sand: I stood like one thunder-struck, or as if I had seen an apparition; I listen'd, I look'd round me, I could hear nothing, nor see any thing, I went up to a rising ground to look farther, I went up the shore and down the shore, but it was all one, I could see no other impression but that one, I went to it again to see if there were any more, and to observe if it might not be my fancy; but there was no room for that, for there was exactly the very print of a foot, toes, heel, and every part of a foot; how it came thither, I knew not, nor could in the least imagine. (Defoe 122)

What Robinson Crusoe observes here, the famous footprint on the beach, has been characterised by Novak as the most influential episode in all of Defoe's writing (206). In the same vein, Hulme has analysed the 'determinedly unrealistic presence of the single, isolated footprint in the middle of the beach' as a 'pure trace of the idea of otherness' rather than 'the actual track of another human being' (201). At any rate, it marks a moment of most intense anxiety for Robinson, who at this point becomes aware that he is not alone and totally isolated on the island but must be wary of the visitors and, potentially, the cannibals who threaten to disturb his solitude. Hence his panic and his increasing efforts to protect himself.

At the same time, though, we should emphatically read this single footprint as a marker of intense desire, too. The 'idea of otherness' that manifests itself in the mysterious mark on the beach signifies the desire of the castaway to reach out toward an other, namely, to find a counterpart or a companion and to establish company, if only as a way of re-establishing himself, long before the moment when Man Friday makes his first appearance. Strictly impossible in a realistic or historical framework of representation, the single isolated footprint therefore is the imprint of the mimetic desire to produce what is lost or lacking and thus to inscribe empty space with compensatory symbolic signs. Again the Caribbean beach here functions as a trope, because the plot in which the footprint figures involves the presence of an absent other and offers the perspective of alterity through which the castaway, the narrator and, indeed, the writer Robinson invests in the economy of literary imagination.

Aligning Defoe's classic English fiction with the literary figurations of postcolonial Caribbean writers raises a fundamental question, however. After all, *Robinson Crusoe* stands for nothing less than the colonial rise of the bourgeois novel. Even though its setting does suggest a Caribbean island, Defoe's narrative of cultural encounter clearly belongs to the other side, the side of the displaced views of record-keeping European voyagers who arrive on New World beaches, whether by design or accident, after crossing the Atlantic into unfamiliar space.

Robinson's entire project on the island, in this sense, is driven by a kind of repetition compulsion, an attempt to turn the strange and threateningly unfamiliar place into a European habitat. Let us therefore now approach his narrative from the other side, as it were, from the defamiliarising point of view in which it figures in the following poem:

> Once we have driven past Mundo Nuevo trace
>   safely to this beach house
> perched between ocean and green, churning forest
>   the intellect appraises
> objects surely, even the bare necessities
>   of style are turned to use,
> like those plain iron tools he salvages
>   from shipwreck, hewing a prose
> as odorous as raw wood to the adze; (Walcott, 'Crusoe's Journal', 92)

These are the opening lines of 'Crusoe's Journal', a central text from Derek Walcott's 1965 collection *The Castaway*. They do not just avail themselves of a particular beach setting, 'perched between ocean and green, churning forest' somewhere on a New World island; they also dramatise the predicament of newness – and of trying to come to terms with newness – through a search for linguistic tools and stylistic instruments that may be useful for this purpose. Significantly, it is as a model, or indeed ancestral figure, of this specific cultural ambition that Robinson Crusoe is invoked here. The third person pronoun 'he' in line 7 refers to Defoe's self-reliant castaway whose narrative is cited in the epigraph and who manages to do just this: salvage whatever he can lay his hands on from the shipwreck and use or recycle what is left of civilisation so as to construct another second-best version of it on the inhospitable island.

The poem's title, quite specifically, refers to Robinson as a writer, that is to say, the journal keeper whose verbal record notes in detail what random objects he finds on the beach: 'In the morning looking towards the sea-side, the tide being low, I saw something lye on the shore bigger than ordinary, and it look'd like a cask' (Defoe 67), one of his characteristic entry reads. 'I roll'd it farther on shore for the present and went on upon the sands as near as I could to the wreck of the ship to look for more' (Defoe 67). Textual examples such as this give evidence that, contrary to much of the reception of his tale throughout the eighteenth century and beyond, Robinson's celebrated civilising project does not start from scratch at all but from the flotsam and jetsam which he happens to find on the beach and in the abandoned wreck, whence he salvages a good many implements and tools. What, however, is the relevance of such entries from Crusoe's journal for postcolonial Caribbean writing and, especially, for Walcott's poem? The opening stanza continues:

> out of such timbers
> came our first book, our profane Genesis

> whose Adam speaks that prose
> which, blessing some sea-rock, startles itself
>   with poetry's surprise,
> in a green world, one without metaphors;
>   like Christofer he bears
> in speech mnemonic as a missionary's
>   the Word to savages,
> its shape an earthen, water-bearing vessel's
>   whose sprinkling alters us
>
> into good Fridays who recite His praise,
>   parroting our master's
> style and voice, we make his language ours,
>   converted cannibals
> we learn with him to eat the flesh of Christ. (Walcott, 'Crusoe's Journal', 92–3)

This is a version of the oft-repeated notion of the New World Adam, a genealogy of cultural production in the Americas that appropriates the Book of Genesis in order to hypothesise a paradise of fresh beginnings. Yet in the particular version of this myth we read here, what seems to be most striking is how clearly the supposed paradise is modelled on the Puritan and work-intensive place of labour we recall from Robinson's adventure, far removed from any marvellous charm or original natural power. Many features of these complex lines would invite more detailed commentary. But for present purposes, one point is crucial: the curious and contradictory acts of self-positioning performed by the poetic persona. Towards the end of the stanza, the persona clearly sides with Friday: the first-person pronoun 'we' (in a sentence such as 'we make his language ours') designates a collective group of Caribbean 'good Fridays' who have taken on their 'master's style and voice' through mimetic acts of 'parroting'. At the same time, the same first-person pronoun suggests rather a different constituency in the earlier phrase 'our first book, our profane Genesis', where the reference is to the 'timbers' and 'tools' which Robinson collected from the wreck, a reference thus including this colonial collector figure into the collective Caribbean cultural effort. In a double strategy, not unlike the one we observed in Brathwaite's Columbus poem, the deictic orientation in Walcott's beach text, we note, is not confined to one side only but tries to comprise both – siding with Friday just as with Robinson, imaginatively overwriting the colonial divisions between master and slave. Both Friday and Robinson are stranded on the island, fatally endangered and thus fatefully bound to each other, almost to the point of an imaginary identification of coloniser with colonised.

Such a provocative move, however, is not proposed in Walcott's poem as part of a sentimental rhetoric of reconciliation. It rather follows from a reconsideration of the concrete historical conditions as a result of which all current Caribbean culture, after the violent erasure of indigenous languages, shares the same predicament: it is built around displacement and mimetic re-creation. The final stanza pursues this line of argument even further, tracing an ongoing process of identification while also staging our reading process of the text as the mimetic repetition of a creation process:

> For the hermetic skill, that from earth's clays
>   shapes something without use,
> and, separate from itself, lives somewhere else,
>   sharing with every beach
> a longing for those gulls that cloud the cays
>   with raw, mimetic cries,
> never surrenders wholly …
> …
>   So from this house
> that faces nothing but the sea, his journals
>   assume a household use;
> we learn to shape from them, where nothing was
>   the language of a race,
> and since the intellect demands its mask
>   that sun-cracked, bearded face
> provides us with the wish to dramatize
>   ourselves at nature's cost,
> to attempt a beard, to squint through the sea-haze,
>   posing as naturalists,
> drunks, castaways, beachcombers, all of us
>   yearn for those fantasies
> of innocence …. ('Crusoe' lines 93–4; emphasis added)

The 'hermetic skill' which here refers to a purported act of clay creation and cultural production – the genesis of something 'without use', however – corresponds to the specific hermeneutic skill we need to read this poem, an artefact produced through complex interplays of mimesis and alterity which 'never surrenders wholly' and yet assumes 'a household use', just as Crusoe's journal does. The climactic and, for the present reading, central line of the poem follows from this as it serves, once more, to widen the constituency of the first-person plural pronoun 'we': 'drunks, castaways, beachcombers, all of us'. With great emphasis and even pathos, it tries to establish yet again a collectivity that comprises the entire Caribbean population, whether settlers or slaves, and in this way naturalises Crusoe to the West Indian locality: the castaway and beachcomber whose creativity and cultural productivity lie in assembling and recycling whatever is at hand, turning it to 'household use' and thus making his entire household from the flotsam and jetsam of the sea.

It is the figure of the beachcomber emerging from this poem which we need to consider in more detail when trying to understand what Walcott has described as 'our profane Genesis' in Caribbean cultural poetics. What might be its significance?

Beach Beginnings

According to the *OED*, the term 'beachcomber' first designated 'a long wave rolling in from the ocean' as if to comb and clear the beach. In a metonymic exchange of cause and consequence, the term then came to be used for the struggling settlers who live along such beaches and try to make their living by collecting whatever such a wave might leave behind. Beachcombing, then, concerns the riches of the poor. It is a cultural labour that draws on contingency and yet attempts to recreate some kind of order by assembling random bits and pieces lost as the result of maritime catastrophes, now washed ashore and soon to be reassembled for new purposes and provisionally reintegrated in different ways. For this reason, beachcombing raises issues of positioning and property. Its social history would have to explore the question who goes out to collect the debris, in what circumstances and with what interests, whether the activity can turn into a means of subsistence or even a profitable business, what sort of legal constraints are imposed on claiming goods found on the beach and several related questions. I cannot answer any of these questions here but would like to point out that the same issues of belonging, control and collection also bear on the economy of cultural production and, especially, of literary creation in the Caribbean. The process of collecting and reusing whatever is at hand, what can be found through random chance or systematic searching and what appears to have arrived from far away, though all traces of its origin may have been washed off long ago by the journey – this process is precisely in what postcolonial Caribbean texts, such as the ones cited and considered here, all engage. They are performances of beachcombing, I contend, products of collecting and recycling literary flotsam, and they often openly display the consequences of these acts so as to suggest an alternative notion of cultural creativity and poetic originality.

This, however, is not a gratuitous strategy but a response to pressing historical predicaments. 'History is built around achievement and creation; and nothing was created in the West Indies' (Naipaul 29). With this notorious polemic, the narrative persona in Naipaul's travelogue *The Middle Passage* once famously described the problem of West Indian culture – an oft-cited and much-resented diagnosis of a social field in which original creativity was long felt to be missing. Yet it would be seriously mistaken to read Naipaul's statement only as expressing elitist, Eurocentric or even racist sentiments. Rather, whatever it expresses follows from the fundamental problem mentioned earlier: the traumatic loss of all indigenous culture in the Caribbean. Nothing was created in the West Indies, in this sense, since the first creators living on the islands were eliminated. It is for this reason that Caribbean literature has long been troubled by questions of originality and its own apparent lack of indigenous tradition or creative genius.

The poetics of beachcombing, then, offer critical redress and set up a counter-model to the aesthetic norms that underwrite a statement such as Naipaul's. They are a poetics of *bricolage* in the sense established by Claude Lévi-Strauss, that is to say, a cultural activity whose rule is 'always to make do with whatever is available', forming 'heterogeneous elements into a new whole in which none of the re-used elements will necessarily be used as originally intended' (Genette 63). To be sure, *bricolage* also constitutes a general concept for other modes of cultural production and the discourses about them, as evidenced in Genette's transfer of the term, which Lévi-Strauss developed for the analysis of myth, into the practices of literary criticism. In an even wider perspective, the same procedure of selecting pre-existing heterogeneous elements and forming them into a composite new whole is the very strategy by which all language users construct sentences in a syntactic matrix. But all these general notions come down to a specific and particularly localised poetic practice in Caribbean literature, where beachcombing emerges as the premise and the promise of a kind of cultural production which is always a kind of cultural reproduction already: recycling, imitating, improvising and inventing by means of debris washed ashore from shipwrecks.

This, at any rate, is my suggestion as to how we should understand what Walcott, in his Nobel speech, describes as 'the basis of the Antillean experience, this shipwreck of fragments, these echoes, these shards of a huge tribal vocabulary' ('Antilles' 70), or what Glissant (passim) describes as the Antillean poetics of relation. And for the best dramatisation of this particular experience, just as for its consequences for Caribbean postcolonial poetics, we should briefly look at Walcott's *Omeros*, his best-known and most daring project, a Caribbean reassembling of the Homeric epics. In a programmatic passage we read how the original and foundational author figure Homer, whose model is rewritten and recycled in Walcott's New World epic, is literally discovered as a piece of flotsam on the beach:

> One sunrise I walked out onto the balcony
> of my white hotel. The beach was already swept,
> and in the clear grooves of the January sea
>
> there was only one coconut shell, but it kept
> nodding in my direction as a swimmer might
> with sun in his irises, or a driftwood log,
>
> or a plaster head, foaming. It changed shapes in light
> according to each clouding thought. …
> …
> I heard my own voice
>
> correcting his name, as the surf hissed: 'Omeros'.
> The moment I named it, the marble head arose,
> fringed with its surf curls and beard, the hollow shoulders
>
> of a man waist-high in water with an old leather
> goatskin or a plastic bag. … (Walcott *Omeros* 279–80)

This is the opening of Book Seven, the final part of Walcott's epic. Just like his poem 'Crusoe's Journal', it stages beachcombing as the enabling cultural condition for a special kind of creativity that lies in re-using lost wreckage in a bricolage of unbelonging parts. That in the new poetic rendering and perception the object found here on the beach also looks like a coconut shell or just a piece of log wood is, of course, entirely appropriate for the creative process that 'Crusoe's Journal' calls 'our profane Genesis'. With *Omeros*, the Homeric original is divested of its place and aura, so that its present reproduction turns indeed into a mimesis that is, in Taussig's words, 'an enactment not merely *of* an original but *by* an "original"' (79; emphases in original).

No doubt, the poetics of fragmentation and fragmentary recreation have long been with us in the literary canon of modernity and have sometimes been championed in a programmatic way. 'These fragments I have shored against my ruins', we read at the end of T.S. Eliot's 'The Waste Land' (79), a declaration that might appear to be quite similar to what we have observed in Caribbean texts – yet with one important difference: the transitive verb phrase 'I have shored' suggests an active and controlled operation establishing, above all, the authority of the speaking persona as director or stage-manager for the poetic process. Such a function and a superior figure remain absent in the Caribbean poetics of fragmentation and recycling – just as absent as the native inside views and the original voices of the islands which can never be retrieved.

In sum, what emerges from my reading therefore is the beach as a central site of autopoetic reflexion. In the case of Caribbean writers, this *poiesis* figures as a mimesis of broken parts, fragments which have been washed ashore. This, finally, would be my answer to the question of how to establish the specifics of the beach trope: we have to look for them in the distinct circumstances of the cultural work performed with it. For the postcolonial writers whose work I have discussed, the crucial point is that each long wave that brings them flotsam from the literary sea also clears the sand, their page of composition, and cleans it from all previous traces and inscriptions. So for them – drunks, castaways, beachcombers all – the specific beach trope is a profane genesis of newness.

Works Cited

Antoni, Robert. *Carnival*. London: Faber, 2008.
Bacon, Francis. 'Of Plantations'. 1625. *The English Literatures of America, 1500–1800*. Ed. Myra Jehlen and Michael Warner. London: Routledge, 1997. 97–9.
Brathwaite, Edward. *The Arrivants: A New World Trilogy*. *Rights of Passage* [1967], *Masks* [1968], *Islands* [1969]. Oxford: Oxford UP, 1998.
Defoe, Daniel. *Robinson Crusoe*. 1719. Harmondsworth: Penguin, 2001.
Eliot, T.S. 'The Waste Land'. 1922. *Collected Poems 1909–1962*. London: Faber, 1986. 61–79.
Genette, Gerard. 'Structuralism and Literary Criticism'. *Modern Criticism and Theory: A Reader*. Ed. David Lodge. London: Longman, 1988. 62–78.
Glissant, Édouard. *Le Discours Antillais*. Paris: Editions du Seuil, 1986.

Greenblatt, Stephen. *Marvelous Possessions: The Wonder of the New World.* Oxford: Clarendon, 1991.

Hulme, Peter. *Colonial Encounters: Europe and the Native Caribbean, 1492–1797.* London: Routledge, 1986.

Matura, Mustapha. *The Coup: A Play of Revolutionary Dreams.* London: Methuen, 1991.

Naipaul, V.S. *The Middle Passage.* 1962. Harmondsworth: Penguin, 1969.

Novak, Maximillian E. 'Fleischlose Freitage: Kannibalismus als Thema und Metapher in Defoes *Robinson Crusoe*'. *Das Andere Essen: Kannibalismus als Motiv und Metapher in der Literatur.* Ed. Daniel Fulda and Walter Pape. Freiburg: Rombach, 2001. 197–216.

Pratt, Mary Louise. *Imperial Eyes: Travel Writing and Transculturation.* London: Routledge, 1992.

Taussig, Michael. *Mimesis and Alterity: A Particular History of the Senses.* London: Routledge, 1993.

Todorov, Tzvetan. *The Conquest of America: The Question of the Other.* Trans. Richard Howard. New York: Harper & Row, 1984.

Walcott, Derek. 'The Antilles: Fragments of Epic Memory'. *What the Twilight Says: Essays.* New York: Farrar, Straus and Giroux, 1998. 65–86.

———. 'Crusoe's Journal'. *Collected Poems, 1948–1984.* London: Faber, 1992. 92–4.

———. *Omeros.* London: Faber, 1990.

Chapter 7

Literary Inscriptions on the South African Beach: Ambiguous Settings, Ambivalent Textualities[1]

Meg Samuelson

South Africa boasts an extensive coastline that stretches over 2,800 kilometres and is alternately caressed and pounded by two oceans, which have produced a chain of golden sandy beaches along its shores. Yet compared to other sites, the beach does not feature very prominently in South African literary culture and is even less visible in literary criticism.[2] The farm, the bushveld and the arid karoo; city, town and village: all have accrued layers of inscription while the beach sits almost silent at the edge of the South African literary and critical imagination.[3] Its relative muteness is at least in part dictated by the lack of space accorded to levity and the ludic in South African letters, burdened as they have been with seeking to bear the weight of the experiences of colonial dispossession and apartheid oppression and of representing struggle and strife.

In everyday life, the beach today – as under and prior to apartheid – is a popular leisure attraction as well as a source of physical and spiritual sustenance. Yet when the beach appears in the national literature it is more often as a contact zone and threshold – inscribed with narratives of encounter and marked by the violence that attended European entry into the southern tip of the African continent – than as a recreational or restorative site. Under apartheid, beaches were conscripted into the

[1] I am grateful to the editors for the invitation to contribute to this collection and particularly for their helpful feedback on earlier versions of this chapter. This work is based on research supported by the National Research Foundation of South Africa (Grant Number 87809). Opinions, findings and conclusions or recommendations expressed herein are those of the author, and the NRF accepts no liability whatsoever in this regard.

[2] This may account in part for the striking absence of South African texts in a growing body of world literature on the beach. For instance, two major anthologies of beach literature – *The Penguin Book of the Beach* (first published as *The Picador Book of the Beach*), edited by Robert Drewe, and *Beach: Stories by the Sand and Sea*, edited by Lena Lencek and Gideon Bosker – include between them only one South African entry: 'The Catch' by Nadine Gordimer, the Johannesburg-based author primarily known for her writing against social injustice under apartheid.

[3] Compare Huntsman's discussion of the discrepancy between the centrality of the beach in Australian everyday life and the mythologising of the bush in its literature.

work of race-making initiated in the colonial contact zone. The segregationist state prescribed separate beaches for the designated population groups of black, white, coloured and Indian, and its Group Areas Act of 1950 alienated local communities from sea and shore, denying them both livelihood and leisure.[4] While the apartheid beach continued to proffer a carnivalesque release from the state's restrictions, it was itself tightly regulated.[5]

Paradoxically, the beach is also experienced as a space of mutation and perpetual motion; of fluidity and flux. And yet – paradox upon paradox – it is precisely this quality of ambiguity and indeterminacy, of ambivalence and mutability or ambiguity and in-betweenness (see Dening, *Islands*; Lencek and Bosker, *The Beach* 5; Mack 165) that has erased or edged out the beach from the field of South African literatures: as an imaginative locale that brings binaries into crisis and breaches boundaries, the beach is relegated to the margins of the national story. Indeed, the metaphorics of the beach – elaborated on its shifting sands and in the to-and-fro movements of the intertidal zone – do not resonate in a political context bound to the 'trurt in black and white', to quote Zoë Wicomb's playful palindrome (*David's Story* 136). Not surprisingly, then, writers such as Wicomb, and others like Lewis Nkosi, who have decried the reductive insights of documentary realism in anti-apartheid protest writing, have turned to the beach in search of nuance and ambiguity.

The ludic quality of the beach is understood here not only as emanating from the spontaneous sport enacted upon it but also as deriving from the play of meaning symbolically invested in it – a playfulness that mocks both the stasis and stability of apartheid race-making and the pious politics of a resistant aesthetic dependent on these same categories. Yet this textual playfulness remains in a state of tension with its opposite: the violence that attends the making and unfolding of South African history. This is a tension inherent in the beach itself, as a social and cultural construct: 'While the beach may be a place of licence and freedom, a place where we disrobe and disport in each other's company, [it] can also be a sinister and threatening place, a place of violence and death' (Hosking et al. ix). The ambiguity of the beach-as-setting is thrown into particular relief in the South African context, in which it has functioned as both borderland and boundary or been cast as a site of regulation and restriction while at the same time signifying a space beyond societal constraint.

---

[4]   Many seaside communities – such as the fishing communities of Simonstown in Cape Town and the Bluff in Durban – were relocated under the Group Areas Act, which identified these residential areas as 'white'. The Reservation of Separate Amenities Act of 1953 granted local authorities the right to define separate beaches for use by white, black, coloured and Indian; typically, the safest and most easily accessible bathing beaches were set aside for white use, consigning black bathers to treacherous surf or strong currents.

[5]   This ambiguity is dramatised in *Buckingham Palace, District Six* (1986), Richard Rive's fictional chronicle of the destruction of an inner-city community under the Group Areas Act: decamping to the beach on one of the big holidays, the denizens of District Six engage in general jollity until two lovers stray across the boundary between black and white beaches and are forcibly reminded of the segregated state they inhabit in a scene that anticipates their forced removal from their homes.

It is precisely the ambiguity of the beach and its ambivalence as a literary figure that this chapter seeks to trace. In the sections that follow, I aim to establish the beach as a significant site in South African literature. I focus entirely on narrative – largely prose fiction but also including an epic and a dramatic poem. Lyric poetry from South Africa encodes the beach rather differently and employs it more regularly if often transiently as setting; it inscribes a set of signifiers on the beach the lie beyond the purview of this paper. In the texts I engage with, the beach is shown to provide the setting for the staging of various narratives of encounter – from the 'contact zone' of the 'voyages of discovery' through the segregated logic of apartheid and to a post-apartheid present that is in an ongoing state of engagement with its past. At the same time, the beach-as-setting will be found to produce or enable a textual ambivalence that – when teased out – might be seen to comprise a more significant thread in South African literary discourse than has as yet been recognised.

Encounters in the Colonial Contact Zone

For all its later comparative absence from South African letters, the beach provides the setting for the first literary appearance of this land in Luís Vaz de Camões's Portuguese national-imperial epic, *The Lusiads* (*Os Lusíadas*, 1572), which charts the rounding of the Cape and the passage to India of Vasco da Gama's fleet in 1497–1499.[6] Although, to archaeologists, shell-middens and rock paintings in caves flanking the beach tell a story of successive waves of human habitation on the coast, the oral records of these non-literate peoples have been scattered and submerged by centuries of colonial devastation and genocide. The beach at the southern tip of this continent enters textual representation during the Portuguese voyages of expansion, and is inscribed through the pens and from the perspectives of European explorers and those memorialising their exploits. In such representations, the beach emerges as what Pratt has defined as a 'contact zone' – a place of 'edgy encounter and ambivalent contact' (Hosking et al. viii).[7] 'Beaches',

---

[6]   I depend entirely on the most recent English translation of the epic by Landeg White; for alternative translations of the scenes I discuss see, for example, Blackmore (*Moorings*), and Klein.

[7]   There is a significant body of literary and literary-critical responses to the poem in South Africa (see Van Wyk Smith, *Shades*; and 'Shades'), but it focuses largely or exclusively on the manifestation of Adamastor, the embodiment of Table Mountain or the Cape itself, to the Lusiads as they round the Cape, rather than the scenes on the beach that precede and follow it; this once again bears out the point advanced in this chapter on the relative obscurity of the beach-as-setting in South African literary culture and criticism: even when this urtext makes its first landing on its shifting sands, it is rather the monumental figure of the mythologised mountain that resonates across the literary field. While enjoying a literary life extending from Roy Campbell's 'Rounding the Cape' in the collection *Adamastor* (1930) to André Brink's *The First Life of Adamastor* (1993), this forbidding and foreboding figure has, however, generally haunted only what Coetzee terms 'white writing' and has been designated 'the white man's creation myth of Africa' by Gray; as Wicomb's narrator notes in her most recent novel, *October*: 'Of course it didn't occur to the poet that

Hoskings et al. note, 'are places of contact, of confrontation and friction: first-comers always arrive on a beach' (vii).

In Camões's Canto Five, the Lusiads make their first landing in the southern hemisphere when they go 'ashore at an open stretch' (5: 26) in the region of what is now St Helena Bay on the southwest coast. Initially, this shore appears a *tabula rasa* across which the sailors scatter joyfully, while the captain 'Stayed on the sandy beach with the pilots ... To fix our bearing on the cosmic chart' (5: 26).[8] In the first lines of its literary appearance, then, the beach is invested with a duality of purpose, signifying both license and fixity. To this ambivalent site the sailors return, bearing 'a stranger with black skin / They had captured' while he made 'his sweet harvest / Of honey from the wild bees in the forest (5: 27). '[T]he mutuality of the encounter', Klein notes, 'finds poetic expression in the chiastic pattern 'Neither did he understand us, nor we him'' (169). Klein concludes: 'The chiastic acknowledgement of a lack of understanding at the moment of encounter is one form in which Camonian poetics offers the maritime experience of the diversity, the coexistence, the simultaneity of cultures' (171). Indeed; though here I would emphasise the beach as setting for encounter as much as the voyage that has transported the Lusiads to this coast.

This first encounter staged on the beach leans towards the mutuality of exchange. The Portuguese mariners offer trinkets to the native honey-gatherer and release him. When more 'strangers' arrive the next day, one of the sailors follows them back to their village to learn their ways. He, however, returns hastily, 'scurrying to the shore' (5: 31). The attempt to cross the beach fails; violent conflict ensues:

> There sprang from ambush a battalion of blacks;
>
> Countless arrows and stones rained
> On the rest of us in a thick cloud
> ...
> But we, as the aggrieved people,
> Returned so superadded a reply
> It was not just those bonnets that they wear
> Were crimson at the end of this affair! (5: 32–3)

---

the Khoi who lived there had a different story for their own sea mountain, Hoerikwaggo as they had already named it' (261). Johnson concludes appositely that Adamastor has functioned as a 'resilient but solipsistic settler myth' (27) in contrast to the fervent if often failed pull towards dialogism that the beach-as-setting is shown to elicit in this chapter. For an alternative reading of the Adamastor episode as an unsettling scene conjuring a melancholic figure that 'will always provoke', see Chapter 3 of Blackmore's *Moorings* (154), this reading has inspired my renewed attention to Adamastor in a forthcoming article, "Rendering the Cape-as-port"; for another excellent recent contribution that addresses the maritime modernity of *The Lusiads* rather than either mountain or beach, see Klein.

[8]   See Blackmore on how 'sight and seeing' is in this scene related to 'the expansionist ethos of *Os Lusíadas*, a dynamic of appropriation of foreign space and the inscription of that space into a Portuguese, maritime gnosis of the world' (*Moorings* 91) that is thrown into relief against the native honey-gatherer, who is presented as 'twisted in sight' (*Moorings* 89).

The blood on the beach of which Camões's Da Gama boasts at the conclusion of his first landing continues to trouble South African letters, as we will see below.

When the Lusiads next come ashore, having rounded the Cape, the beach is more borderland than boundary, bringing 'people together rather than separating them' (Gillis 106). Approached by 'The people who own the country here', Da Gama finds them 'cordial and humane' (5: 62):

> They came towards us on the sandy beach
> With dancing and an air of festival, ...
> These, as their smiling faces promised,
> Dealt with us as fellow humans,
> Bringing sheep and poultry to barter. (5: 62–4)

Yet here, too, exchange founders on incomprehension: 'For all our desire to converse with them, / Neither with words nor signs could we prevail, / So we once again raised anchor and set sail' (5: 64).

The ability to cross the beach and to see it – and the encounters enacted upon it – from the other's perspective is once again negated by the lack of a common language; we are left with only the Lusiads' version of it and the encounters convened thereupon. Yet the beach itself suggests 'another side to the story' (Dening, 'Beaches' 126; see also Samuelson, 'Abdulrazak Gurnah'). More recently, writers such as Ishtiyaq Shukri, Dan Sleigh, and Wicomb have sought to imagine the perspective of those watching from the beach as European ships arrived on the horizon. Revisiting this contact zone from the post-apartheid present, they elaborate Dening's insight on the beach as '[i]n-between place, where every present moment is suffused with the double past of both sides of the beach' ('Deep' 13).

Yet, as one of Wicomb's characters in *David's Story* (2000) reflects while trying to reconstruct from the other side of the beach the moment when the Dutch East India Company (DEIC) ships arrived in the wake of the Portuguese in 1652 to establish the refreshment station that will grow into a colony:

> what do we know of our ancestors, the little people who, loping along the strand
> at the Cape of Storms / Good Hope, watched a smudge on the horizon feed on
> the indeterminate space between sea and April sky, and before whose amazed
> eyes grew steadily, with the help of a conniving wind, the full white sails of a
> Dutch ship? Only that which is passed down by word of mouth, for there was no
> one to record those momentous times. (87)

The version that has been written 'is one that has failed to imagine the world from another's point of view, even if the other were, strictly speaking, the hosts' (87–8).

Sleigh, an archivist who has produced various histories of the DEIC, turns to fiction in *Islands* (2004) precisely in order to conjure up the perspectives of those who watched from the shore as the DEIC settlers arrived to set up shop at the Cape – perspectives that have not been recorded in official archives. In *Islands*, then, the dunes of Table Bay become the setting for a dialogic and heteroglossic (see Bakhtin) account of the origins of the South African nation that *The Lusiads* reaches towards but is ultimately unable to realise.

Similarly, Shukri in *The Silent Minaret* (2005) presents the arrival of history on the beach:

> On 6th April 1652, three ships belonging to the Dutch East India Company, *de Drommedaris*, *de Goede Hoop* and *de Reiger*, dropped anchor in a beautiful bay on the southwest tip of the African continent. … From the shore, their arrival would have been keenly observed by the Goringhaicona. … Autshumao, their self-serving leader, Krotoa, his young, impressionable niece, and the militant, Doman, 'the first indigenous South African resistance leader'. History had arrived on their beach. Forced by it into a new consciousness of themselves, each would respond to it differently. All would be forever changed by it. (68; emphases in original)

All three texts foreground translating and translated figures and seek to restore to what Shukri (66–7) terms a 'whitewashed' history the 'bastard' cultures forged on the beach and within the crucible of a crimson-spotted contact zone.

In these three post-apartheid returns to the beach as a scene of encounter there is, then, an attempt to invest in its sands something other than the blood Camões first portrayed on the South African strand while simultaneously noting and pushing beyond the impediments to the intercourse his Da Gama desires but cannot enact. This is a return to the beach as 'contact zone' with all that this implies and which salvages from this limen between land and sea the creole cultures and social heteroglossia that are also – and as much as the violence and loss that they simultaneously record – a legacy of the first encounters that were played out on the beach.

As a 'contact zone' shaped by 'radically asymmetrical relations of power' yet hosting the mutual constitution of the subjects that meet there, the beach enables ways of reading relations between indigene and interloper 'not in terms of separateness and apartheid, but in terms of co-presence, interaction, interlocking understandings and practices' (Pratt 6–7). The beach, we could say, is put in service to the project of what Sarah Nuttall has evocatively described as 'entanglement' – an approach that seeks to shift the work of culture and theory from the segregated state that has shackled the South African imagination.

Wreckage, Reversal and Recognition in White Writing

Located at the midpoint of their journey and its epic narration, the Lusiads' triumph on rounding the Cape is shot through with foreboding. The mythical and monstrous Adamastor manifests as Table Mountain or the Cape itself, threatening calamity and anticipating the foundering of the *St Joao* that inaugurates a new genre of shipwreck narrative played out on the sands of southern Africa's beaches (see Blackmore, *Manifest*). The poetic vision is apposite. With its treacherous currents, lurking rocks and gale-force winds, the Cape promontory in particular has authored many an episode in 'the tragic history of the sea' (see Boxer). Shipwreck and the fate of those washed up on its shores determined much of the subsequent history of modern South Africa – for it was the wreck of the *Nieuwe Haerlem* in Table Bay in 1647 and the positive reports submitted by its survivors following their repatriation that motivated the establishment of the DEIC settlement at the Cape.

The shipwreck that looms largest in the South African literary imagination – and which for some literary historians inaugurates this national literature (see Glenn) – is that of the *Grosvenor*, an East Indiaman wrecked on the east coast of the Cape Colony in 1782 en route from Calcutta to London. Of the 123 survivors who made it to shore on the Pondoland coast, only eighteen are known to have completed the arduous walk to the Cape settlement (six of whom died in a subsequent shipwreck on their respective return journeys).[9] In contrast to its depiction in George Morland's painting *African Hospitality* (1791; see Glenn 5), the encounter enacted on this beach was apparently shaped by mutual suspicion and antagonism as well as competition – the local inhabitants of that coast took what they could use from the flotsam while offering little assistance to the castaways; the latter in turn received their hosts as savages and offered little succour to one another as the stronger sought to survive at the expense of weaker members of the group. Much of this internal fragmentation – reiterating the foundering of the ship itself – was displaced onto sensationalist stories in the British press of 'white women … carried off by black tribesmen … for which there is no evidence in any of the four contemporary accounts of the wreck' (Titlestad and Kissack, 'Persistent' 203). Such stories can be understood as shoring up a 'hegemonic vision of empire' that the 'shipwreck narrative … troubles' (Blackmore, *Manifest* xxi). As Josiah Blackmore proposes, 'Shipwreck is … the failure of empire and colonization, the moment when a series of power reversals begins' (*Manifest* 53).

The hysterical narrative of white women dragged unwillingly from the beach into the African interior shapes the action of WC Scully's 'The Wreck of the Grosvenor' (1886), in which the wreck found its first overtly literary treatment in the form of a dramatic poem. The genre – with its multiplicity of voices and its arrangement according to scene and setting – is apt: the imperial narrative fractures into a flotsam of speakers on the beach where the ship lies 'strewn in fragments' (5). In a reversal of Da Gama's confident attempt to fix his bearings on the beach, this limen 'Between fierce roaring waves and savage men' (1) confounds imperial certainties and makes a mockery of the captain: 'I know not where we are, nor how to find / A clue to guide us' (2).

Huddling upon 'This barren waste of sand / Between the ocean and the forest dark, / Where roar the beasts of prey' (3), Scully's castaways are brought to uncanny recognitions of their own savagery and animality. The Captain, watching

---

[9]   Different sources claim that between fourteen and eighteen survivors reached the Cape. I have followed James Whyle, who lists "William Hubberly, Thomas Lewis, John Hynes, Robert Price, Jeremiah Evans, John Warmington, Barney Leary, Francisco Delasso, the maids Betty and Hoakim, and the Lascars Allex, Foikan, Roman, Ramat, Imat, Mamaretta, Matthys and Matteroe" (*Walk* 138)

other survivors scavenging for shell-fish, observes 'How like wild animals they seem, – and yet, / Perchance, I am the same. Each one of us / May look with fear upon the others, all / Unknowing that himself is like the rest' (8). Even as the dramatic action – directing readers into the interior in pursuit of the abducted women – shifts from the apprehensions engendered on the beach, the insights obtained reverberate into the future.

Nearly a century later, white writers under apartheid would return to the beach as limen between an intractable white state, on the one hand, and, on the other, a rising tide of Black Consciousness that questioned their ability to speak on behalf of black oppression. Shipwreck offers them a potent trope of 'foundering white identity', accounting for a 'compulsive reiteration of the *Grosvenor* story in [white] South African letters' (Titlestad and Kissack, 'I have' 136). This 'compulsive reiteration' is both evidenced by and dramatised in Sheila Fugard's *The Castaways* (1972), in which 'the narrator experiences a pathological attachment to the metaphorics of shipwreck and the figure of the castaway, which he elaborates as the objective correlative for his sense of alienation as a 'displaced' white South African' (Titlestad and Kissack, 'Persistent' 207).

The Castaway opens with the narration of Christaan Jordan:

> I have always known shipwreck. Deep inside, I know the foundering of the self and the voices of the castaways of the East Indiaman, *The Berkley*, foundering off the coast of Pondoland.
>   Sister took us for a walk along the beach. The gulls, the fiercely agitated sea and the burning sand were all that was there. Yet, I probed the shells looking for secrets. Out of the shells came voices … Captain Middleton … Perels … Mulwena … Dr Locke (the missionary). (1)

Jordan has absconded from the Port Berkley Mental Hospital, where he is a patient, and wanders the beach, reliving the eighteenth-century wreck of the *Berkley* (based on the *Grosvenor*). Walking along the shore, he segues in and out of past and present, haunted by voices from both sides of the beach and enacting the 'in between state' (89) of 'white writing' in Africa (see Coetzee).

'[C]lutching at the debris of shipwreck' (67), Jordan is joined by the self-made black revolutionary, Choma. Choma's desire to plant revolution like seeds in the beach is doomed to failure in this infertile sand (43) – he too is 'an absurd castaway figure in a liminal and shifting beach landscape, desperately signifying revolution' (Titlestad and Kissack, 'Persistent' 207). As Jordan realises: 'Each of us is only a different side of the same coin. Flip the coin and Choma or I will fling ourselves against this burning day, *strandlopers* of the great white beaches, our very bodies falling into submission to nature' (46; emphasis in original). Cast into species-being by the enormity of nature stretching before them on the beach, they will here enact a Hegelian struggle for recognition, joined by the spectres from both sides of the beach of those present at the wreck of the *Berkley*.

A hallucinatory narrative that resists clarity of explication and is defined by its indeterminacy, *The Castaways* uses the beach as setting precisely in order to throw meaning into flux and assigned racial positions into crisis. Set in predetermined positions of antagonism, Jordan and Choma achieve brief moments of recognition on the beach, and in their footprints in the sand, before each is numbed by the forces of an oppressive state and the monologic command manual of an oppositional movement, both of which silence the qualities of heteroglossia and dialogism the novel bestows on the beach.

Also produced in the political moment that defines the *The Castaways*, André Brink's *An Instant in the Wind* (1976) turns to a stretch of beach on the same coast to stage a story set in the mid-eighteenth century. Rather than suffering maritime disaster, Elizabeth Larsson is cast away when her explorer husband dies during their 'fateful voyage into the hinterland' (11); she is found there by Adam Mantoor, who has escaped slavery at the Cape and banishment to Robben Island for assaulting his 'master'. Initially they are each trapped in the social roles ascribed to them by the colonial state and the Cape slavocracy. As they head toward the sea, however, the boundary erected between them permeates, and once they find themselves on the mutable sands of the beach itself – this margin between nature and culture – they enter an Edenic space.

Ignoring the portent of the snake, they create on the beach an 'intimate landscape of happiness. … Everything permissible; everything possible' (111). Yet their idyll is doomed. Although Elizabeth imagines that they can 'live here' like the 'strandlopers' (127) who have left their marks on the cave they inhabit, the encroaching winter sees them withdrawing from the beach, their thoughts returning to the Cape. During their torturous overland journey back to civilisation, the conclusion of their entwined story is iteratively prefigured as loyal or vulnerable animal companions are dispatched for sustenance, each betrayal condoned by the need to survive. When they finally arrive at the Cape they spend a last night together, again on the beach. Calling him by his own rather than his slave name – Aob rather than Adam – Elizabeth is both true to her lover's appeal that she bear him 'a son who will be free one day' (213) and treacherous to the 'paradise' – the 'instant in the wind' – they had found on the beach: waiting for her in the bush the next morning, Adam realises she is not among the approaching group; instead, his fate of strangulation as anticipated in the prolepsis is foreshadowed as the colony's guards restrain him. In bringing him back to the town where he is received as a fugitive, Elizabeth has decided his end; the paradise created on the beach cannot be transported to the social world of the Cape. The novel's epigraph, from Eldridge Cleaver, is left to resonate across the beach that both hosts their conjoining and marks their separation from one another within the colonial economy: 'We recognize each other. And, having recognized each other, is it any wonder that our souls cling together even while our minds equivocate, hesitate, vacillate and tremble?'

It is to this fraught scene of recognition that Nkosi also turns in *Mating Birds* (1987) as he renders the beach a stage on which to present the bleak South African drama of apartheid or separateness. Once again a white woman is cast as 'the site of desire and transgression' (Kossew 127), yet Nkosi is more adept than either Scully or Brink in opening up the contradictory meanings that cluster around 'woman as sign' (Driver) as he produces an ambivalent textuality out of the ambiguity of the beach setting.

Prohibition and Transgression on the Apartheid Beach

Segregated beaches became symbolic of the simultaneously arbitrary, absurd and ruthless nature of apartheid: a line drawn on the sand consigning 'non-whites' to strands with dangerous currents or rocky and inaccessible shores, beach apartheid was as banal as it was oppressive and potentially deadly. Yet, while it exemplifies the excess and inanity of apartheid, the beach also represents a space of freedom from constraint, and particularly from societal regulation.

It is on these shifting sands that Nkosi sets *Mating Birds*, in which Ndi Sibiya reflects from death row on the chain of events that will culminate in his extinction. With flashbacks to a childhood and youth over which the net of segregation and apartheid has been cast and tightened, his narrative centres on the beach, elaborating it into an extended manifestation of and metaphor for the plethora of laws that composed apartheid, such as those enforced under the Reservation of Separate Amenities, Group Areas and Immorality Acts. 'African youths', he reports, 'combed the beach every day for lost or discarded articles', including the infrequent 'worthier trophy – a young body lying spent and motionless on the warm white sands to be gazed at by us, the silent forbidden crowds of non-white boys in a black, mutinous rage' (2–3). It is here that he first sees Veronica Slater, 'the English girl', 'lying on an empty stretch of Durban beach as though washed up by the tide after an all-night storm' (3).

The metaphorics of shipwreck along with the license of the beach and its ontological edginess between apparently opposed states have drawn Sibiya up against the 'limits … of what is known as the 'Whites Only' bathing area' (4) and allowed him to recognise 'what White Authority, with the aid of so many laws and legal penalties, had forbidden me to see. Another human being. A woman with a body that was soft and round and desirable. And within reach' (6). However, as a white woman, she is marked by the prohibitions of the apartheid state: 'behind the girl's inert body was the inevitable notice board bearing the legendary warning: BATHING AREA – FOR WHITES ONLY!' (6).

The mercurial geography of the beach itself makes a mockery of apartheid and becomes an extended sign of the hypocrisy of a system that depends on black labour in the most intimate sphere while propounding 'separate development'. Recalling how 'the English girl' would 'cross the small stream that divided her side of the beach from mine' (127), Sibiya reports:

> She would walk so close to where I lay on the sand I could see the fine pores of her skin on her shaved, gliding legs, smooth like polished wood. I could even sniff the gusts of perfume emanating from her body as it sauntered past me. …
> She would walk so close that had I reached out my hand, I could have touched

her. … So near yet so far, for all the proximity we shared we might as well have been in different parts of the universe. (127)

Erected on the beach's mutable surface, the segregating sign is as ineffectual as it is imperious – far from presiding over separation, it bears witness to an intimate proximity of bodies.

Veronica's own marginal position – on the beach and on the edge of the white beach – reads as an invitation as well as a mirror of Sibiya's own sense of liminality: of no longer belonging to the African world of his forefathers – a world which has itself 'fallen apart' (62) under the repeated blows of colonial and apartheid rule – while living, 'resentfully, on the fringes of a white world that tried to keep me out' (101). In turn, this liminality brings with it a recognition of the impermanence and provisionality of the ruling state: 'the white world … is built on so much shifting sands. It will not last. It will be swept away. That is what history teaches us' (101).

For now, however, on these shifting sands betrayal follows recognition, as it does for Brink, and Fugard. The 'English girl', who lies 'white, limp, drowsily sunbathing in a no-man's-land between the 'Whites Only' section and the rock-strewn 'Non-Whites' bathing area' (38) will charge him with rape and consign him to death row. The sequence of events leading to this conclusion that Sibiya presents to the reader sees them first simulating intercourse on the beach, transgressing the boundary drawn by the apartheid sign's 'mocking warning: BATHING AREA – FOR WHITES ONLY' (143):

> She was lying on her side, facing me. I, on my side of the beach, lay facing her … We came together, dragged by the retching flesh across the space of prohibition and taboo that separated us. … That is how it was between Veronica and me. *Apartheid?* We had defeated apartheid. We had finally perfected a method of making love without making contact, utilizing empty space like two telepathic media exchanging telegraphic messages through the sexual airwaves. (147–50; emphasis in original)

Later, Sibiya reports, he followed her home and entered her bungalow in response to an implicit invitation.

Veronica's contrasting version of events, which she presents before the court, is also tendered in the novel. The result is ideological quicksand in which critics have struggled to secure a footing as they oscillate between the positions of black man and white woman. Yet ultimately, such vacillations seem part of the point of the novel as it throws these very categories into crisis. Whereas 'black peril' – the myth of the black rapist preying on white womanhood (see Samuelson, *Remembering* 140–52) – has been evoked since the *Grosvenor* wreck to fix identities and uphold colonial and then apartheid rule, it is the work of *Mating Birds* to relocate it onto shifting sands. Encapsulated in its beach setting, then, is the novel's own transgressive and unsettling ambivalence – an ambivalence that pushes readers beyond the binary terms that have organised cultural and political meaning in South Africa and which continues to resonate today as we reach towards a post-apartheid aesthetic.

Beaching after Apartheid

Stretched taut between site of narration and narrated site – between death row and the beach as pleasure zone – *Mating Birds* begins to locate this tension within the beach itself as an ambiguous setting. Some of this ambiguity is taken up by subsequent fiction that begins to reflect on and perform a post-apartheid cultural politics. Such a cultural politics often takes as its launching pad Njabulo Ndebele's intervention in the mid-1980s when he first issued his call for a 'rediscovery of the ordinary', which has become a critical guide in thinking through what it might mean to write beyond apartheid. A more recent theoretical beacon is that established by Nuttall, with her notion of 'entanglement' to which I have referred earlier regarding post-apartheid returns to the 'contact zone' convened on the beach. Nuttall inflects the term with various implications, including historical entanglements between subjects who have been racialised as distinct and temporal entanglements between past, present and future; as a 'means by which to draw into our analyses those sites in which what was once thought of as separate – identities, spaces, histories – come together or find points of intersection in unexpected ways' (11). The concept can also be applied to the entanglement of human and animal or nature and culture, as well as of South Africa and the world. It is my contention here that the beach provides a literary setting that elicits and enables a post-apartheid aesthetic by providing a setting in which to imagine the emergent state. As Gillis suggests, '[i]t is at the edge of the sea that we imagine both the birth of new worlds and the death of old ones' (157–8).

Like the beach itself much post-apartheid fiction is 'suffused with the double past of both sides' (Dening, 'Deep' 13) and infused with an ambiguity of tone that is simultaneously rhapsody and dirge, and that entwines such tonal variance into a key able to carry the complexity of becoming post-apartheid. For instance, Wicomb's *David's Story* turns to the beach to mark the jubilation that attends the imagining of a new world while simultaneously surfacing on its sands the return of repressed pasts that come to haunt the post-apartheid polity and cloud the promise of this new day with death and dismemberment (see Samuelson, 'Oceanic Histories').

In what initially seems a jarring antinomy, *Absolution* (2012) by US-British author Patrick Flanery stages torture on the South African beach through the narrative constructions of the protagonist – an aging writer at least in part a composite of Nobel laureates Nadine Gordimer and J.M. Coetzee. Trying to imagine the fate of her daughter, who disappeared during the anti-apartheid struggle, Flanery's writer-protagonist envisions cages lined up on the strand, each occupied by a captured comrade left to fry in the sun or dragged in and out of the water; those who will not 'break' are exposed to the sharks in a 'clean' and 'ecological' disposal system (185). Quotidian memories of family beach outings intrude into this scene of torture, now infused with horror: even nostalgic recollections are tarnished with political violence as the space of play is overwritten with the brutality of the regime. Though the protagonist later reveals her awful apparitions to be 'nothing but a vision' (318), an atmosphere of dread continues to hang over the beach:

> They say sharks have been spotted in False Bay, sharks the size of helicopters or dinosaurs, sharks the size of minibuses, sharks as big as nuclear submarines. One does not know what to believe. Marie will not go within twenty metres of the ocean so convinced is she that sharks are destined to start coming out of the water and taking their prey from land. (268)

Notable in *Absolution* is the way in which the non-national writer identifies the persistent saturation of the South African imagination by a 'spectacular' narrative that banishes or at least tempers an 'ordinary' engagement with the beach (to use Ndebele's terms). Yet, even when the grand political narrative that has dominated the South African imagination recedes from view, as in Henrietta Rose-Innes's *Shark's Egg* (2000), a first novel lauded for its rendering of the 'ordinary', the beach remains a site of treachery and betrayal, of death and indifference. It is from the beach that a young man is swept out to sea and on its sands that his corpse washes up; years later, the girl who callously abandoned him to his fate returns to the beach to steal away the lover of the protagonist as she had previously stolen the attentions of the drowned boy. In both Flanery's novel, which signals and reflects upon the predominance of spectacular representation, and Rose-Innes's, which seeks to turn from the political spectacle in search of other domains of experience, the sunny surface of the beach is cast into shadow by the menacing threat embodied by the shark lurking in the bay.[10]

The tension between the 'ordinary' and the 'spectacle' that is endemic to South African literary culture finds a most felicitous setting on the beach. If Wicomb's *Playing in the Light* (2006) evokes an ending in which two women 'saunter' companionably along the beach, 'shrieking when the icy water creeps up, lapping at their ankles' (215), these 'ordinary' manifestations of the beach as leisure location will not stick and cannot bring the novel to closure. Too much history intervenes, as do persistent social and economic inequalities and the vexed question of narrative perspective and control: of who will write whose story, and from which side of the beach. Here we observe the push and pull – the incoming and outgoing tides – of the 'ordinary' and the 'spectacle' and find inscribed on the shifting sands of the beach the proposition that even this binary is inadequate to the South African experience: Wicomb suggests in this and the subsequent scene of the novel that these terms themselves are best received as entangled. As in *David's Story*, moreover, the tide of history in this novel does not simply retreat from the shores of the present but returns incessantly, creeping up in an action simultaneously erosive and constructive that produces the beach as a location resistant to closure.

---

10   See Kluwick's chapter in this volume, which explores the representation of sharks for what it reveals about the relation between human and nature on the beach.

As it reflects from the beach on dugongs and mermaids, *Playing in the Light* also teases out the entanglement of nature and culture that this limen encodes and that for Scully's shipwrecked captain marks the undoing of the imperial subject. In the most recent return to the wreck of the *Grosvenor*, and thus perhaps also to Adamastor's curse, James Whyle's *Walk* (2013) turns away from the emblematic figure of the white woman that animated previous versions of this story to present a harrowing account of the castaways' walk from the coast of Mpondoland to the Cape. Their abjection scrambles the categories of civilised and savage, human and animal, living and dead. These 'ambiguous figures' (77) make their way along the beach or collapse upon it 'like things discarded there by the high tide' (47). If the castaways are repeatedly described as 'things' (for example 51, 76), the wreck that jettisoned them from the known world to this strange shore is understood to signal 'a prodigious shift in the nature of things' (4) and thus, to follow Brown's 'Thing Theory', in the 'subject-object relation' (Brown 4).

This relation and that between nature and culture is also the major preoccupation of Zakes Mda's *The Whale Caller* (2005), in which the eponymous protagonist enters into an erotic relationship with a Southern Right, Sharisha, whom he summons and courts with his kelp horn, '[b]lowing louder and louder as the tide responds by receding in time to the staccato of his call' (2).[11] When Sharisha later beaches on the shore, where she is euthanised with dynamite, the beach is infused with 'the strong stench of death' (291) that recalls the 'two hundred year old stench' (18) of whale hunting earlier remarked upon by the novel: more blood on the beach.

Sharisha's beaching is said to result from the degradation of the ocean and the overdevelopment of the shoreline, which has in turn expelled and sought to expunge the very memory of those who inhabited it before. To the eyes of the Whale Caller, however, the beach is a palimpsest on which prior human histories and human-animal relations surface. It is inscribed with the footprints of 'the strandlopers of old' (129); beneath the sands on which tourists sprawl are mnemonic traces of prior occupants:

> When the Whale Caller is in a happy mood he can see the weather-beaten fishermen shrouded in the mists of time, taking to sea in their fleet of small boats. … He can see even deeper in the mists, before there were boats and fishermen and whalers, the Khoikhoi of old dancing around a beached whale. Dancing to Tsiqua, He who Tells His Stories in Heaven, for the bountiful food he occasionally provides for his children by allowing whales to strand themselves. But when there are mass strandings the dance freezes and the laughter in the eyes of the dancers melts into tears that leave stains on the white sands. (2–3)

In contrast to the communion forged on the beach between Khoikhoi and whales is the current scenario in which tourists hound birthing and nursing Southern Rights in chartered boats – the Whale Caller likens them to harpooners. As the town

---

[11]   See Richter's chapter in this volume, which explores human-whale encounters in this and other narratives.

is converted into a whale watching mecca, moreover, 'ordinary' people are once more exiled from the beach (14): the eviction from the beach of *strandlopers* and fishermen by colonial genocide and apartheid segregation continues in the present in compliance with the demands of international tourism.

This complex of problems is also reflected on in Mda's earlier novel, *The Heart of Redness* (2000), which recalls spiritual relations to the sea and practices of subsistence foraging on the beach that were interrupted under colonial and apartheid rule. Under the new dispensation, the seaside village of Qholorha is presented with the prospect of 'progress' in the form of a tourist resort development. The threat posed to their way of life is acutely analysed by the character Qukezwa:

> This whole sea will belong to tourists and their boats and their water sports. Those women will no longer harvest the sea for their own food and to sell at the Blue Flamingo.
>> Water sports will take over our sea! (117–8)

Far from being a local phenomenon, this is part of a global pattern in which 'coastal people [are] expelled from all but the most undesirable parts of the beach' (Gillis 149). As Taussig (97–109) explains: while the unification of the world into One Big Market renders human civilisation more reliant on the sea than ever before, the advent of containerised shipping means that the sea as an element of nature has disappeared from everyday life and has become invisible; the rising popularity of the beach as leisure location since the mid-twentieth century is part of its fantasmatic recovery. In the process, the beach has been transformed from an ordinary place into prime real estate in a reversal of value that alienates the poor from the sea. *Moxyland* (2008) – Lauren Beukes's cyberpunk fiction set in Cape Town in 2018 – projects the next manifestation of this process of alienation into a future in which the ruling corporati have privatised the city beaches. Here, then, we observe on the beach the return of apartheid by another name, as neoliberal property rights trump those appealed to in the Freedom Charter and the tide of segregation and social regulation rises again on the shore of this brave new world. Marked with the exclusions particular or peculiar to South Africa, the beach as margin of the world ocean is simultaneously shown to be subject to global forces: it is both of the nation and not, in an ambivalent state that has characterised its inscription through the history of South African literatures.

Conclusion

The beach emerges in these narratives as a setting that resists closure and muddies categories, that convenes encounter and stages scenes of recognition and that figures simultaneously both prohibition and transgression. Spotted crimson during the colonial encounter while infused with thwarted desire for communicative exchange, inscribed with the regulatory zeal of apartheid and haunted by bloody apparitions of its aftermath, the beach equally calls into question the binaries and definitions that have determined both everyday life and cultural representation in this place, producing resonant forms of textual ambivalence. It is instructive to surface its often submerged presence as a literary setting, for it is from the beach in all its ambiguity that a literary strand offering alternative positions to those produced out of a politics of difference that have been available to writers in this state might begin to be grasped, and thereafter entangled into new cultural forms. At the same time, just as South African literary studies may benefit from paying more attention to the beach than they have done to date, so too beach studies may find valuable orientation points in the field of South African literature, with its carefully calibrated analytics for engaging with the forms of prohibition and exclusion and the negotiations of alterity that are an increasing feature of beaches across the world today.

Works Cited

Bakhtin, M.M. *The Dialogic Imagination: Four Essays*. Ed. Michael Holquist. Trans. Caryl Emerson and Michael Holquist. Austin: U of Texas P, 1981.

Beukes, Lauren. *Moxyland*. Johannesburg: Jacana, 2008.

Blackmore, Josiah. *Manifest Perdition: Shipwreck Narrative and the Disruption of Empire*. Minneapolis: U of Minnesota P, 2002.

———. *Moorings: Portuguese Expansion and the Writing of Africa*. Minneapolis: U of Minnesota P, 2009.

Boxer, C.R., ed. *The Tragic History of the Sea, 1589–1622*. 1958. Minneapolis: U of Minnesota P, 2001.

Brink, André. *The First Life of Adamastor*. London: Secker & Warburg, 1993.

———. *An Instant in the Wind*. 1976. London: Flamingo, 1983.

Brown, Bill. 'Thing Theory'. *Critical Enquiry* 28.1 (2001): 1–22.

Camões, Luís Vaz de. *The Lusiads*. 1572. Trans. Landeg White. 1997. London: Oxford UP, 2008.

Campbell, Roy. *Adamastor*. New York: Harper, 1930.

Coetzee, J.M. *White Writing: On the Culture of Letters in South Africa*. New Haven: Harvard UP, 1988.

Dening, Greg. *Beach Crossings: Voyaging Across Times, Cultures, and Self*. Philadelphia: U of Pennsylvania P, 2004.

———. 'Beaches of the Mind'. *Readings/Writings*. Melbourne: Melbourne UP, 1998. 85–146.

———. 'Deep Times, Deep Spaces: Civilizing the Sea'. *Sea Changes: Historicizing the Ocean*. Ed. Bernard Klein and Gesa Mackenthun. London: Routledge, 2004. 13–36.

———. *Islands and Beaches: Discourses on a Silent Land, Marquesas 1774–1880*. Honolulu: U of Hawaii P, 1980.

Drewe, Robert, ed. *The Penguin Book of the Beach*. Camberwell: Penguin, 2006.

Driver, Dorothy. ''Woman' as Sign in the South African Colonial Enterprise'. *Journal of Literary Studies* 4.1 (1988): 3–20.

Flanery, Patrick. *Absolution*. London: Atlantic, 2012.

Fugard, Sheila. *The Castaways*. 1972. Johannesburg: Ad Donker, 2002.

Gillis, John R. *The Human Shore: Seacoasts in History*. Chicago: U of Chicago P, 2012.

Glenn, Ian E. 'The Wreck of the *Grosvenor* and the Making of South African Literature'. *English in Africa* 22.2 (1995): 1–18.

Gordimer, Nadine. 'The Catch'. 1954. *The Penguin Book of the Beach*. Ed. Robert Drewe. Camberwell: Penguin, 2006. 287–307.

Gray, Stephen. 'The White Man's Creation Myth of Africa'. *Southern African Literature: An Introduction*. Cape Town: David Philip, 1979. 15–37.

Hosking, Susan, Rick Hosking, Rebecca Pannell and Nena Bierbaum. Introduction. *Something Rich & Strange: Sea Changes, Beaches and the Littoral in The Antipodes*. Ed. Hosking et al. Kent Town: Wakefield Press, 2009. vii–xi.

Huntsman, Leone. *Sand in Our Souls: The Beach in Australian History*. Melbourne: Melbourne UP, 2001.

Johnson, David. *Imagining the Cape Colony: History, Literature, and the South African Nation*. U of Cape Town P, 2012.

Klein, Bernard. 'Camões and the Sea: Maritime Modernity in *The Lusiads*'. *Modern Philology* 111.2 (2013): 158–80.

Kossew, Sue. 'From Eliza to Elisabeth: André Brink's Version of the Elisa Fraser Story'. *Constructions of Colonialism: Perspectives on Eliza Fraser's Shipwreck*. Ed. Ian J. McNiven, Lynette Russell and Kay Schaffer. London: Leister UP, 1998.

Lencek, Lena, and Gideon Bosker. *The Beach: The History of Paradise on Earth*. New York: Penguin, 1999.

Lencek, Lena, and Gideon Bosker, ed. *Beach: Stories by the Sand and Sea*. New York: Marlowe, 2000.

Mack, John. *The Sea: A Cultural History*. London: Reaktion Books, 2011.

Mda, Zakes. *The Heart of Redness*. Cape Town: Oxford UP, 2000.

———. *The Whale Caller*. 2005. Johannesburg: Penguin Books, 2006.

Morland, George. *African Hospitality*. 1791. Mezzotint. Private Collection.

Ndebele, Njabulo S. 'The Rediscovery of the Ordinary: Some New Writings in South Africa'. 1984. *Rediscovery of the Ordinary: Essays on South African Literature and Culture*. 1991. Pietermartizburg: U of KwaZulu Natal P, 2006. 31–54.

Nkosi, Lewis. *Mating Birds*. Johannesburg: Ravan, 1987.

Nuttall, Sarah. *Entanglement: Literary and Cultural Reflections on Post-Apartheid*. Johannesburg: Wits UP, 2009.

Pratt, Mary Louise. *Imperial Eyes: Travel Writing and Transculturation*. London: Routledge, 1992.

Rive, Richard. *Buckingham Palace, District Six*. Cape Town: David Philip, 1986.

Rose-Innes, Henrietta. *Shark's Egg*. Cape Town: Kwela, 2000.

Samuelson, Meg. 'Abdulrazak Gurnah's Fictions of the Swahili Coast: Littoral Locations and Amphibian Aesthetics'. *Social Dynamics: A Journal of African Studies* 38.3 (2012): 499–515.

————. 'Oceanic Histories and Protean Poetics: The Surge of the Sea in Zoë Wicomb's Fiction'. *Journal of Southern African Studies* 36.3 (2010): 543–57.

————. *Remembering the Nation, Dismembering Women? Stories of the South African Transition*. Pietermaritzburg: U of KwaZulu-Natal P, 2007.

Scully, W.C. 'The Wreck of the Grosvenor (A Dramatic Poem)'. *The Wreck of the Gosvenor and Other Poems*. Alice: Lovedale, 1886. 1–18.

Shukri, Ishtiyaq. *The Silent Minaret*. Johannesburg: Jacana, 2005.

Sleigh, Dan. *Islands*. Trans. André Brink. London: Secker & Warburg, 2004. 97–118.

Taussig, Michael. 'The Beach (A Fantasy)'. *Walter Benjamin's Grave*. Chicago: U of Chicago P, 2006. 97–120.

Titlestad, Michael, and Mike Kissack. "'I have always known shipwreck': Whiteness in Sheila Fugard's *The Castaways*'. *African Renewal, African Renaissance: New Perspectives on Africa's Past and Africa's Present*. Conference Proceedings. Crawley: U of Western Australia, 2004. 1–15.

————. 'The Persistent Castaway in South African Writing'. *Postcolonial Studies* 10.2 (2007): 191–218.

Van Wyk Smith, Malvern. *Shades of Adamastor: Africa and the Portuguese Connection – An Anthology of Poetry*. Grahamstown: Rhodes U & NELM, 1988.

————. 'Shades of Adamastor: The Legacy of *The Lusiads*'. *Cambridge History of South African Literatures*. Ed. Derek Attridge and David Attwell. Cambridge UP, 2012. 113–37.

Whyle, James. *Walk*. Johannesburg: Jacana, 2013.

Wicomb, Zoë. *David's Story*. Cape Town: Kwela Books, 2000.

————. *October*. Cape Town: Umuzi, 2014.

————. *Playing in the Light*. Cape Town: Umuzi, 2006.

Chapter 8
Food for Sharks:
Abjection on the Beach

Ursula Kluwick

In the Western cultural imagination, the beach features prominently as a site in which humans seek to realise their fantasies of a return to nature, however short-lived; at the same time, reactions to encounters with dangerous wildlife there indicate that our cultural investment in the beach as vacationscape jars with our awareness of humanity as always already a part of nature. When sharks attack, the beach becomes a site of abjection, a zone where divisions so laboriously upheld by humans collapse. It is up to cultural mediation to repair what has been breached, and to mould the account of the shark attack into familiar narratives, thereby channelling our gory fascination with the fact that humans can be eaten and saving us from the full impact of the realisation that when sharks eat human flesh they do not merely devour individual human subjects but threaten our self-perception on a larger scale.

This essay looks at the representation of sharks in order to determine what it reveals about the relationship between humanity and nature on the beach. I begin with the source of our human fascination with sharks and propose how one might account for ambivalent attitudes towards shark attacks and their representation. The appeal of abjection which I locate here features prominently in the popular science books I discuss. This genre is interesting because, even though they convey facts about shark behaviour, popular science books are really more concerned with cultural perceptions, a prime concern being to rectify the image of the shark as far as possible. Such cultural images are at the core of the final part of my essay, which analyses two films, Steven Spielberg's *Jaws* (1975) and Danny Boyle's *The Beach* (1999), in which shark attacks significantly shape the plot, as well as the characters' attitudes towards nature. In this concluding section of my essay, I also probe the concept of the beach as such by suggesting that the shark attacks in these two films reveal the complex dynamics between beach and shore.

The Shark as an Agent of Abjection

The statistical insignificance of shark attacks is well documented: according to Leatherman, '[o]n average, only one person a year is killed by sharks in the United States' (2), while the International Shark Attack File records, for instance, 80 attacks in 2012, 7 of which were fatal.[1] By contrast, the 2012 *National Coastal*

---

[1]   See International Shark Attack File 'ISFA Statistics'.

Safety Report for Australia records 119 coastal drowning deaths in Australia alone for the season of 2011/12 (3). Clearly, the prominence of the shark attack in our mental list of sea and shore hazards is a matter of representation. The rarity of shark attacks stands in stark contrast to the media hype that habitually surrounds them when they do happen, or when the specifics of a human-shark encounter become known. Fear of sharks is often linked to the first screening of *Jaws*, but both this fear and its exploitation in the media are phenomena of long standing. In New Jersey, for instance, 1916 is known as the infamous 'Year of the Shark' (Leatherman 4), and the Jersey Shore shark attacks of that year are frequently included in accounts of shark incidents, as one of the most gruesome examples:[2] during 'Twelve Days of Terror' (Leatherman 4), a shark claimed two victims off the coast of New Jersey, even swimming up a tidal creek and killing three people eleven miles inland (Leatherman 3) before being caught. This must certainly have been a traumatic series of attacks, particularly in light of the shark's unexpected foray inland. In spite of this, human reactions seem to have been extreme, as Leatherman reports: 'as a result, hundreds of sharks were caught and slaughtered along the mid-Atlantic coast' (4). Shark attacks seem to spark deep-rooted human fears about being at the mercy of forces beyond human control. Hence a single man-eating shark is enough to trigger widespread panic, despite the infrequence of shark attacks and despite the fact that it is human agency that has turned many subspecies of sharks into endangered species, not the other way round.[3]

The disproportionate reactions to man-eating sharks described above are part of the same phenomenon as the sensationalism of media coverage of shark attacks, in particular when these are fatal or near fatal for humans: both point to a fearful fascination with sharks. Indeed, the International Shark Attack File specifically highlights the propensity to sensationalise shark-attack-related information and has declared its data sensitive material, announcing on its website that 'duplication of the File's contents is forbidden since it contains such confidential items as physician reports, autopsies, victim's interviews and photographs that might be characterised as "sensational" if they fell into the wrong hands'.[4]

Reactions to sharks and to shark attacks are determined by a variety of factors, many of which are culturally contingent. But even for the particular perspective which I am analysing – that of Western holidaymakers on a beach perceived as vacationscape – fear is by no means the only emotion called forth by shark attacks. In this essay, I am interested in four distinct, though interlocking, responses to the danger of the shark: fear, horror, fascination and desire. Shark attacks elicit shock

---

[2]   See, for instance, two recent newspaper articles by Rosenfeld and by Golgowski.

[3]   Only very recently – in March 2013 – various species of sharks were added to Appendix II of the United Nations-backed Convention on International Trade in Endangered Species of Wild Flora and Fauna in a move intended to provide better trade protection (UN News Centre).

[4]   International Shark Attack File, 'Access'. The expression 'wrong hands' is, of course, interesting, as it points to a perceived discrepancy between scientific and popular interpretations of data.

and *fear* because they evoke the dangers of the ocean and its unstable boundaries. Fear gives rise to *horror* at the idea of being eaten alive, an emotion which partly relies on identification with the shark's human victim and, hence, on the adoption of an internal view of the attack. At the same time, fear and horror also call forth a *fascination* with the violence of the attack. This fascination tends to be connected to the assumption of an external point of view, a safe vantage point from which the attack can be voyeuristically enjoyed,[5] as in the consumption of sensational accounts of shark attacks. *Desire*, finally, is the result of the translation of fear into attraction and, as such, is linked to sublime awe. The very perception of sharks as potentially lethal arouses the desire for (a safe form of) closeness to these majestic creatures. Guided swimming-with-sharks packages are an example of this phenomenon.

Fear, horror, fascination and desire – obviously, the Western beachgoer's response to sharks is shaped by a paradoxical mix. In order to unravel this complicated set of reactions, Kristeva's concept of 'the abject' is helpful in that it sketches a similar dance of fascination and repulsion:

> There looms, within abjection, one of those violent, dark revolts of being, directed against a threat that seems to emanate from an exorbitant outside or inside, ejected beyond the scope of the possible, the tolerable, the thinkable. It lies there, quite close, but it cannot be assimilated. It beseeches, worries, and fascinates desire, which, nevertheless, does not let itself be seduced. Apprehensively, desire turns aside; sickened, it rejects. ... But simultaneously, just the same, that impetus, that spasm, that leap is drawn toward an elsewhere as tempting as it is condemned. (1)

Attraction, here, appears as an intrinsic element of abjection. The abject 'fascinates desire', but a desire that wants to resist and withdraw, unable, however, to separate itself completely from what it finds nauseating. Kristeva's description is singularly appropriate for human reactions to shark attacks, which are characterised by a similar 'vortex of summons and repulsion' (1). As my discussion of photographic and film material below shows, textual, and in particular visual, evidence of shark attacks can indeed be highly disturbing. The revulsion with which the viewer reacts tends to cause an instinctive shrinking from its source, a form of self-protection which renders the subject safe by separating it from what repels it (see Kristeva 3), literally forcing it to turn 'to the side and ... away from defilement' (Kristeva 2).[6] The resulting distance helps the subject protect itself from chaos, the

---

5   The horror genre plays with such variations in perspective. Both in *Jaws* and in *The Beach*, scenes of shark attacks are characterised by alternating points of view, with suspense deriving from point-of-view shots which variously show the unsuspecting victims from the point of view of the sharks and from the limited view of the victims, who remain unaware of the fact that the shark's perspective has already turned them into prey. By necessarily assuming the proffered point of view, the audience veer between identification with the victim and adoption of the predator's perspective.

6   See also the reaction of the shark's first victim's would-be lover in *Jaws*: when a policeman takes him to Chrissie's remains on the beach, he turns aside and vomits.

central danger immanent in the abject, which 'draws [the subject] toward the place where meaning collapses' (Kristeva 2).

Reading the shark as an agent of abjection following Kristeva reaffirms the protective impetus of disgust. For the shark attack indeed brings chaos to perceptions of human beings which suppress the fact that humans can be food. Of course, they serve as food in a variety of ways, one of the most obvious being the ingestion of dead human matter by animals in relation to burial rites (worms and insects in cultures where inhumation is practised, vultures in Parsi funeral rites and so on). But in Western societies, both the human corpse and its disposal frequently constitute a taboo as unpleasant signifiers of our final decomposition. As Kristeva contends, the repugnance provoked by the injured or dead human body is related to the need to ignore reminders of one's own materiality as a safeguard against the constant consciousness of death, which would imperil life:

> The corpse (or cadaver: *cadere*, to fall), that which has irremediably come a cropper, is cesspool, and death; it upsets even more violently the one who confronts it as fragile and fallacious chance. A wound with blood and pus, or the sickly, acrid smell of sweat, of decay, does not signify death. In the presence of signified death – a flat encephalograph, for instance – I would understand, react, or accept. No, as in true theater, without makeup or masks, refuse and corpses *show me* what I permanently thrust aside in order to live. (3; emphases in original)

The physical remains of the human body are disgusting because they call into question the autonomy, indeed the very vitality, of the living human subject. Faced with the visual evidence of mortality, the subject recoils from the actual presence of death. As I have already suggested, however, there is an additional reason for abjection when it comes to shark attacks. On the one hand, survivors shrink from the victim's mutilated body as from any corpse or injured person. Yet, on the other hand, the shark's victim also evokes disgust because it has visibly become food. Thus the shark attack and its victim challenge views of humans as existing outside the food chain, and they serve as unpleasant reminders of the fact that human flesh can also be meat. That this is a highly disturbing thought can also be seen in reactions to cultural practices which turn the human body into food. The widespread abhorrence of cannibalism characteristic of most human societies clearly shows that what for many is fairly unproblematic when it happens to animals is unacceptable when it concerns humans: while a considerable percentage of the world animal population seems to exist solely in order to provide meat for human consumption,[7] and while we accept it as natural that animals hunt and eat each other, the swallowing of human flesh is regarded as abnormal. The very eagerness with which some anthropologists have embraced views of 'cannibalism as a mere product of the European imagination' (Lindenbaum 476) can be regarded as symptomatic of the status of cannibalism as a taboo. And

---

[7]   With J.M. Coetzee (*The Lives of Animals*) and Jonathan Safran Foer (*Eating Animals*), two important contemporary writers have addressed ethical aspects of meat-eating and vegetarianism.

cannibalism is not solely a phenomenon of the 'colonial discourse of otherness' (Beaver 673) either, as becomes apparent, for instance, in Louise Noble's recent book on medicinal cannibalism, which depicts 'a cultural fascination, almost to the point of obsession, with the medical recycling of corpse matter' (2) in early modern Europe. However, the ingestion of bodily matter for medical purposes is fundamentally different from its ingestion as food. While medicinal cannibalism relies on the belief 'that the human body contains a mysterious healing power that is transmitted in ingested matter such as mummy' (Noble 2), and while it is thus related to the occult, seeing human corpses as food turns the human body into pure nutriment, thus demystifying it and robbing it of its imagined categorical difference from other flesh.[8] This is how attacks by wild predators cause chaos in human self-perceptions. They stand for 'a reality that, if I acknowledge it, annihilates me' (Kristeva 2), or, if one extends Kristeva's phrase, a reality that, if acknowledged, annihilates the perception of our human identity as a species conceptually different from all others because situated outside the food web. In the case of the shark attack, this is all the more shocking, since the littoral environment of the attack is inconsistent with violence and danger in the tourist imagination. A victim of a bear in Alaska or of a lion in the African savannah is likely to have entered the wild predator's habitat fully aware that in doing so, they were putting themselves at risk. But as many of the essays in this collection suggest, in the Western cultural imagination the beach features prominently as a realm of relaxation and regeneration, and though it is not incompatible with death, this popular perception of the beach as vacationscape seems far less compatible with images of mangled and half-devoured human remains. I relate this phenomenon to slippages between beach and shore in my film analysis below.

What might seem paradoxical about the human response to real encounters with sharks is less strange when experience is transposed into cultural production. In addressing the question of why 'anyone [would] *want* to be horrified, or even art-horrified' (33; emphasis in original), Carroll acknowledges the different trajectories of desire in what he calls 'everyday life' (33) as opposed to its cultural representation. For 'a key element in the emotion of art-horror is repulsion or disgust' (Carroll 33), and hence audiences are attracted by the representation of what they would ordinarily avoid. Indeed, a familiar feature of the horror genre in literature and film is that it 'gives every evidence of being pleasurable to its audience … by means of trafficking in the very sorts of things that cause disquiet, distress, and displeasure' (Carroll 33). Carroll relates this to 'the narrative structure in which the presentation of the monster is staged' (34), which is driven by the urge to disclose the unknown. Horror in literature and film often takes the form of 'narratives of discovery and proof' (36) in which the central secret, or monster, is something that falls outside our schemes of classification, an interpretation which is indebted to Mary Douglas's theory of impurity. As a result, disgust, in Carroll's reading of horror, is a central feature of the genre, and predicated on the nature of the monster:

---

[8]   As the examples listed by Beaver suggest, cannibalism has rarely been practised solely for the purpose of nourishment, except in cases of dire necessity (672, 674–7).

> It is not that we crave disgust, but that disgust is a predictable concomitant of disclosing the unknown, whose disclosure is a desire the narrative instills in the audience and then goes on to gladden. Nor will that desire be satisfied unless the monster defies our conception of nature …. [A]rt-horror is the price we are willing to pay for the revelation of that which is impossible and unknown, of that which violates our conceptual schema. The impossible being does disgust; but that disgust is part of an overall narrative address which is not only pleasurable, but whose potential pleasure depends on the confirmation of the existence of the monster as a being that violates, defies, or problematizes standing cultural classifications. (37)

Carroll's theory works well for a horror film such as *Jaws*, which is indeed characterised by the narrative structure he proposes. Here the existence of a shark as huge as the great white in question beggars belief, and this is strengthened by Spielberg's trick of not showing the shark until towards the very end of the film. The attempts to capture and kill the shark, therefore, can readily be seen in terms of the typical narrative of disclosure which Carroll regards as intrinsic to the horror genre. His theory offers a less convincing tool for the analysis of films such as *The Beach*, however, which incorporate elements of horror but in which the role of the monster is much more diffuse. While the great white clearly functions as the monster in *Jaws*, the shark in *The Beach* does not fit this category; nevertheless, as I argue below, the effects of the shark attacks are similar, with sharks forming agents of abjection in both films.

In order to enhance the usefulness of abjection for my analysis of popular science books and films, it is still necessary to tease out the relationship between abjection and desire. In this context, Slavoj Žižek's reading of Lacan provides a useful intervention, in particular his distinction between object and object-cause of desire. Following Lacan, Žižek separates the cause of desire from the object of desire, commenting on how commonly accepted concepts of the trajectory of desire tend to confuse the two:

> While the object of desire is simply the desired object, the cause of desire is the feature on account of which we desire the desired object – some detail of which we are usually unaware and which we sometimes even misperceive as an obstacle, in spite of which we desire the object. (212)

Žižek takes this further when he claims that 'being deprived of its obstacle/ cause … desire itself will wane' (212), thus suggesting that what we desire is not so much particular objects but conditions in which desire can develop, and hence desire itself. Applied to human encounters with sharks, this dynamic indicates that while, due to its popularity as a fictional character, the shark might appear as an object of desire in popular cultural production, it is, in fact, the danger emanating from the shark that can be seen as the cause of desire. We would neither enjoy meeting a real shark on the beach nor encountering a toothless shark on film, or even in an aquarium. The shark has to be dangerous, but we want to experience its danger from a safe remove. The shark's attraction lies in the *idea* of danger, and hence in the menace it embodies, a menace which finds its confirmation in the shark's mutilation of other human bodies (never our own!) and in the aversion that we feel when confronted with the traces this violence leaves behind.

But human fantasising about shark attacks, both in pseudo-scientific texts and in cultural products such as novels and films, has an additional function. The telling and consumption of stories about shark attacks creates a narrative which becomes familiar through repetition. Thus abjection is couched in familiar contexts. In Žižek's terms, 'fantasy serves as the screen that protects us from being directly overwhelmed by the raw Real' (222). The story of the shark attack is popular because it conveys the danger of the shark and produces abjection, while remaining a recognisable story. Narrativity serves as a membrane that separates the real event from the audience, protecting them from the Real horror of human mortality even when the narration is based on actual occurrences, and hence keeping the Real at bay.

The Shark in Popular Science

Popular science publications derive their appeal from ambiguous human attitudes towards sharks. While their ostensible purpose is mostly to deflate the myth of the ferocious shark in order to reassure beachgoers, they frequently, if implicitly, reaffirm fears of sharks, which lie at the heart of the marketing success of the shark as a commodified creature. Terry Deary, for instance, though apparently committed to elucidating shark behaviour and defusing human terror of sharks, nevertheless exploits such fears in the very title of his book: *Terry Deary's Terribly True Shark Stories*. In this respect, the references to Spielberg's *Jaws* with which most books commence are also noteworthy, as they show that this film is recognised as the single most powerful influence on popular representations and perceptions of sharks. Cerullo and Rotman, for instance, describe how audience reactions to *Jaws* in the 1970s spilt over onto real beaches, in the form of fear and panic, because the film 'scared audiences so much that many people stopped swimming in the ocean after seeing it. In some seaside resorts, police had to patrol beaches where there had never been a shark attack to look out for sharks, just so beachgoers would feel safe' (25). Indeed, the tenacity of the images evoked by *Jaws* tends to stimulate accounts of sharks which directly oppose the film, and which use it as a template against which one has to position oneself with 'true' information about sharks.

Such examples demonstrate how our perception of sharks and of their presence on the beach has been shaped by particular cultural models. And, as statistics show, it is indeed the beach and its offshore waters that have become contested ground as the liminal zone which separates the shark's territory from a realm safe for humans.[9] Fear of sharks is all about fear of entering a space in which humans are at a considerable biological disadvantage. In addition, it is also about defining

---

[9]   According to the *International Shark Attack File*, '[m]ost attacks occur in nearshore waters' ('How, When, & Where').

to whom the beach belongs, whether it is human or shark territory or whether it ought to be regarded as a collision zone.

Xavier Maniguet's *The Jaws of Death*, one of the most sensational books about sharks explicitly describes beaches as hunting grounds for sharks, relying, once again, on a comparison with *Jaws*, yet stressing, in this instance, the validity of the situations presented in the film (224). The implication that we might quite possibly encounter a shark comparable to the one depicted in *Jaws* is in tune with the general trajectory of Maniguet's book, which seeks to sensationalise and frighten under the guise of providing (pseudo-)scientific information. Most interesting, in this respect, is the visual aspect of the book, already highlighted on the front cover by the following caption: 'WARNING. This book contains disturbing photographs'. If the book here activates the anticipation of abjection as a cause of desire, it initially disappoints. A first browse-through reveals nothing but the usual photographs of shark-attack victims with well-healed scars and bite-marks. On closer scrutiny, however, Maniguet's book contains a special photographic section, suitably sealed and even captioned:

> WARNING: The photographs contained in this sealed section are liable to shock the sensitive reader. They have been selected by the author according to their demonstrative value, and correspond in the text to a scientific explanation or to a real-life event. … To open tear CAREFULLY along the perforated edge.

The pages in question are even unpaginated, and while the abject is thus contained at the very core of the book, it is simultaneously also characterised as external, since the pages devoted to it do not appear in the final page count. In spite of being the source of the appeal of Maniguet's book, the abject nevertheless remains a foreign element. It is up to each reader whether he or she wants to ignore or face it, and so an individual thrill is added as a cause of desire. The photographs themselves are gruesome, consisting of pictures of severely injured people, torn and mauled human limbs, as well as the chewed remains of recovered human corpses.[10]

---

[10]   Other instances where humans were devoured by predators, for example bears, are naturally also very shocking. A well-known example is the case of Timothy Treadwell and his girlfriend, documented in Werner Herzog's film *Grizzly Man*. Herzog used found footage produced by Treadwell himself, including the sound recording of the lethal attack by a grizzly bear. This 'audio-abject' is both contained and sealed off within the film: the cries of the dying couple are not heard; instead, we see Herzog with headphones, listening to the sounds of the couple's death throes with a horrified face. In contrast to Maniguet's book, the 'voyeuristic offer' is here withheld from the audience. While the emotional impact of documentations of bear attacks on humans is probably similar to that of shark attacks, there is, however, no similar 'bear scare' industry. Individual bears that harm people and domestic animals are killed (such as the brown bear M13 in Grisons, Switzerland, in 2013), but there are no exterminatory raids against the whole species, as in the cases discussed in the beginning of this essay. In addition, as already suggested, reactions to attacks are influenced by the various cultural meanings carried by the different settings in which they occur.

I only want to focus on the final sequence of pictures in this section, which consists of close-ups of an opened stomach in which one can clearly see the remains of a man – head, legs, arms and all – as they are being retrieved and reassembled on the ground. The pictures draw much of their shock value from the fact that the man's face is basically unharmed and hence distinctly recognisable, while the manner in which he is pressed into the animal's now open stomach recalls ancient rites of burial. The visible proof that a human being has been completely devoured is upsetting and is sure to elicit the intended effect of abjection.

What is most interesting for my purposes, however, is the fact that the animal in question is not a shark but a crocodile. Maniguet's book explicitly deals with sharks, not crocodiles, which is also clear from its title: *The Jaws of Death: Shark as Predator, Man as Prey*. But as this title also suggests, Maniguet wants to construct a narrative of monodirectional threat, in which sharks are the hunters, humans the hunted. No matter that statistics speak quite a different language,[11] and no matter that humans have managed to render sharks yet another endangered species, cultural myth insists on casting sharks in the role of villains. As the example of Maniguet's book shows, this version of human-shark relations can be upheld against surprising odds: when sharks have not been 'cruel' enough and when shark footage is too tame, a crocodile is made to pose as a shark.

Sharks as 'Jaws'

The films under discussion here display a similar focus on the shark as hunter rather than hunted; indeed, Drummond talks about the 'animal enemy' in connection with *Jaws* (234). In both films, human characters consciously seek out nature – either in an attempt to escape from civilisation and return to a vision of pristine paradise or as a national pastime intimately connected with the celebration of national identity – but come to experience it as antagonistic. *Jaws*, of course, is the ultimate shark horror film. Set on Amity Island, it depicts a beach resort which becomes a man-eating great white shark's feeding ground in the run-up to the 4th of July and is only rendered safe once the shark has been killed by three brave men. *The Beach* focuses on a community of Western tourists who aim for idyllic unity both with each other and with nature on the perfect beach on a secluded island. Their community begins to disintegrate when they prove unable to cope with the presence of the surviving victim of a shark attack and send the severely injured man off into the forest, de facto abandoning him to his own devices. Thus they escape the living reminder of their own physical frailty, as well as of the threat lurking in their supposed beach paradise.

Both films engage with the complexities which humanity-nature interactions and the human desire for contact with nature entail. The shark functions as a figure of intercession here: it exposes human fears of encounters with animals and

---

[11]   Deary quotes *The Times*: 'The balance sheet reads: Man, about 25 deaths each year. Shark, about 100 million deaths each year' (111).

simultaneously poses a challenge to the concept of a nature-culture binary. As a radical reminder of the artificiality of this binary, the shark attack constitutes an act of literal reincorporation of humanity into nature. As humans are reintegrated into the food web, becoming one with nature emerges as something significantly less harmonious than envisaged. The beach is a contact zone, not a cuddle zone, a realm in which the violent side of inter-species encounters becomes fully apparent. Indeed, the brutality of these encounters becomes particularly obvious on the beach because it is mostly here that their product, the mutilated human body, becomes visible. As long as the chewed body disappears inside the ocean or inside the shark, its 'foodness' is mercifully hidden. When it is washed up on the beach, however, the fact that humans can be turned into food can no longer be disguised. As human characters' reactions in both films demonstrate, this is particularly disturbing when it clashes with visions of the beach as vacationscape. In point of fact, it is useful to distinguish between two terms here: shore and beach.[12] In its primary form as vacationscape, the beach is characterised by an imagined absence of dangerous wildlife. Visions of the perfect holiday beach might entail the presence of colourful fish for the purposes of snorkelling but are unlikely to include lethal jellyfish; they might tolerate a few quaint crabs but will probably not include poisonous scorpions; and only rarely, for very specific forms of adventure tourism, will the perfect holiday beach be the territory of predators likely to feed on humans. Instead, the beach offers a culturally constructed version of nature in which the illusion of a Disneyfied unity with the natural world can be enacted in a commodified setting. In *Jaws*, for instance, the beach forms an essential component of the practice of celebrating Independence Day. The beaches have to remain open, as this holiday is unthinkable without the favourite national pastime of relaxing on the beach. That the beach is part of a commodified scenario here is clear: the decision to ignore the implications of Chrissie's death is largely contingent on the importance of Amity Beach for tourism. Similarly, in *The Beach*, the commodified and romanticised aspect of the beach community's attitude towards beach life is obvious despite their belief in their own difference from what they regard as 'mainstream' backpackers' tourism. After all, it is its mythical seclusion that renders 'their' beach the ultimate object of desire in the context of Western tourists' craving for the collective exclusiveness of access to the last pristine remnants of unspoilt nature.[13]

In contrast to the beach, the shore promises a rawer version of nature in which encounters between humanity and nature can take place outside the setting of vacationscape. As a geological and evolutionary site, the shore reaches back to deep time,[14] and as such it entails a different perspective on the position of

---

[12]   Kylie Crane also makes this distinction in an unpublished essay, and I am grateful to her for sharing her thoughts on this issue with me.

[13]   In this context, see also Annesley's reading of the manner in which *Lonely Planet* authors, heavily criticised by characters in *The Beach*, 'position themselves as gatekeepers of the world's delicate cultures' (555) when they decide not to include locations as a means of protecting them.

[14]   Zwierlein discusses the notion of deep time in relation to the beach in this volume.

humanity within nature. This does not mean that the shore is less of a cultural construction than the beach; but it does offer a broader vista of humanity-nature relationships. And, while it follows that we do our utmost to ignore death on the beach as a result of our investment in it as a vacationscape,[15] death is an essential component of the history of the shore.

Much of the chaos the shark attack brings to the beach in *Jaws* and *The Beach* is rooted in the fact that the half-devoured human remains which re-enter the beach from the direction of the ocean result in a slippage between these two concepts: the shore here infringes on the beach. In both films, the beach can be read as a space of imagined human sovereignty in which nature features as an agent of human delight, and as Richard's killing of a shark in *The Beach* suggests, this is by no means incompatible with sublime awe and fear. But with the emergence of the abject, it becomes evident that this view of the relationship between humanity and nature is jeopardised by the continued presence of the shore beneath the surface of the beach.[16] The partial collapse of the beach into the shore also exposes the naïvety of conceptualisations of humanity-nature interactions as harmonious. In *Jaws*, the population of Amity react with panic and with raids that lead to the eventual extermination of the great white. In *The Beach*, the shark's injured victim is viewed as a destructive element that needs to be ostracised. What the film sharks leave in their wake, therefore, is a profound unease concerning the relationships both between humans and between humanity and nature. As such, the shark attack opens up a space for the interrogation of what it means to be human, in relation to nature as well as to other humans.

This is strikingly obvious in the consequences of the fatal shark attack in *The Beach*. Indeed, the consequences are the only thing we see, as the shark attack itself is never shown. Instead, we witness Richard registering shouts from outside and see him almost stumble across the corpse of Sten, whom a shark has just killed, as he leaves his hut. Human horror at the vision of human vulnerability is palpable. The camera work emphasises this, shifting from close-ups of Sten's mutilated body to Richard's shocked face. The vision of Sten's material remains transports him to 'the border of [his] condition as a living being' (Kristeva 3), forcing him to face up to the reality of physical decay permanently present beneath the celebration of sensual beach life. The remaining members of the beach community react with horror, shock and disgust; the physical evidence of human mortality is abject, an unbearable demonstration of the precariousness of human life. In forcing the beach dwellers to recognise their own vulnerability, both as physical bodies and as a community, what seemed the epitome of the tourist's beach-fantasy reveals its propinquity to the shore.

---

[15] In *Jaws*, the attempt to ignore Chrissie's death on the beach results in further deaths.

[16] The trailer of *Jaws* explicitly plays with the notion of deep time in the voice-over which accompanies the shark's point-of-view shot of the ocean bed with which the trailer starts: 'There is a creature alive today who has survived millions of years of evolution without change, without passion, and without logic'. The shark is here stylised as a prehistoric animal in comparison with whose very length of unaltered existence humanity is rendered an insignificant evolutionary player (see *Jaws* 'The Original Theatrical Trailer').

Repugnance at Sten's corpse is one cause of abjection; the fact that he has been turned into food is another. The shark's bite-marks on Sten are very visible, and chunks of his body are missing – the shark has chewed away his physical boundaries. As such, it has also breached the barriers of his human identity: 'The abject confronts us … with those fragile states where man strays on the territories of *animal*' (Kristeva 12; emphasis in original). It is the fragility of the border between animalness and humanity that is exposed by the shark attack. The shark does not recognise the human as intrinsically or fundamentally other than its normal prey, and so its bite-marks reveal the flimsy construction of biological difference upon which the distinction between humans and animals rests. Hence the shark draws the human into a 'zone of indetermination and uncertainty, "something shared or indiscernible", a proximity "that makes it impossible to say where the boundary between the human and animal lies"' (Deleuze and Guattari 301). Deleuze and Guattari's challenge to the border between humans and animals here goes even further than Kristeva's by foregrounding the aspects of being they have always 'shared'.

In *The Beach*, it soon transpires that it is the living residues of the body that are the real problem for the beach community, more difficult to accommodate than the corpse – for Sten can quickly be buried. As the film reveals and as Richard's voice-over stresses, however, the wounded body of the second, surviving, victim of the attack poses a more serious threat. Unable either to recover or die, Christo remains in the liminal zone between life and death, and as such he serves as a perpetual physical reminder of human vulnerability and of 'an inhuman connivance with the animal'(Deleuze and Guattari 302). For the beach community, his presence becomes insufferable, abject, as it reminds them of their own precarious identity – social, cultural and material. As a community, these escapees from Western consumerism cling to the notion that they are at one with nature, but Christo's decaying body clearly exposes the romanticising inadequacy of this beach vision, as his cries, sighs and smells begin to infect the atmosphere in the communal hut. Thus it is through Christo's dissolving body that horror seeps in, both in thematic and in generic terms.[17] The members of the beach community react in a way that Kristeva describes as a natural instinct: the 'body extricates itself, as being alive, from that border' which jeopardises its 'condition as a living being' (Kristeva 3) because it renders visible the limits of life and of the living body. Unable to deal with the presence of Christo's half-chewed body in their midst, the other members of the beach community extricate themselves from recognition of their own mortality by dispatching him to a tent in the forest. Yet in denying Christo the right to remain,

---

[17]   See Tudor on 'the characteristic ambiguity and fluidity of bodily boundaries in modern horror', which he relates to 'postmodern "experience[s] of social fragmentation and to the constantly threatening confrontation between embattled 'selves' and the risky and unreliable world they inhabit" (Tudor, 1995:40)' (51). Since in our post-postmodern and post-humanist moment risk and unreliability are frequently related to environmental concerns, it is not surprising that Christo's bodily ambivalence is also couched in terms that evoke the troubled relationship between humanity and the rest of nature.

of course, they ultimately aggravate their communal identity crisis by opening up questions concerning their humaneness. Thus the shark attack holds the seeds of the end to their sojourn on the island, and the dream of perpetual beach life becomes unsustainable. Not because the island becomes more dangerous but because the shark attack and human reactions to it reveal the fault lines within the community's relations with nature, as well as within the community and its way of life itself.[18]

In *The Beach*, the shark attack is represented only by its products, the two mutilated human bodies. The attack itself is witnessed neither by the protagonists nor the audience. In *Jaws*, by contrast, the second fatal shark attack, in which a young boy is killed, takes place in the midst of a throng of beachgoers. The shark here enters a '*zone of proximity*' (Deleuze and Guattari 301; emphasis in original) with a whole group of humans, creating chaos as meaning collapses and the boundaries between humans and animal become unclear. Terrifyingly, even though the actual attack happens right before our eyes, the shark is nowhere to be seen, neither for us as spectators nor for the human characters in the shallow waters of the beach. Horrified, the bathers become a confused herd, trying to escape the dangerous waters but unable to distinguish between animal and human amidst the hysterical thrashings of limbs around them. Once again, the shark attack challenges the conceptual boundary between humans and animals.

It is, of course, precisely the shark's virtual absence that makes this scene so effective. Spielberg here, as in most of the early shark-attack scenes, uses the 'subjective camera' technique, representing the attack 'from the point of view of the unseen *antagonist*' (Gordon 31; emphasis in original). Visually influenced by Hitchcock (see Gordon 33), Spielberg makes his audience gaze at characters from the point of view of the shark. In effect, of course, this entails another border crossing, since the audience, by sharing the shark's point of view, symbolically merges with it. Interestingly, this point-of-view shot, so often quoted in films which depict people in the sea, was not Spielberg's original choice for the film. He wanted to show the shark much earlier, but the three mechanical sharks built for the film notoriously failed to function during much of the production: 'Each proved to be disastrous when put to the test: One exploded, one sank, and the third just wouldn't function properly' (Parish 41–2). For the film, of course, the resulting absence of the killer shark turned out to be extraordinarily effective. As Parish remarks, 'in many scenes in *Jaws*, the killer shark's presence is felt rather than actually seen. ... [T]his psychological point of view heightened the on-screen sense of terror' (42). Due to its visual absence, the threat to human autonomy that the shark embodies is unspecific and seems to come from the environment as such rather than from one of its individual components. Nature itself has become a dangerous space, precisely because it refuses to be locked in.

In his discussion of Spielberg's oeuvre, Drummond distinguishes between animal and machine films (207), but as the case of the mechanical shark shows,

---

[18]   In this sense, *The Beach* is a typical example of island fiction in the vein of Golding's *Lord of the Flies*, which, in its portrayal of an isolated community and its fall from paradise to hell, explores the notion that what is inhuman 'is a terrifying excess which, although it negates what we understand as humanity, is inherent to being-human' (Žižek 220).

this opposition is untenable. Indeed, the shark we see in *Jaws* is both animal and robot, as real sharks were also used in the film. And just as the malfunctioning of the mechanical shark decisively influenced the filming process, so the one scene containing live shark footage did not go according to plan either. Towards the end of the film, the ichthyologist Hooper enters a shark cage out on the open sea in order to shoot the great white, which, however, attacks and destroys the cage. During production, a small dummy was placed inside the cage in order to scale up the sharks. Yet the sharks filmed for this scene were not interested in the cage. The footage eventually used in the film was of a shark whose snout got caught in the chain of the cage by accident and which subsequently destroyed the cage. As the latter was empty at the time, however, the script had to be rewritten, and so the story was changed by the shark's involuntary intervention (see *Jaws* 'The Making of *Jaws*'): in contrast to the novel, Hooper now escapes as the shark attacks the cage and thus survives in the film. Once more, the film's protagonist, now in the shape of real sharks, refused to cooperate and changed the filmic outcome.

What complications such as those accompanying the production of *Jaws* highlight is that, rather than collapsing the nature-culture binary by harmoniously fusing the two sides of the equation, films about the beach show to what extent each is already implicated in the other. The controversy surrounding the ecological impact of filming on Maya Bay, the setting of *The Beach* on Phi Phi Lee Island, is another example: in order to turn it into the paradisiacal beach fantasy required for the film, the crew altered the original beach, bulldozing sand dunes, planting palm trees and removing local flora that failed to reach the necessary standard of picturesqueness. To some extent, this is a logical consequence of constructions of the beach as vacationscape. The beach cannot exist as vacationscape without the presence of humans who use and possess it for purposes of leisure, and the vision of pristine nature on the beach always presupposes its human observer. The true psychological fallacy of the crew of *The Beach*, therefore, was not so much the idea that it was fine for them to alter the geographical and ecological make-up of Maya Bay but, rather, the belief that they would be able to restore the damage by returning the beach to its original state after filming. Such a notion, of course, is necessarily oxymoronic, and it points to the complexities of relations between the natural and the cultural, the original and the technological, and of our investment in these concepts.[19]

As regards its representation, any vision of pristine nature necessarily remains elusive because it can only be conveyed in cultural and technological terms. In this sense, film sharks emerge as perfect protagonists of the horror genre. Not only do they breach the dividing line between shore and beach, thus attacking one of the favourite tropes of Western cultures of leisure, but if we follow Carroll's reading of Douglas and take into account the mechanics of the sharks' production, they also turn out to be monsters singularly difficult to reincorporate into stable systems

---

[19]   Incidentally, it is not fully clear from media footage what raised more concern: the environmental effects of the film crew's alterations to the original beach or the economic consequences of these effects in their impact on tourism (see 'Fears for Di Caprio's Beach'). For more precise information on the reconstruction of the beach, see Vidal.

of classification. Both in *The Beach* and in *Jaws*, it is almost impossible to deduce what exactly the sharks are in any one shot: live sharks, robots or products of computer animation. The filmic littoral settings in which encounters with sharks happen mirror and enhance this existential fuzziness through their own ambivalent position between beach and shore, humanity, artifice and nature, paradise and hell. As the example of audience reactions to *Jaws* shows particularly well, however, together with the cultural baggage of shark representations which I have outlined in my reading of popular science books above, this indeterminacy is translated on screen into abjection, and off screen into the productive mix of emotions which turns the consumption of horror into pleasure.

Works Cited

Annesley, James. 'Pure Shores: Travel, Consumption, and Alex Garland's *The Beach*'. *Modern Fictions Studies* 50.3 (2004): 551–69.

Beaver, Dan. 'Flesh or Fantasy: Cannibalism and the Meanings of Violence'. *Ethnohistory* 49.3 (2002): 671–85.

Carroll, Noël. 'Why Horror?' *Horror, the Film Reader*. 2002. Ed. Mark Jancovich. Taylor and Francis e-Library, 2006: 32–45. Kindle.

Cerullo, Mary M. *The Truth about Great White Sharks*. Photogr. Jeffrey L. Rotman. Illustr. Michael Wertz. San Francisco: Chronicle Books, 2007.

Coetzee, J.M. *The Lives of Animals*. Ed. Amy Gutmann. The University Centre for Human Values Series. Princeton: Princeton UP, 1999.

Deary, Terry. *Terry Deary's Terribly True Shark Stories*. London: Scholastic, 1995.

Deleuze, Gilles, and Félix Guattari. *A Thousand Plateaus: Capitalism and Schizophrenia*. Trans. Brian Massumi. London: Continuum, 2004.

Drummond, Lee. *American Dreamtime: A Cultural Analysis of Popular Movies and Their Implications for a Science of Humanity*. Lanham: Littlefield Adams Books, 1996.

'Fears for DiCaprio's Beach'. BBC News. 10 Feb. 2000. Web. 23 Mar. 2013. <http://news.bbc.co.uk/2/hi/entertainment/637965.stm>.

Foer, Jonathan Safran. *Eating Animals*. 2009. New York: Back Bay Books/Little, Brown and Co., 2010.

Golding, William. *Lord of the Flies*. 1954. London: Faber and Faber, 2002.

Golgowski, Nina. 'REVEALED: The 1916 shark attacks off the Jersey coast that was the inspiration for Jaws'. Daily Mail. 11 Aug. 2012. Web. 23 Mar. 2013. <http://www.dailymail.co.uk/news/article-2187103/Jaws-The-1916-shark-attacks-Jersey-coast-inspiration-film.html>.

Gordon, Andrew M. *Empire of Dreams: The Science Fiction and Fantasy Films of Steven Spielberg*. Lanham: Rowman & Littlefield, 2008.

Grizzly Man. Dir. Werner Herzog. Revolver Entertainment, 2006. Film.

International Shark Attack File. 'Gaining Access to The International Shark Attack File'. Florida Museum of Natural History. Web. 7 July 2011. <http://www.flmnh.ufl.edu/fish/sharks/isaf/access.htm>.

International Shark Attack File. 'How, When, & Where Sharks Attack'. Florida Museum of Natural History. Web. 7 July 2011. < https://www.flmnh.ufl.edu/fish/sharks/attacks/howwhen.htm>.

International Shark Attack File. 'ISAF Statistics for the World Locations with the Highest Shark Attack Activity (2004–2013)'. Florida Museum of Natural History. Web. 25 July 2014. <http://www.flmnh.ufl.edu/fish/sharks/statistics/statsw.htm>.

Jaws. Dir. Steven Spielberg. Perf. Roy Schneider and Robert Shaw. Universal, 2004. Film.

Jaws. 'The Original Theatrical Trailer'. Dir. Steven Spielberg. Perf. Roy Schneider and Robert Shaw. DVD Extras. Universal, 2004. Film.

Jaws. 'The Making of *Jaws*'. Dir. Steven Spielberg. DVD Extras. Universal, 2004. Film.

Kristeva, Julia. *Powers of Horror: An Essay on Abjection*. Trans. Leon S. Roudiez. New York: Columbia UP, 1982.

Leatherman, Stephen P. *Dr. Beach's Survival Guide: What You Need to Know About Sharks, Rip Currents, and More Before Going in the Water*. New Haven: Yale UP, 2003.

Lindenbaum, Shirley. 'Thinking about Cannibalism'. *Annual Review of Anthropology* 33 (2004): 475–98.

Maniguet, Xavier. *The Jaws of Death: Shark as Predator, Man as Prey*. Trans. David A. Christie. London: HarperCollins, 1992.

National Coastal Safety Report. *2012 National Coastal Safety Report: Preventing Coastal Drowning Deaths in Australia*. Surf Life Saving Australia. Web. 25 July 2014. <http://sls.com.au/sites/sls.com.au/files/NCSR_2012_LR.pdf>.

Noble, Louise. *Medicinal Cannibalism in Early Modern English Literature and Culture*. New York: Palgrave Macmillan, 2011.

Parish, James Robert. *Steven Spielberg: Filmmaker*. New York: Ferguson (imprint of Facts on File), 2004.

Rosenfeld, Everett. 'Jersey Shore Attacks, 1916'. *Time Magazine*. 1 Aug. 2011. Web. 23 Mar. 2013. <http://www.time.com/time/specials/packages/article/0,28804,2085822_2085823_2085948,00.html>.

The Beach. Dir. Danny Boyle. Perf. Leonardo DiCaprio and Daniel York. Figment Films, 2000. Film.

Tudor, Andrew. 'Why Horror? The Peculiar Pleasures of a Popular Genre'. *Horror, the Film Reader*. 2002. Ed. Mark Jancovich. Taylor and Francis e-Library, 2006: 45–55. Kindle.

UN News Centre. 'UN-backed forum extends protections for sharks, manta rays and precious timbers'. Web. 25 Mar. 2013. <http://www.un.org/apps/news/story.asp?NewsID=44379&Cr=endangered&Cr1=#.UVMl7RykrCc>.

Vidal, John. 'DiCaprio Film-Makers Face Storm over Paradise Lost'. *The Guardian*. 29 Oct. 1999. Web. 23 Mar. 2013. <http://www.guardian.co.uk/film/1999/oct/29/news.johnvidal>.

Žižek, Slavoj. 'Psychoanalysis and the Lacanian Real: Strange shapes of the Unwarped Primal World'. *Adventures in Realism*. Ed. Matthew Beaumont. Malden, MA: Blackwell, 2007. 207–23.

Chapter 9
'Where things meet in the world between sea and land': Human-Whale Encounters in Littoral Space

Virginia Richter

Constructing Littoral Space: Sites, Practices and Agents

Whales have a long history of interaction with human coast-dwelling communities. As whales have continued to approach the same regions on the Atlantic and Pacific shores in the course of their long-distance oceanic pilgrimages, they have become sources of food and fuel, mythological and literary figures and, finally, symbols of human ruthlessness and ecological endangerment. Some recent creative works, notably Witi Ihimaera's novel *The Whale Rider* (1987, 2005), Niki Caro's film adaptation *Whale Rider* (2002) and Linda Hogan's *People of the Whale* (2008), depict this complex web of human-cetacean relations, paying particular attention to indigenous coastal communities' negotiations of tradition, economic viability and cultural regeneration predicated on their connection to whales. These encounters between humans and whales happen in what I will be calling 'littoral space': the interconnected terrestrial and maritime space on both sides of the shoreline. In the works under consideration here, littoral space includes various sites: the beach, the strip of land between – and close to – the tidelines, the human dwelling places nearby, the coastal waters including the fishing grounds, and the immediate hinterland. Such sites are not simply 'there': they are constituted both materially and symbolically through the interactions of the various human and non-human inhabitants of littoral space. In this essay, I look at the way encounters between humans and whales – specifically, whale strandings and the resumption of indigenous subsistence whaling – shape the conceptualisation of littoral space in postcolonial fiction and film.

Encounters with animals play a major role for human practices within littoral space.[1] Shore dwellers and visitors alike engage with marine and coastal animals on a multitude of levels – the cultural, the aesthetic, the material and the economic. Many origin myths of coastal peoples feature animals as creators, ancestors, protectors and totem animals, and they continue to provide a frame of reference for modern experiences of, and narratives about, the shore. At the same time, fish,

---

[1]   These are not always pleasurable and regenerative. For an analysis of human-animal encounters based on fear and abjection, see Kluwick's contribution on the subject of sharks in this volume.

shellfish and cetaceans have always been a source of sustenance and wealth for littoral communities. Conversely, the continuing decimation of marine fauna is one of the causes for economic decline that is only in some regions compensated by the rise of tourism.[2] The progressive imbalance between the various shoreside populations – an overabundance of human coast dwellers and seasonal visitors, a scarcity of animals that sustain, or used to sustain, littoral communities – constitutes an important aspect of the ecological discourse on the seashore.[3] Increased settlement of the seashore has resulted not only in a transformation of its physical geography but, equally importantly, in a change of the social composition and economic basis of coastal communities. In consequence, social practices and, with them, the cultural meanings of the seaside have changed as well.

In its use of the term 'practice', this essay follows Henri Lefebvre's assumption that social practice and social space co-emerge and constitute each other's meaning (73). In this sense, practice is both 'conservative', containing the memory of how things were done in the past, and open to new gestures and actions: 'Itself the outcome of past actions, social space is what permits fresh actions to occur, while suggesting others and prohibiting yet others' (73). However, Lefebvre defines 'practice' somewhat narrowly as 'labour' in the Marxist sense (69), thereby excluding the agency of nature. For Lefebvre, space is a social product. Nature, in consequence, 'is now seen as merely the raw material out of which the productive forces of a variety of social systems have forged their particular spaces' (31). It is in this respect that his spatial theory appears most dated. As Bruno Latour has since persuasively argued, agency cannot be restricted to social labour, nor can (Western) culture be seen as the exclusive bearer of agency. Lefebvre implicitly subscribes to the logic of what Latour called 'the Great Divide', 'the absolute dichotomy between the order of Nature and that of Society' (Latour 40), a logic that aligns modern Western culture on one side of the divide and so-called primitive peoples, animals and nature on the other. It is precisely this dichotomy that is critically questioned in the texts under consideration here. An understanding of how littoral space is constituted through the interaction of various human and non-human agents thus warrants a more inclusive view of 'practices of everyday life', as developed for instance by Michel de Certeau in relation to walking in the city as a 'speech act' (91–9). Accordingly, littoral space is the result of past and present practices such as fishing, whaling, recreation, traffic, building and storytelling. Individual and collective agents have a certain, albeit not unlimited, range of possibilities to reinterpret these practices and perform them in new, creative ways.

---

[2]   The biodiversity of coastal regions, and a resulting diet rich in proteins and nutrients such as iodine, has always attracted humans to the seashore (see Gillis 32). In consequence, the depletion of the seas hits fishing communities particularly hard. For an analysis of the conflicting interests of fishermen and environmentalists, see Johnson.

[3]   Non-fictional ecological writings about the sea and the shore have a long tradition; see, for example, Rachel Carson's seminal texts *The Sea around Us* (1951) and *The Edge of the Sea* (1998). On the global increase of coastal populations, see Gillis 1. Today, shore settlements are also endangered by climate change and the resulting rise of the sea level; see Weik von Mossner's contribution in this volume.

As will be shown below, agency in littoral space – at least where the creative works discussed here are concerned – is not restricted to human agents: animals and even the sea itself 'do' things – move around, transform the material space – and in that sense have agency.

Whales have always had a special status for many littoral cultures. In the myths of both the Makah and the Māori, the collective protagonists of Hogan's and Ihimaera's novels discussed below, whales figure as the ancestors of the coastal people in question. Similar mythical narratives and rituals appear across many coastal cultures (see Van Ginkel). However, the conceptualisations of and concrete interactions with the world's largest mammals not only differ in various cultures, they have also changed significantly over the last couple of centuries, not least due to the dramatic decimation of cetaceans during that period. Whaling, in the nineteenth century 'an extractive industry of global scope' (Buell 205) famously anatomised in Melville's *Moby-Dick*,[4] supplied raw material that literally fuelled the industrial revolution.[5] Due to technological developments such as the invention of the grenade harpoon, whaling reached a truly planetary scale between the 1920s and 1960s and resulted in the near-extinction of many cetacean species. For example, blue whales, the largest cetacean species, were decimated: 'In all, more than 350,000 blue whales were killed in the south; by 1958 there were only 4,000 left in all the southern oceans' (Roman 143). Rather belatedly, the status of whales in public discourse has changed; cetaceans are now recognised for their 'importance both as part of the marine ecosystem and as a symbol of past excess and newfound respect for the earth' (Johnson 4). Whaling has become a highly contested practice, openly pursued by only a few nations under the guise of scientific interest.[6] Concomitantly, whales have been reconceptualised, from dangerous leviathans and sources of whale oil and baleen to highly intelligent, friendly and endangered fellow mammals.

Today, the whale has become one of the iconic animals of conservationism:

> In post-industrial cultures today – with some obvious exceptions – whales are protected collectively because the rarity of some species vividly embodies the fragility of ecological biodiversity. And individual cetacean lives are valued

---

[4]   Melville's *Moby-Dick, or The Whale*, first published in 1851, continues to provide an important frame of reference for cultural studies on cetaceans. See, in particular, Hoare's *Leviathan or, The Whale*.

[5]   On the history of whaling and the importance of whale oil and baleen for industrial production, see Hoare; Roman; Dolin; Francis; and Mawer. On current controversies, see Kalland.

[6]   In 1986, the International Whaling Commission (IWC) introduced zero catch limits for commercial whaling, allowing only a few exceptions, especially for indigenous subsistence whaling, the legal grounds for the Makah whale hunt. However, the IWC also authorises national governments to grant special permits 'to kill, take and treat whales for purposes of scientific research' (IWC Resolution 1986-2), the basis for the continued whaling of nations such as Japan and Russia. On the Japanese position, which is more complex than usually represented in international media, see Watanabe.

because their mammalian characteristics, along with their purported intelligence and benignity, invite in humans a sense of kinship all the more distinctive because it coexists with other features that embody radical otherness: their sometimes colossal proportions; their morphological similarity to an utterly different order of creatures; their occupation of an 'alien world' in the oceans. (Armstrong 104)

Even former whale-hunting countries, such as New Zealand, have enlisted in the ranks of cetacean conservationists, acknowledging that the whale is not only a valuable member of the marine ecosystem but also part of the nation's cultural heritage.[7]
While many of these processes unfolded on the high seas – or were decided upon in far-away boardrooms – rather than close to the shore, the history of whaling has had a deep impact on life in littoral space. Coastal communities have had to adapt to the disappearance of the whale as well as to its changed symbolic meaning. In many coastal towns, whale watching has become a major source of income and, in fact, an important factor in global seaside tourism.[8] The inhabitants of such places – for instance, Hermanus on South Africa's western Cape, the setting of Zakes Mda's novel *The Whale Caller*[9] – have to reconcile the various historical and narrative layers that produced the current image of the fishing village as traditional, and set apart from modernity (see Gillis 77–8), with the contemporary exigencies of economic survival. The latter demand precisely such a romanticisation of the past and of the shore as an unspoiled natural space to attract sufficient numbers of visitors. In the case of coastal towns and villages whose populations are of predominantly non-European descent, a history of cultural and political expropriation, which in part obliterated indigenous traditions further, complicates the communities' attempts at a viable redeployment of their forces in cultural as well as economic terms.
Contemporary creative treatments of non-Western communal life on the seashore emphasise the complex positioning of such communities as – willing or reluctant – participants in processes of globalisation, consumerism, and catering for the tourist industry while simultaneously engaging in contested efforts to reconstruct their identity and recapture agency under such new conditions. In a spate of recent novels, it is the various communities' relationship not only to the sea – as a source of life and cultural origins – but also to whales that provides

---

[7]   See the exhibition on *Whales/Tohorā* organised by the Museum of New Zealand Te Papa Tongarewa, Wellington, now on tour internationally (*Whales/Tohorā*).

[8]   Starting in the 1950s, seaside visitors have been attracted in growing numbers to watch migrating whales. According to Roman, eighty-seven countries host whale-watching excursions, and nine million people went whale watching in 1998 alone, 'spending more than a billion dollars on tours, tickets and souvenirs' (171). As conservationists argue, 'the value of seeing a whale brings in more tourist dollars than a dead one ever could' (171).

[9]   In addition to Ihimaera's and Hogan's fictions discussed below, Mda's *The Whale Caller* (2005) is frequently named as a third in this by now almost classical group of postcolonial cetacean novels. For a reading of Mda's novel in the context of South African beach fictions, see Samuelson's contribution in this volume.

a focal point for attempts at collective rebirth and redemption. The fictions and film by Ihimaera, Caro and Hogan considered here do not simply posit modernity and tradition as mutually exclusive terms. Rather, in each case the functions of traditional narratives, rites and roles have to be renegotiated under the conditions of a modernity that entails unemployment, poverty and lack of political empowerment. In the coastal communities of the Māori of New Zealand and the Makah of the American Pacific Northwest – fictionalised as the A'atsika tribe in Hogan's novel – marine myths of origin and, in particular, each people's relationship with whales play a central role. However, it is not the aim of this essay to engage with Māori and Makah culture from an anthropological perspective – mythology only plays a role in so far as it is invoked through the magical realist mode employed in the fiction. Rather, the two novels and Caro's film will be considered as narratives that address precisely the interaction between present material conditions of life, the diegetic use and often conflicting interpretation of whale-centred mythology and tradition, and the communities' specific topographic location on the shore.

As Stenwand has pointed out, Ihimaera and Hogan, while addressing the plight of the respective ethnic groups from an informed inside perspective,[10] also aim at engaging an international audience: they 'negotiate their liminal positions as cosmopolitan global cultural ambassadors with specific connections that allow them access to the lives of the insiders who dwell more permanently in the localities in question. Their audiences also include cosmopolitan readers lured by the postcolonial and the ecopastoral exotic' (185). A divergent position is stressed, however, by Huang who reads *The Whale Rider a*nd *People of the Whale*, together with the novel *Eyes in the Sky* by Tao author Syaman Rapongan (2012), as examples of a 'transpacific and transindigenous ecopoetics' (121). This entails that the Great Divide between human and non-human animals underpinning Western conceptions of the natural world, as described by Latour, be replaced by a multispecies continuum: 'The interchanges between the human and ocean species shape the multiple, divergent communities of the waters. The boundary – or, rather, the binary relationship – between human and nonhuman is perpetually blurred in the presence of a multispecies world' (Huang 128). Whales, as marine mammals and mythical ancestors of the human communities, are to a high degree representative of this erasure of the divide between the human and the natural world. Through the invocation of myth and the description of close encounters with the creatures, the novels offer redemption to 'human animals, giving them a place in the cosmos, and materialize the dialogues between human and sea animals' (127).

The idea of the shore as a place of regeneration is thus approached from a different angle to that of Western views that are predicated on the separation between civilised and natural space. Nevertheless, the transindigenous position claimed by Huang intersects, I would like to suggest, with an emplacement in the modern world of globalised traffic, trade and tourism, thus creating a

---

[10] Linda Hogan is a member of the Chickasaw Nation. Her work covers the life of Native Americans in various parts of the USA. Witi Ihimaera is of Māori descent and is considered the first Māori writer to publish a novel (*Tangi*, 1973).

'hypercomplex' space in which, according to Lefebvre, various concrete places – the local, the national, the worldwide – are 'intercalated, combined, superimposed' and 'traversed by myriad currents' (88). In other words, littoral space, which forms the focus of my following discussion of Ihimaera, Caro and Hogan, is constituted by the practices of local agents but also impacted by events elsewhere – in the remote metropolis as well as the deep ocean.

As stated at the beginning, littoral space is not a uniform site but can be subdivided into different topographical areas, such as the beach, the coastal waters and the land near the shore. These areas differ not only materially, for instance regarding their geological structure, but also in respect of their use: different agents do different things on, say, the beach and in the water. In the three examples considered here, the beach, the inhabited shore and the sea are constructed in distinct ways. In particular, there is a striking contrast between the conceptualisations of the beach in Ihimaera's novel and Caro's film. This is due partly to the different exigencies and possibilities of the respective media but also to the distinct marketing needs of the film, an international co-production, on the one hand and of the novel on the other.[11] All three examples place their emphasis on the life of the coastal communities in question and on individuals for whom the beach functions as a theatre of their alienation from, as well as reconciliation with and reintegration into, the multispecies natural world. However, in varying degrees these communities are shown to be part of a modern nation state and of an international geopolitical constellation, an interaction effected partly through media such as television and newspapers. One function of the media in Hogan's and Ihimaera's novels is to reflect on the constructedness and the contested quality of tradition – significantly, this is a dimension missing from the film where tradition is naturalised. Through the various movements, acts and discursive exchanges on, through and beyond its topographies, littoral space emerges as a complex site that, like the beach itself, undergoes constant change.

Whales on the Beach: Ihimaera's and Caro's Versions of *Whale Rider*

While beached whales used to signify bounty or spectacle,[12] today they stand for an ecological disaster that is not fully understood. It may be man-made, the effect

---

[11]   The success of the film has, however, influenced the marketing strategies of the novel as well. As Eckstein has shown, the novel was reissued and, in fact, rewritten by Ihimaera to make it more accessible to an international audience. The edition referred to in this essay is the most widely available 'international' Heinemann edition of 2005, in which some of the Māori terms used in the original have been replaced, without acknowledgement, by English translations.

[12]   As Roman notes, for the Māori as well as other coastal peoples, 'stranded whales once provided a vast amount of meat and oil, a gift from the god of the sea' (179). In Europe, beached whales were a spectacle that attracted the curious, and, in fact, their carcasses were the first specimens of cetaceans that could be examined in full by naturalists (see Hoare 253–4).

of sound pollution,[13] but it has the impact of an inexplicable tragedy. For whales, the beach is a thanatotope: they come to the beach only to die, thus profoundly disturbing our vision of the beach as a site of regeneration. In view of the drastic decimation of some cetacean species, mass strandings constitute a significant threat to their genetic diversity and, in the long run, their chances of survival. With the reconceptualisation of whales from human prey to objects of environmental engagement, these fatal mishaps engage the affects of human beholders on various levels: empathy, ecological and practical concerns (how to dispose of the huge carcasses?), as well as sensationalism. The emotional power of these huge creatures, lying helplessly on the beach and dying slowly if they do not receive human help certainly contributed to the international success of the film *Whale Rider* directed by Niki Caro, a low-budget New Zealand-German co-production. The film culminates in a sequence in which the people of Whangara try to save a pod of beached southern right whales. The rescue operation is only successful when Pai (short for Paikea), an eleven-year-old Māori girl – a direct descendent of the mythical ancestor Paikea who came to shore on the back of a whale – rides the alpha whale back into the surf. She almost drowns in the process but is miraculously saved and finally recognised by her grandfather Koro Apirana as Paikea's true heir.

Whangara is situated close to the sea. Several scenes in *Whale Rider* take place on the beach, culminating in the dramatic stranding and subsequent rescue of the whales. But despite the prominence of this setting, the people's ancient association with the ocean has been weakened. As Mack has stressed, the account of their maritime origins continues to be crucial for the Māoris' present sense of identity: 'Such assertion of ancestral connection to the sea is in itself one of the ways in which people "inhabit" it, even if they are otherwise largely terrestrial' (18). In the film, however, only Pai and her grandfather exhibit this connection. The beach as part of the littoral space that connects the now terrestrial people of Whangara with their maritime past has to be regained. Nor is the seashore depicted as a workplace: only Koro is seen to be working on a boat, if not actually fishing. [14] With few exceptions, the inhabitants of Whangara do not seem to know what to make of their proximity to the ocean: 'The beach in *Whale Rider* ... encapsulates the intermediate, boundary state that characterises the local community trapped between modernity and primitivism, culture and nature' (Leotta 127). The meaning of the beach is reduced to a single dimension: it is a place of waiting. The film thus disregards other functions of littoral space, as a workplace, a dwelling and so on. The Whangaras' alienation from the ocean is shown metaphorically: the ceremonial canoe Pai's artist father had started to carve has never been finished; an initiation rite in the sea fails, partly because the candidates cannot swim, partly because they lack the stamina to dive deep enough to retrieve the symbol of

---

[13]   On anthropogenic noise as a possible cause of whale strandings, see Hoare 304–5.

[14]   According to Leotta, in films made by Māori directors such as Barry Barclay the beach is depicted as a workplace (107), partly to counter the earlier stereotype of 'happy Māori' living in an ahistorical space unconnected to the real New Zealand (24).

leadership, a *rei puta* (a pendant carved from a whale tooth) Koro had thrown overboard to determine the future leader.

Among the younger generation, Pai is the only one who is shown to be close to the sea, often sitting on the beach and contemplating the ocean. She is also the only one who succeeds in completing the tasks in which all others fail, including – in secret – the retrieval of the *rei puta*. But her relationship to the sea is deeper and mystical: repeated juxtaposition of underwater whale footage and close-ups of her face suggests that she is able to hear the whales, and conversely it is in response to her call that they come to the beach. It is in fact Pai's spiritual connection to the whales that causes the catastrophe; it is her self-sacrifice that averts it. This constitutes a major departure from Ihimaera's novel, where the whales' behaviour has both a modern and a mythical cause: on the one hand, they are disoriented by human intervention in the marine ecosystem, specifically nuclear testing in the Pacific (44); on the other hand, their leader, the original whale of the myth, is driven by his mourning for his 'golden master' Paikea (45). The social structure of this whale population reduplicates the patriarchal organisation of Whangara, with the alpha whale's nostalgia and stubbornness leading to a similar near-catastrophe as Koro's traditionalism. For Pai, who claims agency and female leadership[15] by virtue of her ride on the whale, the beach enables multiple positive transgressions of boundaries: the union between an animal living in the sea and an earthbound human being, between nature and culture, between the sacred past and the profane present, between patriarchy and the reinterpretation of tradition from a female point of view. The result of Pai's seaward ride that reverses the whales' movement onto the beach is the moral renewal of the community and its ancient relationship with the ocean, a happy ending that has been applauded by audiences all over the world.

However, *Whale Rider* has also been sharply criticised from a postcolonial point of view. Critics such as Prentice or Hokowhitu have pointed to the absence of any political and social context. The villagers' troubles seem to be due to their neglect of tradition rather than a long history of colonisation and dispossession, or to more recent factors such as economic and educational disadvantage. Whereas, as Prentice has argued, there is a high investment in the referentiality and 'authenticity' of the location and the cast, the film's worldwide success can partly be explained by its efficient positioning of the non-materialist lifestyle and communal values of Whangara for aesthetic consumption by a global audience. In other words, the film has been so successful precisely because it grafts a Western notion of the beach – as a natural space opposed to modern, urbanised spaces – onto its representation of a Māori community. This includes what Prentice calls the 'fetishisation of landscape' through the camera work, experienced vicariously through 'the virtual tourism of the film' or the real tourism promoted by many New Zealand films (261).

---

[15]   See Gonick's reading of the film as a fable of female agency that resonates with audiences across different cultures: 'the figure of the girl in *Whale Rider* is used as a "glocalizing" factor, one which ties the indigenous public sphere to global cultural processes and at the same time re-articulates new discourses of agentic girlhood through its decolonizing of the screen' (310).

In short, both the community and the landscape are dehistoricised. The beach is construed as an archaic space where a mythical past can eventually be accessed. The whales play an important role as conduits for this communal healing. They stand for a living, throbbing nature that can be touched and that, despite the animals' obvious vulnerability, is the source of a tremendous power of renewal. It is significant, however, that while real footage of southern right whales was used in several scenes, the stranded whales are the results of animation technology. For the climactic beach scene, animatronic models, some with a human operator inside, were used and subsequently digitally enhanced, with very convincing results. The emotional impact of this scene cannot be disputed, although the models are smaller than actual right whales would be (see Roman 179). At the same time, however, the animatronic models, proudly presented in the documentation included on the *Whale Rider* DVD, underscore both the ecological consciousness of the production and its technological sophistication. The result is complete control: of the film whales' response to Pai's advances and of the audience's emotional reaction. The scene that engages the viewers most deeply on an emotional level is the one that is least 'natural'.[16]

The politics of global consumption that determine the representation of the beach and whales in *Whale Rider* become even more evident if the film adaptation is compared to Ihimaera's novel. In the film, Pai is the main focaliser and speaks the voice-over that introduces the myth of the whale rider, thus establishing a 'rhetoric of the natural' (Prentice 259). Not least because of this adoption of a young person's perspective, 'Whangara assumes many of the characteristics of a Disney fantasyland – a timeless, childlike world, free from the hegemony of the powerful adult' (Hokuwhitu 128). By contrast, in the book, the narrative is told by her uncle Rawiri, in other words from an experienced, adult perspective. It is through Rawiri that the community is connected to a wider South Pacific network of travel, labour and cultural exchange. In fact, it is this figure that has undergone the greatest transformation in the adaptation. Whereas in the film Rawiri is completely passive and only reluctantly discloses his potential as Pai's mentor and an important member of the community, in the novel he is conspicuously associated with modernity, mobility and the wider world: he is a biker, a zealous worker, and he has just returned from a four-year stay in Australia and Papua New Guinea – the very opposite of the film's stay-at-home, amiable sluggard.

Like the film, the novel culminates in the girl's (called Kahu in the book) ride on the whale, which she experiences as a re-enactment of, and a merging with, the founding myth and its protagonist:

> She was the whale rider. … She was Kahutia Te Rangi. She felt a shiver running down the whale and, instinctively, she placed her head against its skin and closed her eyes. The whale descended in the shallow dive and the water was like streaming silk. … She was Paikea. (106)

---

[16] See also Kluwick's analysis of Spielberg's use of animatronic sharks in *Jaws*, in this volume.

Despite her mortal danger, Kahu experiences an intimate connection with the animal on whose back she rides; for a fleeting moment, the whale and the girl overcome the divide separating human from animal. Significantly – and this narrative level has not been reproduced in the film – Kahu's experience of merging, with Paikea and with the animal that carries the whale rider, is also described from the bull whale's perspective: 'Ko Paikea, ko Paikea. … I am carrying my Lord, Paikea' (110). That this is in fact an error, and that the supposed golden master has to be restored to the surface, is spotted by the 'old mother whale' (111). It is the female whale's intervention that saves Kahu's life (whereas the girl's survival is not really explained in the film).

Like the film, the book establishes a connection between the survival of the whales and that of Whangara, and it ends on an equally hopeful note – 'the whales are still singing' (122) – but, as Huggan and Tiffin have argued, 'without suggesting that the cultural renaissance [the happy ending] implies is anything other than temporary, or that the ecological crises it alludes to are definitively resolved' (65). The happy ending is not that of a fairy tale: while magical elements such as the mother whale's intervention contribute to it, other, more naturalistic factors also play a role. Ihimaera creates a complex framework that disallows any facile acceptance of the 'mythical' solution to social problems, even while the myth is authorised as the Whangara's founding narrative through magical realist elements such as interspersed passages narrated from the whales' perspective, in which naturalistic descriptions – the whales' sonic mode of communication – are intermingled with references to the Paikea myth, suggesting that this myth is as real for the whales as it is for the Whangara:

> *The bull whale had become handsome and virile, and he had loved his master. In the early days his master would play the flute and the whale would come to the call. Even in his lumbering years of age the whale would remember his adolescence and his master; at such moments he would send long, undulating songs of mourning through the lambent water. … In a welter of sonics, the ancient bull whale would communicate his nostalgia.* (8–9; italics in original)

As this passage suggests, the bull whale who leads the pod to Whangara, and to near-certain death, is the original whale of the myth, set some millennia ago. He is driven to the fatal shore by his nostalgia for his master, the whale rider. At the same time, a different explanation is added to this magical level of the narrative – the whales are disoriented by nuclear testing in the Pacific: '*Sparkling like a galaxy was a net of radioactive death. For the first time in all the years of his leadership, the ancient whale deviated from his usual primeval route*' (45; italics in original). According to Huang, the inclusion of the whales' perspective on its mythological and modern – ecological – levels contributes to the emergence of a multispecies, rather than anthropocentric, littoral space without obliterating the environmental deterioration caused by human intervention (134).

In the film, the Paikea myth is the only frame of reference for the Māori relationship with whales: for the most part, viewers who are not familiar with

Māori culture learn about the myth from Pai's voice-over. By contrast, the novel gives more scope to the myth, which is told both from the whales' and the people's points of view but also adds a historical narrative that does not shrink from disturbing aspects such as the implication of indigenous peoples, including the Māori, in industrial whaling.[17] Koro is sensitive to the continuing temptation of commercialism and the ensuing dangers for both the community and the natural environment: 'We have to place prohibitions on our fishing beds, boys, otherwise it will be just like the whales – ... *Listen how empty our seas have become*' (39; emphasis in original). Koro himself contributes to this critical historicising, a stance in contrast with the film's naturalisation. Despite his present regret, Koro is still 'mesmerised' by the memory of the whale hunt in which he participated in his youth (40). His physical proximity to the whales – 'I was able to reach out and touch the skin. ... I felt the ripple of power beneath the skin. It felt like silk. Like a god'. (40) – evokes awe but does not erase the thrill of the chase, nor, naturally, does it prevent the continuation of the hunt. His touching of the whale's silk-like skin thus differs significantly from Kahu's experience; while both feel the whale's beauty, strength and divinity, the child entrusts herself completely to the marine creature whereas Koro is still ready to treat it as prey.

In addition, the killing of whales for sport is not safely confined to the past. The novel juxtaposes reverence for the marine ancestors to an approach to whales as spectacle that can take a turn toward a voyeuristic savouring of violence. Beached whales become a spectacle through the dissemination of images by the media. The ambivalent responses to strandings are explored in an episode that prefigures the culminating whale rescue and that is completely omitted in the film. Two hundred whales strand – and eventually die – on Wainui Beach, not far from Whangara. The initial stages of this event are not immediately witnessed by the narrator Rawiri but, rather, are mediated through newspaper, radio and television coverage. In fact, the novel emphasises that this is a media event as much as something really happening in the neighbourhood. The most fascinating piece of media coverage is also the most gory and repulsive:

> One particular sequence of the news film will remain indelibly imprinted on our minds. The camera zooms in on one of the whales, lifted high onto the beach by the waves. ... The whale is on its side, and blood is streaming from its mouth. The whale is still alive. Five men are working on the whale. They are splattered with blood. As the helicopter hovers above them, one of the men stops his work and smiles directly into the camera. The look is triumphant. He lifts his arms in a victory sign and the camera focuses on the other men, where they stand in the surging water. The chainsaw has just completed cutting through the whale's lower jaw. The men are laughing as they wrench the jaw from the butchered whale. (79–80)

Here the beach becomes the site of deliberate killing; more than that, of the deliberate inflicting of pain on a helpless animal. The five men literally bathe in the

---

[17] See Hoare 102–3; Mawer 165–78. On hostile relations between local Māori and foreign whaling crews, see Francis 75–6.

whale's blood to recapture the visceral experience of killing big game. Rather than celebrating a fusion with nature, they underscore their mastery and the whale's status as a thing. The framing by the TV camera enhances the meaning of this act: a gesture of human dominance, of defiance. The men completely lack Koro's awe for the godlike animals he helped kill in his youth, as well as his recognition of their godlike grandeur, not to mention Kahu's merging with the animal and magical world during her ride on the whale.

It is not quite clear who these men are, but there are indications that they are also Māori, which would disrupt the binary opposition between indigenous people immersed in a multispecies community and Western people who assert their dominance over the natural world. The coastal community's response to the scene of butchery is equivocal: 'Some would have argued that in Maori terms a stranded whale was traditionally a gift from the Gods and that the actions could therefore be condoned' (80). However, this 'traditional' stance is contradicted by the 'feelings of sorrow and anger among the people on the Coast', and the love they feel 'for the beasts which had once been our companions' (80). This emotional connection to the whales – every bit as much a traditional position – is enhanced by a new ecological awareness: 'Nor was this just a question of one whale among many; this was a matter of two hundred members of a vanishing species' (80). The Māori's stance towards whales has become heterogeneous, no longer prescribed by tradition and tribal identity. Rather, the rescue party from Whangara, including Rawiri's tough biker friends, forms an ad hoc coalition with the locals from Wainui, many of whom are elderly residents of European descent: 'By that time many of the locals were out on the beach. Some of them still had their pyjamas on … it was amazing to see them trying to stop younger men from pillaging the whales' (82). As these unlikely allies struggle together to save the whales, a new, transient community emerges that is not determined by traditions and lines of descent, but by their spontaneous reaction to the whales' plight. While their joint attempt to save the whales is ineffective, and they disperse soon after, something enduring has happened on this bloody beach. Rawiri and the boys have chosen a life-affirming practice and, concomitantly, rejected the destructive act of the five men. By doing so, they have also opted for an interpretation of littoral space that emphasises the community of living creatures, including Māori, Europeans and animals. Perhaps, this has been a first step towards the communal regeneration that is then symbolically enacted through Kahu's ride on the whale.

Littoral Space in Hogan's *People of the Whale*

Linda Hogan's *People of the Whale* shares various features with Ihimaera's novel, not least the interweaving of magical elements with a harsh social realism. For example, a great drought in the last part of the novel is described as an ecological disaster that has dire economic consequences for the A'atsika, and simultaneously as Nature's punishment for their transgression against the whale. The drought is ended with the help of a rainmaker who transforms himself into an octopus – the second totemic animal who plays an important role next to the grey whale. Both narrative modes are connected to the novel's setting, the North Pacific coast and the littoral village of Dark River. The prologue already highlights the importance of the sea, and of living on the shore, for the Dark River community's sense of identity:

We live on the ocean. The ocean is a great being. The tribe has songs about the ocean, songs to the ocean. It is a place where people's eyes move horizontally because they watch the long, wide sea flow into infinity. Their eyes follow the width and length of the world. … The nearby fishing towns are now abandoned, as is the sawmill in disrepair, the forest missing. Down the beach a ways to the south, white piles, shining piles of clam and oyster shells were left behind by the earlier people, the Mysterious Ones, who were said to have built houses of shells, perfectly pieced together. These places truly existed, the secret houses were made of shells. Royal ships once anchored there; those who kept journals said the houses were made of pearls. No one sees them now except as a memory made of words. One man passing by at sunset wrote, in 1910, that they were made of rainbows, but of course no one believed him. This was also the year the deadly influenza arrived with the white whalers. The houses of shells were covered in a mudslide that same year. (9; italics in original)

In this opening paragraph, history, space and narrative are closely interlinked. The very corporeality of the shore dwellers, the way they move about and use their senses, is formed by the topographical disposition of ocean, shoreline, islands and human habitations. This place is thus not simply the setting of the narrative but is ascribed agency in its own right, just as the ocean is described as a living being. The endless horizon of the Pacific guides the beholders' eyes into the distance, into infinity. This temporal and spatial limitlessness suggests the dissolution of boundaries. However, it immediately becomes clear that the eternal flow of the sea does not render the inhabitants of its rim immune to historical change. On the contrary, historical and economic processes – the contact with explorers and whalers (and the diseases they bring), the economic slump suggested by the abandoned fishing villages and sawmill – as well as natural events – the mudslide – form the coast and transform the lives of those who live there. The present identity of Dark River emerges as a network of superimposed traces: the material leftovers of derelict buildings, the much less tangible memory of the mysterious shell houses, written records and oral tradition. The introductory lines of the novel thus firmly place the A'atsika people as participants in history rather than an ahistorical nature people. At the same time, Western concepts of history and time are not the only determining frames of reference. The Western idea of time as linear and countable is juxtaposed with the *longue durée* of tribal memory, passed on through oral tradition but also vulnerable to obliteration.

As for the Māori, for the A'atsika the animal populations of the coastal waters are of crucial importance, as a source of food and income, as symbolic providers of communal coherence and as ancestors and fellow creatures regarded with curiosity and affection. In the hierarchy of totem animals, the grey whale of the Northern Pacific ranks before all others: 'All their stories clung like barnacles to the great whale, the whale they loved enough to watch pass by. They were people of the whale' (43). Through direct encounters and the repetition of the traditional narratives and rites, a rich, interconnected littoral world emerges. In former times, even killing the whale, if done in an appropriate, respectful way, did not profoundly disturb this relationship. Traditionally, the whale hunt used to be an activity in which the whole community was involved and which demanded thorough preparation, ritual cleansing, fasting and praying.[18] Witka, the grandfather of the novel's protagonist Thomas Witka Just, was the village's chief whale hunter and possessed an innate affinity to the ocean: 'At night he dreamed of the way it changed from day to day. They were beautiful dreams and he loved the ocean world' (19). In the present generation, however, this deep connection to the sea has been broken. Only a few individuals have stayed in touch with the old ways and with nature: the Old People who are the guardians of tradition; Thomas's wife Ruth, a professional fisherwoman who knows and loves the sea; and their son Marco, who has inherited his great-grandfather Witka's calling. Representing the A'atsikas' past, present and potential future, these persons endeavour to revive the spiritual life of the community.

The community's present crisis is in part due to the moral failure of its adult men. For the generation of Thomas Witka Just, the trauma of the Vietnam War further contributes to their state of disorientation. Thomas, missing in action for years, eschews returning to Dark River and acknowledging his son. Only when he reads in a San Francisco newspaper that, after decades of interruption, a new whale hunt – admissible, despite the IWC moratorium of 1986, as a case of aboriginal subsistence whaling – is planned does he decide to return home. He hopes that the hunt will prove to be the road to his personal salvation as well as that of his tribe: 'We are going to return, he thought. We are going to be a people again' (70). However, as Thomas eventually finds out, there is no simple dichotomy between a wrong life in modernity and a good life lived according to tradition, nor is the imagined return so easy. While the community's leaders 'argued treaty rights, and their return to tradition' (68), they are partly motivated by pecuniary interests – a secret agreement to sell the whale meat to Japan – and partly by a desire for violence for its own sake that is a legacy of their Vietnam experience.

The decision to resume whaling is opposed by the A'atsika women, with Ruth acting as their chief spokesperson. As a fisherwoman, Ruth knows the coastal waters better than the council members who work on land; like Koro in *The Whale Rider*, she knows how empty the ocean has become. She is also motivated by a genuine love for the whales and a recognition of the spiritual dimension of the world they symbolise: 'When she saw them rise and return to the sea, when she saw them breathe spray, she was aware that there was at least one god' (65). In the conflict, both parties enlist the help of the media and NGOs. Animal protection

---

[18]   On the Makah whale hunt, see Van Ginkel 67–92. Linda Hogan was one of the opponents of the resumption of Makah whaling in 1999; before addressing the conflicts surrounding this event in fiction, she co-authored a non-fiction account of the controversy with Brenda Peterson, *Sightings: The Gray Whales' Mysterious Journey.* See also Schweninger 202–17.

groups intervene on behalf of the whales, while others who support the A'atsika right to hunt romanticise the supposedly primitive people: the reporters, 'especially the white men, thought the tribal hunters were men of mystery and spirit, foreign enough to their own America to be right' (68). What appears as a support of the tribe's autonomy is in fact an exoticising gesture.

When the hunt is finally carried out, it becomes an inept butchery. Far from being a communal endeavour following the ancient rites, the self-styled traditional whalers in their canoes are guided by 'speedboats and a helicopter, the pilot spotting the whales so the men wouldn't have to wait for them or search' (87). Instead of harpoons, they use automatic rifles, in fact the very guns some of them had learned to fire at human targets in Vietnam. The hunt is no longer an affair of the community but a media event that attracts various groups of onlookers: 'Newspeople and watchers from outside, from other tribes who swore later that they themselves would never whale, and the many protesters from San Francisco and thereabouts. It was a spectacle' (87). Finally, the hunters' ineptitude is revealed when they need to enlist these outsiders' help to drag 'the sand-covered, bloody, weed-covered whale up the ancient dragging beach' (91) – a public sign of failure, of their deep-seated alienation from tradition rather than their return to it. Far from restoring the A'atsika to their roots, the whale hunt further alienates them from their natural surroundings as they become aware that the sacred ties with nature have been broken, and their world has lost its spiritual dimension: 'They think about the whale and what they've done, who they have become in time, each person examining their own world. They do not feel the spirits that once lived in the fogs and clouds around them. The alive world is unfelt. They feel abandoned' (128).

The perversion of this staged return to tradition becomes obvious when it eventually transpires that Marco, who had gone missing after the hunt, had been killed by the tribal leader and main agent behind the whaling expedition, the Vietnam veteran Dwight. As one of the few who had been properly initiated in the ancient rituals, Marco, while participating in the hunt, had opposed the killing of a whale that was much too young, and he had been secretly dispatched in the confusion following the whale's death struggle. Instead of bringing the expected salvation, the disastrous whale hunt exacerbates Thomas's trauma and widens his alienation from his former life. While he remains at Dark River, he symbolically enacts his withdrawal from love and life by turning, literally, away from the sea. He occupies his grandfather Witka's house on the shore, but he builds a high fence that prevents him from seeing the sea or being seen by it: 'He builds it taller than himself so he can't see the eyes of the ocean watching him. He doesn't want to look at the creator of life, the first element' (113).

As the novel's prologue suggests, the sea has agency. Even as men draw boundaries and erect fences on land, the movement of the waves, the erosive powers of the wind, and the spiritual lure of the sea undermine anthropogenic structures of separation.[19] Thomas's fence does not suffice to keep the teeming

[19]   See Weik von Mossner's comments on the detrimental effects of seawalls, in this volume.

life of the shore at bay. Even as he turns his back on the ocean, Thomas cannot avoid hearing its sounds, smelling it even as he sits in his shuttered house, and, finally, remembering his grandfather's intimate connection to the deep. Slowly, as his armour is cracked by this sensory invasion, Thomas begins to re-enact Witka's practice of diving, and he finally follows not only the path of his grandfather, his ancestors, but also of his murdered son: he seeks out the Old People to become purified, and to relearn his people's ancient practices (281). Finally his tranquillity is restored, and he is ready for a different encounter with the whale, one in which the human does not seek to be a master but recognises his creaturely vulnerability, his smallness in face of the sea:

> In all the green beauty Thomas … hears the sounds of all the life in water, the clicks and ticking, and for a while time changes. It seems he was there listening, hearing what almost amounted to words and now he no longer needs to breathe. He hears a low rumble, the kind Ruth describes, the low rumble of a whale and it comes to him and it looks at him with its wise old eye and he knows everything in that gaze. He knows how small a human is, not in size, but in other ways. As he rises to the surface, it helps him, pushes him slowly and it exhales a breath as he surfaces, too, gasping for air. … He comes out of the water and sits down on the beach where things meet in the world between sea and land. (183)

In the deep of the ocean, immeasurable natural time supersedes linear, countable time and allows the diver to perceive the world differently: to become aware of infinity. As Thomas finally emerges from this liminal space, he not only has become whole again but also is ready to assume the role inherited from his grandfather and, paradoxically, his son, and to lead the people of Dark River into a future where they live again in harmony with nature: 'We are going to be better people. That is our job now. We are going to be good people. The ocean says we are not going to kill the whales until some year when it may be right' (183).

So far, the narrative of Thomas's redemption deploys the beach and even more so the coastal waters as a liminal space in the anthropological sense elaborated by Arnold van Gennep and Victor Turner, as a zone into which a subject must venture to undergo a rite of passage, and then to return strengthened and transformed into his community (see Turner). Having first returned to the shore, Thomas then must move further, onto the beach and finally into the ocean. Due to the properties of water – its fluidity, the way it carries sound and filters out light, its ability to lighten bodies immersed in it – he re-emerges as a different being. The beach then becomes the site on which this transformative experience is consolidated into a social stance: Thomas is ready to convey his experience to the A'atsika. Because of the specific characteristics of littoral space such as the synaesthetic engagement of the senses on the beach, the properties of water and the dissociation from life on land experienced in the womblike depth of the ocean, it functions as a privileged site of regeneration and rebirth.

Thomas's ultimately successful search for his lost self thus follows the trajectory of many beach stories across different cultures and, in fact, seems to subscribe, despite the novel's resistance to such labelling, to the notion of indigenous people's innate 'closeness to nature' and the possibility to return to a holistic pre-modern life.[20] However, this comforting story is complicated by the novel's ending. Despite Thomas's injunction to leave off whaling for the foreseeable future, a second whale hunt is decided upon. This time, the whalers have prepared themselves in the ancient ways, and the media are absent. It is, they claim, an expedition in search of strength, not of prey. Like his grandfather and his son before him, Thomas joins the crew, teaches them how to paddle, how to sing. However, the collective path to regeneration on which Thomas believes to be leading his people is closed: at the very moment when Thomas is ultimately transformed into 'something else, not one of the conquered any longer' (286) nor a conqueror, he is shot through the heart by Dwight. Although this second murder does not go unpunished, and Thomas's spiritual healing is not negated by his death – while clearly dead, he continues to be a conciliatory, ghostlike presence on the last pages of the novel – the hope of collective regeneration is undermined. As long as material interests continue to govern people's actions, a return to the past that does not take into account the burden of the present appears as ineffectual at best.

In Hogan's novel, the coastal zone is constructed as a spiritual space in which encounters between humans and animals outside a framework of violence and exploitation can be achieved. For people like Ruth, and Thomas in the last stage of his life, to see and to listen to the creatures of the sea opens a window to a sacred dimension of the world and allows them to overcome the binary divide between human and non-human animals. At the same time, however, the novel insists on the social dimension of littoral space which often cuts across this holistic vision. History and the material conditions of life substantially determine the practices and attitudes of coastal communities, and render the hoped-for return to nature a precarious endeavour. As in Ihimaera's *The Whale Rider*, the beach in *People of the Whale* is simultaneously a liminal space in which transformation and regeneration are possible, and a site of violence against animals. While Caro's film focuses too exclusively on the regenerative dimension of littoral space at the expense of social reality, the two novels show a greater degree of scepticism about attempts to construct the beach as a site where the return to nature and nature-based traditions will be instrumental in overcoming social ills. Nevertheless, Hogan's and Ihimaera's novels hold out the hope that a multispecies community of the waters is not beyond human reach. Both present littoral space as a complex site where human practices and the forces of nature meet and mix, just as the sea and the land do on the beach.

Works Cited

Armstrong, Philip. *What Animals Mean in the Fiction of Modernity*. London: Routledge, 2008.

---

[20]   Throughout her work, Hogan explores the relationship between humans and the natural world while resisting the stereotyping of Native Americans as 'keepers of the land'. For various studies on her earlier writings, see Cook.

Buell, Lawrence. *Writing for an Endangered World: Literature, Culture, and Environment in the U.S. and Beyond*. Cambridge, MA: The Belknap P of Harvard UP, 2001.

Carson, Rachel. *The Edge of the Sea*. Boston: Houghton Mifflin, 1998.

———. *The Sea around Us*. New York: Oxford UP, 1951.

Cook, Barbara J., ed. *From the Center of Tradition: Critical Perspectives on Linda Hogan*. Boulder: U of Colorado P, 2003.

De Certeau, Michel. *The Practice of Everyday Life*. Trans. Steven Randall. Berkeley: U of California P, 1988.

Dolin, Eric Jay. *Leviathan: The History of Whaling in America*. New York: Norton, 2007.

Eckstein, Lars. 'Think Local Sell Global: Magical Realism, *The Whale Rider*, and the Market'. *Commodifying (Post)Colonialism: Othering, Reification, Commodification and the New Literatures and Cultures in English*. Ed. Rainer Emig and Oliver Lindner. Amsterdam: Rodopi, 2010, 94–108.

Francis, Daniel. *A History of World Whaling*. Markham: Viking, 1990.

Gillis, John R. *The Human Shore: Seacoasts in History*. Chicago: U of Chicago P, 2012.

Gonick, Marnina. 'Indigenizing Girl Power: *The Whale Rider*, Decolonization, and the Project of Remembering'. *Feminist Media Studies* 10.3 (2010): 305–19.

Hoare, Philip. *Leviathan or, The Whale*. London: Fourth Estate, 2008.

Hogan, Linda. *People of the Whale*. New York: Norton, 2009.

Hokowhitu, Brendan. 'The Death of Koro Paka: 'Traditional' Māori Patriarchy'. *The Contemporary Pacific* 20.1 (2008): 115–41.

Huang, Hsinya. 'Toward Transpacific Ecopoetics: Three Indigenous Texts'. *Comparative Literature Studies* 50.1 (2013): 120–47.

Huggan, Graham, and Helen Tiffin. *Postcolonial Ecocriticism: Literature, Animals, Environment*. London: Routledge, 2010.

Ihimaera, Witi. *The Whale Rider*. Edinburgh: Heinemann, 2005.

IWC Resolution 1986–2. Web. 23 July 2013. <http://iwc.int/cache/downloads/5q49gv1uutssss4sgksocsg8o/Resolution%201986.pdf>.

Johnson, Tora. *Entanglements: The Intertwined Fates of Whales and Fishermen*. Gainesville: UP of Florida, 2005.

Kalland, Arne. *Unveiling the Whale: Discourses on Whales and Whaling*. New York: Berghahn Books, 2009.

Latour, Bruno. *We Have Never Been Modern*. Trans. Catherine Porter. Cambridge, MA: Harvard UP, 1993.

Lefebvre, Henri. *The Production of Space*. Trans. Donald Nicholson-Smith. Malden, MA: Wiley-Blackwell, 1991.

Leotta, Alfio. *Touring the Screen: Tourism and New Zealand Film Geographies*. Bristol / Chicago: Intellect / U of Chicago P, 2011.

Mack, John. *The Sea: A Cultural History*. London: Reaktion Books, 2011.

Mawer, Granville Allen. *Ahab's Trade: The Saga of South Seas Whaling*. New York: St. Martin's P, 1999.

Mda, Zakes. *The Whale Caller*. New York: Farrar, Giroux and Strauss, 2005.

Melville, Herman. *Moby-Dick, or The Whale*. New York: Penguin, 1988.

Peterson, Brenda, and Linda Hogan. *Sightings: The Gray Whales' Mysterious Journey*. Washington: National Geographic, 2002.

Prentice, Chris. 'Riding the Whale? Postcolonialism and Globalization in *Whale Rider*'. *Global Fissures, Postcolonial Fusions*. Ed. Clara A.B. Joseph and Janet Wilson. Amsterdam: Rodopi, 2006. 247–67.

Rapongan, Syaman. *Tiankong de yanjing* (*Eyes in the Sky*). Taipei: Lianjing, 2012.

Roman, Joe. *Whale*. London: Reaktion Books, 2006.

Schweninger, Lee. *Listening to the Land: Native American Literary Responses to the Landscape*. Athens: U of Georgia P, 2008.

Stenwand, Jonathan. 'What the Whales Would Tell Us: Cetacean Communication in Novels by Witi Ihimaera, Linda Hogan, Zakes Mda, and Amitav Ghosh'. *Postcolonial Ecologies: Literatures of the Environment*. Ed. Elizabeth DeLoughrey and George B. Handley. Oxford: Oxford UP, 2011. 182–199.

Turner, Victor. 'Betwixt and Between: The Liminal Period in *Rites de Passage*'. *Symposium on New Approaches to the Study of Religion*. Ed. Melford E. Spiro. Seattle: American Ethnological Society, 1964. 4–20.

Van Ginkel, Rob. *Coastal Cultures: An Anthropology of Fishing and Whaling Traditions*. Apeldoorn: Het Spinhuis, 2007.

Watanabe, Hiroyuki. *Japan's Whaling: The Politics of Culture in Historical Perspective*. Trans. Hugh Clarke. Melbourne: Trans Pacific P, 2009.

Whale Rider. Dir. Niki Caro. Perf. Keisha Castle-Hughes, Rawiri Paratene and Vicky Haughton. South Pacific Pictures, 2002.

Whales/Tohorā. Museum of New Zealand Te Papa Tongarewa. Web. 3 July 2011. <http://collections.tepapa.govt.nz/exhibitions/whales/default.aspx>.

Chapter 10
Slow Violence on the Beach: Documenting Disappearance in *There Once Was an Island*

Alexa Weik von Mossner

Briar March's 2010 documentary *There Once Was an Island: Te Henua e Nnoho* opens with a shot from a camera that is half-submerged in seawater.[1] It is followed by a sequence of stunningly beautiful images of the south-western Pacific at sunset filmed from a traditional fishing boat and accompanied by soft music and the sounds of a male voice singing in what to most ears will be an unknown language. A palm-tree-covered island appears on the horizon, a text insert informing us that what we see is Takuu, a small atoll 250 kilometres north-east of Bougainville in Papua New Guinea. The atoll might look like a Western tourist's dream vacation spot, but we quickly learn that Nukutoa, the atoll's only inhabited island, is home to 'a Polynesian community of 400' that generally does not allow foreigners to set foot on it. It is a home that is only 0.5 kilometres long and only 1 metre above sea level, and, as a result of global warming and sea level rise, it is slowly disappearing into the waters of the Pacific Ocean.

The places that are at the forefront of this gradual disappearance are Nukutoa's beaches – that sandy, wave-washed part of the shoreline that in the Western imagination so often figures as a space of leisure and recreation.[2] The beach, as John Mack reminds us, 'is a place where everything transformational in the cultures of coastal peoples begins and ends' (165). All beaches are subject to complex physical and political processes that depend not only on geographical location but also on human intervention both at the local and the global level. Space, cultural geographer Doreen Massey has claimed, is always 'constituted through interactions, from the immensity of the global to the intimately tiny' (9). Rather than 'a coherent, closed system within which … everything is already related to everything else', we are confronted with 'a space of loose ends and

---

[1] Portions of this essay have been previously published in my article entitled 'The Human Face of Global Warming: Varieties of Eco-Cosmopolitanism in Climate Change Documentaries' in *Revista Canaria de Estudios Ingleses* (2012).

[2] 'The beach', explains marine scientist Carl Hobbs, 'is a specific, physical environment' (3) that is not identical with the shore. Properly defined as 'a deposit of unconsolidated sediment, ranging from boulders to sand, formed by wave and wind processes along the coast', the beach 'extends from the dunes, cliff face, or change in physiography seaward to the low-tide line' (3).

missing links' (11). Space is never a neat and potentially controllable system of interrelations among local actors of all kinds. Instead it is radically open to outside forces, and this is particularly obvious in the case of the beach. Throughout history, beaches have been spaces of arrival and departure, of contact and trade, and they are also subject to ecological forces such as sea-level rise. In fact, the long-distance effects of climate change are a particularly dramatic instance of the complex interactions that constitute littoral space and make it vulnerable to outside forces.[3] The coastal regions we see in *There Once Was an Island* are the result of such complex interactions between global forces and local spaces. Because of the changing climate, Nukutoa's beaches are in a constant state of disappearance, its shoreline a – literally – fluid boundary between land and sea, constantly moving inland as the shape and size of the island changes.

It is important to remember, however, that this climate-change-related transformation of coastal space is not just the result of 'natural' processes. Rather, it is a direct consequence of the failure to reduce carbon emissions elsewhere, a case of climate injustice and of what the postcolonial ecocritic Rob Nixon has called 'slow violence': 'a violence of delayed destruction that is dispersed across time and space' (2). As Nixon points out, slow violence might include forms of what the Norwegian mathematician and sociologist Johan Galtung has called 'structural violence' – the vast societal and economic structures that enable individual acts of direct violence. However, 'it has a wider descriptive range in calling attention, not simply to questions of agency but to broader, more complex descriptive categories of violence enacted slowly over time' (11). Climate change is a prime example of slow violence because of its wide spatial and temporal scope and the resulting distance between culprits and victims.

Through her directorial choices, March foregrounds such processes of delayed destruction in her documentary, thereby making visible and comprehensible the gradual and long-distance modes of 'environmental violence' (Nixon 8) that all too often occur 'out of sight' (2). *There Once Was an Island* is an 'environmental documentary' in Helen Hughes's definition of the term because March made 'a film about the environment, understood as a political subject' (5). The documentary not only places the ecological degradation of Nukutoa's beaches in the context of global emissions but also turns viewers' attention to the environmental justice dimension of that degradation by looking at this slow violence on the beach from the perspective of its human recipients: people living locally who cherish their traditional culture and struggle to grasp fully the larger ecological, economic and political processes of which, in a globalised world, they must inevitably be part. However, rather than evoking pity for these 'poor people' on their low-lying island, *There Once Was an Island* shows a community of individuals who – in very diverse and different ways – are aware of what is at stake and try to come to terms with the fact of their disappearing home, considering the advice of scientific experts and the possibility of continuing their lives elsewhere. These complex

---

[3]   For detailed information on the effects of climate-change-induced sea-level rise on low-lying islands, see Hunter, Allison and Jakszewicz's *ACE SLR Report Card Sea Level Rise 2012*. Hunter's visit to Nukutoa is documented in March's film.

processes of ecological, economic and cultural interaction and transformation are all encapsulated in the film in the haunting image of the vanishing beach and the resulting intrusion of the ocean into the islanders' gardens and homes.

Where Land Turns to Sea: The Beach as Space of Transformation

Documentaries have a peculiar relationship to the geographical spaces in which they are filmed. When films are shot on location, Gorfinkel and Rhodes remind us, they 'take actual places – take images of places, record impressions of the world's surfaces – and archive them on celluloid' (viii). Of course, nowadays celluloid is increasingly replaced by digital data, but the fact remains that many films, especially if they are documentaries, 'act as archiving agent[s]' (viii), recording the images of actually existing environments at a given point in time. They are snapshots, so to speak, of constantly changing geographical spaces. *There Once Was an Island* is particularly interesting in this regard because it captures images of a geographical space that is not only changing but also literally vanishing from sight as it slowly drowns in the Pacific Ocean. With the sea encroaching from all sides, it is only a matter of time until all of Nukutoa becomes a swash zone, until its many palm trees are no longer able to hold on to the eroding ground, disappearing in the salty water one by one. The film's title even suggests that the island is *already* gone with only the recorded images of its beaches, trees, houses, animals and people awakening back to life whenever the film is screened. It is this temporal framing that gives the film's spatial organisation a particular edge. March has stated in an interview that she sees 'the island as an allegory for the whole planet' (Chase). Her film indeed suggests that not only is the local ecosystem it depicts constituted, shaped and ultimately destroyed by global interactions but also it also serves as a symbol of the Earth as a whole at a time of increasingly rapid climate change. 'Just by looking at the microcosm of the macrocosm', says March, 'you can speak about all of these issues' (Gnanalingam), and so the disappearing beaches of a remote island become a symbol for the slow violence of climatic changes that is at work constantly, everywhere on the planet, changing local places in often catastrophic ways.[4]

The makers of environmental documentaries, Hughes has suggested, tend to understand themselves 'as not only engaged but involved' (5), and March is no exception. March is a filmmaker from New Zealand who stumbled upon her story when reading an article by the ethnomusicologist Richard Moyle that mentioned Takuu's eroding beaches.[5] She was lucky that at the time when she

---

[4]   There are also other documentary films which have tried to connect the fate of low-lying islands to larger ecological and geopolitical processes, most notably Paul Lindsay's BBC documentary *Before the Flood: Tuvalu* (2004) and Jon Shenk's *The Island President* (2011) about former president of the Maldives, Mohamed Nasheed, and his efforts to help the world tackle climate change.

[5]   March explains this in a brief promotional video for the 2012 Sea Level Rise Summit in Florida (see 'Filmmaker Interview').

became interested in the topic, the local people were worried enough about the ecological changes on their island to request 'that someone comes and documents things' (Gnanalingam), thus loosening their restrictive visiting policies.[6] After having been invited onto the island, March and her crew embarked on the 18-hour boat trip to Takuu, knowing that they would only be able to leave again several months later on the next available boat. Her situation as filmmaker was therefore almost a case of participant observation in that she to some degree shared the life of the people she was portraying and also experienced some of the environmental changes on Nukutoa's beaches first-hand. This does not mean, however, that we should understand her film as a simple 'recording' of these changes and the ways in which they affect the local population.

The special appeal of the documentary form lies in its very power to seduce us into believing that we are watching an 'objective' account of the events presented to us. Like fiction films, however, documentaries are the product of directorial choices. 'To take the documentary film as a mere photographic document', argues film scholar Carl Plantinga, 'ignores the "creative shaping" that is an ineluctable element of all documentary films' (495). Although documentaries may make use of documents, maintains Plantinga, it is a problem if we reduce them to the provision of documentation, because such an understanding neglects the manifold ways in which documentary filmmakers actively frame and shape the filmic worlds they present to their audiences. In the case of *There Once Was an Island*, such framing and shaping was in part a collaborative effort, since the Takuu people were closely involved in the making of the film. March intertwines the visual documentation of the ecological changes on Nukutoa's beaches with the personal stories of the three people who are at the centre of her documentary – Satty, Endar and Telo. Rather than speaking for them, March lets her protagonists speak for themselves and uses no other form of narration than that which is provided by the occasional text inserts. Nevertheless, the material that is included in the film is the result of a careful selection process, a selection that is guided by March's intention to make an environmental documentary and the community's interest in raising global awareness of their dire situation.

Hughes has suggested that it is helpful 'to place documentary in the context of communication rather than aesthetics' and that this choice implies 'tak[ing] sides on the question of agency or intentionality in film and possibly to claim intentionality as a fundamental for environmental documentary' (5). March's intention, as stated in several interviews and in the 'What You Can Do' section of her film's website, was to turn her viewers' attention to the issue of climate change and its effects on the ecologies and inhabitants of small islands. Her foregrounding of the personal stories of some of the Takuu people helps viewers to

---

[6]   To protect their indigenous practices and religious sites, the people of Takuu have been highly restrictive about visits from outsiders. Only in recent years has their policy become a little more liberal, which is why March and her team were allowed to visit the atoll twice, once in 2006 and once in 2008.

develop an interest in them as individuals rather than just see them as victims or as providers of information about the ecological changes along the island's shoreline. March encourages her audience to see the ecological changes *in relation* to these individuals and, therefore, to understand their immediate and long-term impact on the community and its traditional culture.

The first person who speaks in the film is Satty, a 30-year-old fisherman who relies on Takuu's traditional fishing methods to put food on the table for his wife, their five children, and everybody else in the community who might need some. That, he explains, 'is all I do here'. Having been largely isolated from the Papua New Guinea mainland culture due to their relatively remote location, the islanders have been able to retain an egalitarian culture where people work for the common good and resources are shared equally. Satty seems to be in good spirits as he pulls out the fishing line with his bare hands, evidently looking forward to the evening meal. To him, the palm-rimmed sand beach close to his house is less recreation area than the place where he keeps his boat, an integral part of his working environment. From here the film cuts to a long shot of a different part of the shoreline. Viewers must assume that it is high tide, since the seawater is now so close to the shoreline that it is leaping up the trunks of the island's palm trees. Even if they know very little about marine ecology, they are likely to realise that the complete lack of a dry backbeach must be somewhat unusual.[7] Unlike the water-washed foreshore, this portion of the beach is almost horizontal and functions as a natural protection from storm flooding. In the case of the beaches we see in March's film, however, this protective area is almost completely missing, exposing the island's palm trees and houses to the encroaching sea.

The beach is thus introduced not only as a working environment between land and sea but also as a transformational space of environmental risk, a space where global warming and sea level rise have lead to observable ecological changes that threaten the livelihood of the islanders. March shows their attempts to keep the water away from their houses with the help of simple seawalls made of stone, netting and pieces of wood. The images are not accompanied by any kind of explanatory commentary or even music. Because of the slow pacing of the editing, however, viewers have enough time to ponder on them and notice the gradual collapse of distance between village and ocean as a result of the vanishing beach. The sequence thereby effectively establishes the theme of disappearance and foreshadows the much greater assault that will come later on.

Endar, the second person who introduces herself in March's film, insists that Takuu's disappearing backbeaches are the first forebodings of a much more dangerous future. One of the few islanders who have spent time on the Papua New Guinea mainland, Endar is married to a Papua New Guinean in Bougainville and has returned to the island only temporarily to help her sister take care of their

---

[7] 'The backshore or backbeach', explain Davis and Fitzgerald, is the supratidal part of the beach that 'extends from the berm crest' – which separates it from the water-washed foreshore – 'landward ... to the next physiographic feature' (120).

elderly father.[8] A converted Christian and the first woman of Takuu who has gone overseas to work, Endar admits without hesitation that it would be 'worse for [her] to stay on this island compared to [her] life in Port Moresby with [her] husband', and she is a staunch advocate of the Bougainville Government's plan to relocate the islanders to the mainland. While it is clear that, because of her religious beliefs, Endar is not as attached to Takuu's traditional culture as Satty and many other people in the community are, her advocacy of relocation is also grounded in her understanding of the larger forces at work on Nukutoa's beaches and the long-term danger they pose for the island's inhabitants. 'The sea level is rising', she declares, 'and destroying the whole island'. Another unsteady shot from the half-submerged camera reminds viewers of this very real danger.

Once again, March establishes the connections between words and image solely through the way in which the film is edited. There is no narrator or text insert that would provide additional information. A long shot of the island's shoreline shows a serious looking Endar standing close to a line of palm trees whose root systems are being slowly laid bare by the breaking waves. The film communicates visually the potentially disastrous transformation of coastal space, documenting not only the disappearance of the protective backbeach but also that of domestic space when Endar points to the ocean beneath her, explaining that 'when I was living … in this house, this is where my kitchen [was]. … Now the sea has washed the place'. She then proceeds to describe the other rooms of her old house, which used to stand where now there is nothing but water. 'It is very sad to see', she adds, 'that the children growing are not seeing what we have seen before'. When Endar asks her sister's little sons where they will go when the sea has taken away all of Nukutoa, they name the neighbouring island of Amotou and look lost when she answers that that will be no solution 'because Amotou will be destroyed, too'. The magnitude of the changes ahead of them exceeds the scope of their imagination.

The third protagonist to introduce himself is Telo, who, as a father of six, embraces the traditions of the community. Telo is distraught by the increasing intrusion of seawater into the soil of the nearby 'garden island' and the fact that the changing salinity levels are killing the giant taro, a slow-growing food plant that plays a central role in the community's traditional ceremonies.[9] He leads the filmmakers into the garden – a thick forest filled with millions of mosquitoes – explaining that two generations ago it was already 'affected by salt

---

[8]   Gnanalingam has expressed his relief about the fact that *There Once Was an Island* 'avoids a 'noble savage' kind of stereotype, with the island's inhabitants well aware of what was at stake' (Gnanalingam). He quotes the film's producer Lyn Collie (who accompanied March to Nukutoa for the shooting) stating that '[t]he island itself has three PhD graduates, and a number of expats living in Port Moresby and Australia. … There's movement on and off the island, insofar as the boat allows, so it's not as if these are people wearing grass skirts, they do get technology' (Gnanalingam).

[9]   Giant taro is a staple food for many communities in tropical areas. All parts of the plant are edible, from the enormous leaves that can reach 10 feet across to the stem and corm (see 'Super-sized').

water'. Telo, too, shows his awareness of the global context and the limitation of the community's power to address it when he declares that, because of sea level rise, 'in the future all these gardens will be all affected. And there is nothing we can do now'. March contextualises Telo's pessimistic prognosis with a text insert that states that '[i]ncreasingly the islanders have become reliant on food supplied by the Autonomous Bougainville Government. However, it only comes sporadically, making planning difficult'. The viewer is thus informed that the islanders can no longer sustain themselves with local crops and that, in spite of its relatively remote location and ancient culture, Takuu is subjected to various outside forces and agents. Not only is the geographical space of the atoll exposed to sea level changes that are themselves the result of the melting ice in very different and spatially remote places but these changes also make its inhabitants dependent on the goodwill of people outside of that space, people who still have access to food and other vital resources.

Despite his awareness of the changing ecology of the island, however, Telo cannot see himself moving away from the island unless relocation becomes absolutely necessary. 'It is not right for us to move to another place', he explains, because 'it is going to be very difficult for [us] to take our culture with [us]'. Like others in the community, he is worried about the future because he fears that his people's Polynesian culture will not survive once they have been relocated. The prospect of moving to the mainland scares most of them, not least because they believe that they will be chased away by the local landowners regardless of what the government promises them. And even if they were indeed allowed to stay, they would have to get used to an entirely different culture – Bougainvilleans are Melanesian – and to the pressures of a money-based economy. At the same time, Telo has come to understand that the seawalls that they have been building along the shoreline will not be sufficient. The powers that are at work in this transformational space between land and sea are much too great to be contained by seawalls made of stone and netting.

Through the three people that she has placed at the centre of her film, March offers viewers insight into various indigenous perspectives on climate change, sea level rise and their consequences for the Takuu people. Not all are as radical as Endar is with her suggested solutions, but even the most traditional among the islanders understand that their local knowledge is only of limited help in addressing the larger problem and that the seawalls they have been building along their eroding shoreline will eventually be washed away with everything else. 'When I was a little kid', remembers Satty, 'I used to play around the beach fronts. … There was white sand. Since we've started to make the seawalls we have no white sand'. Not only is Satty well aware of the gradual disappearance of the island's backbeach areas; he also draws a clear link between the community's preventive actions – the building of seawalls – and that disappearance. Like Telo and many others, he does not want to leave his home or relocate to Bougainville, and so the Takuu people gradually realise that they will have to rely on help from outside. Only few of them believe that this help will come from a benevolent God, and their trust in the Bougainville Government, which has been exceptionally ineffective in its support, does not seem to go much farther. Most of them think that bringing in international scientists is their best option if they want to gain a better understanding of the larger dimensions of their problem and of possible solutions.

Because they realise that Takuu's vanishing beaches are part of much larger ecological processes, the islanders have begun considering a new and different level of exchange and interaction that will allow them to understand the local changes they observe in a more abstract and scientific way. The formerly secluded community has begun to develop what Heise has called 'eco-cosmopolitan awareness' (90). It is expressed in the people's increasing attention to the complex interferences of global forces in the ecological processes along their shoreline and their willingness to combine their concrete experiential knowledge of the changes on the island with the abstract knowledge of scientific experts in order to address their problems. Like postcolonial thinkers, proponents of eco-cosmopolitanism insist on 'the inseparability of the current ecological crisis from historical legacies of imperialistic exploitation and authoritarian abuse' (Huggan 702), and they thus pay attention to the power structures that are typically involved in interactions of the local with the global. At the same time, however, they believe in the possibility of new forms of exchange and engagement that reach 'for an understanding of both cultural and ecological differences and connectedness' (Heise 90). The development of such eco-cosmopolitan modes of exchange and engagement, and their relevance for the environmental practices and concerns of the Takuu people, is what March chronicles in the second half of her film.

Slow Violence and Local Resistance: Documenting the Environmentalism of the Poor

When March returns to Nukutoa for her second shoot in 2008, she shares the boat with Endar, who brings along two new visitors to the island: the Australian geomorphologist Scott Smithers and the British-Australian oceanographer John Hunter. Endar has arranged for the two scientists to accompany her so that they can take some measurements and counsel the islanders; she also hopes that listening to the scientists will convince her people that they have to accept the offer of the Government and relocate to Bougainville. Smithers and Hunter plan to provide the community with 'some fairly simple, easy to understand resources' as well as 'some advice … on what some of their options are'. At their first community meeting, Hunter offers an explanation for the observed sea level rise that underlines its complex spatial and political dimensions. He explains that 'at the moment the world is warming up because of other people in the world … burning things like diesel fuel in large amounts' which 'cause[s] the world to warm'. This describes exactly the form of long-distance 'violence that is neither spectacular nor instantaneous, but rather incremental and accretive' that, according to Nixon, 'impacts the environments – and the environmentalism – of the poor' (2).

As Nixon reminds us, the recipients of such violence are often 'triply discounted: discounted as political agents, discounted as long-term casualties' of this type of aggression, 'and discounted as cultures possessing environmental practices and concerns of their own' (2). All of this is the case for the Takuu people, who, as a Bougainville Government official puts it, must realise that their only option 'is to move to the mainland'. They are already being treated as refugees, as landless and rightless people, who must be grateful for anything that is offered to them. No one seems to be accountable for their losses, and no one expects them to demand adequate compensation or revolutionary changes in the way in which the world is run, simply because they do not have the political or economic means necessary to make such demands.

However, there is more for the islanders to learn from the scientists than the global reasons for their local environmental problems. Satty tells Smithers about their local practice of building seawalls against the encroaching sea water, only to learn that, in the long run, these will actually 'impede the island's ability to cope with sea level rise'. The vanishing beaches he bemoaned earlier in the film are in fact – at least in part – an unintended consequence of the community's attempt to protect their houses from the water. Smithers explains that a wave that comes up a natural beach and swashes over its berm – the upper part of the beach's wet foreshore – will deposit sand as it retreats and partially drains into the ground. The seawalls, which keep the water separate from the land behind, prevent such natural build up of washed-up sand and thus contribute to further shoreline erosion. This important information confirms Satty's vague notion that the seawalls might have something to do with the disappearance of the island's sandy backbeaches, which, as he now understands, were not only an aesthetic pleasure but also an important part of the island's ecology and an (insufficient) protective mechanism against storm floods. He begins to think about what can be learned from this lesson and decides that they should move their houses further inland 'so that the sand can build up and the shoreline can rebuild'. The beach, he believes, must be allowed to grow back so that it can protect them from the rising sea.

Satty's local understanding of the island's ecology is therefore further enriched and partially transformed in an eco-cosmopolitan process of exchange and learning that values both physical experience and 'the abstract and highly mediated kinds of knowledge and experience that lend equal or greater support to a grasp of biospheric connectedness' (Heise 62). The same is true for Telo, who now has a better understanding of the physical dimensions of the processes he has observed on the community's garden island as well as the global forces that drive those processes. March uses a fly-on-the-wall approach for her portrayal of all these interactions between scientists and islanders, presenting their conversations as if they occurred naturally without any camera present. Of course, such interactions can never be quite natural whenever there is a camera around that captures everything on film. March's situation as a participant-observer who lived with the local population over several months enabled her to avoid situations that seem staged for the most part, but that does not mean that she does not carefully frame individual shots. When Smithers and Satty talk about the seawalls, they do so standing knee-deep in the ocean. The setting of the shot not only visually communicates the subject of their conversation; it also reminds viewers that they have planted their feet into the water where the beach should have been. Mack has argued that the tides 'emphasize the liminality of the beach as parts of it are successively revealed and then swamped by tidal action' (165). In this shot, however, the beach is permanently submerged under several feet of water, thus losing not only its liminality but also its protective capacity.

Both the filmmakers and the scientists are still on the island when it is hit by an unusually high tide – a so-called 'king tide' – that arrives more or less out of the blue. March captures the moment with a shot of a woman who stands in the open door of her house. The camera is inside the house, showing the silhouette of the woman against the ocean. As the camera slowly pans down, it reveals that the seawater is coming up right to her doorstep, almost covering her feet. The next wave suddenly raises the water to the woman's thighs; all she can do is turn around and look on helplessly as the ocean enters her house. This momentary transformation of domestic space into waterfront, however, is only the beginning. One of the following shots shows Satty and his family standing next to the beach, watching anxiously as the water keeps rising, reaching the second line of palm trees, then the third. The scene is overarched by a disconcertingly blue sky. There is no storm in sight, just an unusual tidal range, lifting the water way above its normal high tide level. People are busy moving their boats away from the beaches, carrying furniture and other valuable possessions out of the most exposed houses. However, the waves – seemingly for no reason – are growing higher, causing the water to move further and further inland. It effortlessly spills over the community's seawalls and floods many of their houses, including the island's only schoolhouse, which loses most of its teaching materials. We see people running away in surprise from the oncoming tidal waves, see the astonishment and shock in their faces as they try to comprehend what is happening. Never before has a tide wave come this far inland without there being some sign of a storm.

The camera is in the middle of all this, showing water on all sides, allowing the viewer a subjective look at the spectacle and giving a sense of what it must feel like to experience it on the ground. Not only are the protective beaches now gone; it is no longer possible to distinguish between island and surrounding sea. The shoreline is transforming before the viewer's eyes into a liminal space that is made up of water and land, seemingly at the same time. The disorienting quality of the sequence is further enhanced by the unchanging blue sky that simply does not seem to match what is happening on the ground. March later remembered how she was standing with the encroaching water reaching up to her chest, capturing the important event on film while at the same time desperately trying to keep the camera above the waves (see Chase). Even as she was filming it, she knew that this would become the climax of her film, the moment that visually captures the threat of total annihilation, of disappearance. Watching the sea climb up the island, covering with several feet of water what minutes before was dry and solid ground, is impressive and frightening, and these images communicate Takuu's perspective on the problem of global warming better than any scientific report ever could. Most viewers of the film are likely to be among the perpetrators of slow violence, regularly 'burning things like diesel fuel in large amounts', and they are now given the opportunity to see what normally happens 'out of sight' (Nixon 2) and consider the long-distance consequences of their everyday actions. As Powell points out in his review of the film, *There Once Was an Island* 'successfully connects the viewer to the plight of Takuu by highlighting our part (insignificant though it may seem) in its slow but steady submersion'. And so it will likely be with very mixed feelings that such viewers watch the Takuu people wading ankle-deep in water as they wait for the sea to withdraw completely from their village and for their shoreline to reappear.

However, it is not only the retreat of the water that is on the minds of the islanders. They are also waiting anxiously for some outside help. We learn that '[d]uring the four days of the flood, it has been too dangerous to fish or harvest taro' and that the community is therefore running low on food. Not only has the beach ceased to function as a bastion against storms, king tides and other flooding events; it can no longer be used by the fishermen or gardeners of the community either, thus further weakening their ability to sustain themselves autonomously. Telo listens to the radio news, hoping that the reports about the regional king tide will mention the events on Takuu. But he is disappointed. 'Nothing about the Mortlock people', he declares, 'still forgotten'.[10] His frustration is evident, and it is quite understandable. Although the National Disaster Service coordinator has promised relief for those who have been affected by the flooding, the islanders wait in vain for food or medical assistance. Telo voices the principal fear of many in the community: 'One day when we have the real problem and when we ask the Government, and if the Government doesn't do it immediately, maybe they'll find nobody on this island. We'll all be gone'. Complete disappearance, Telo understands, is indeed a possibility not only for Nukutoa's beaches but for its people as well. This is a scary prospect, and it is dangerously real since it is only a matter of time until the next abnormally high flood tide will hit the island.

As oceanographer Hunter explains to the community, unusual flooding events such as the one they have just experienced 'may be happening three to ten times more often' in the future, 'just because of sea level rise'. Given the inertness of the climate system, these environmental changes would have to be expected even if the world community *did* take significant steps to mitigate climate change. However, as Smithers points out, sea level rise is not the only contributing factor to the island's vulnerability: 'There is the issue of climate change here, but there is also simply an issue of money and resources'. Unlike the inhabitants of some other low-lying islands, such as Tuvalu or the Maldives, the Takuu people have no dotcom domain to sell and no tourism revenue to speak of, and they are therefore even less well equipped to deal with the ecological changes that are affecting

---

[10]   The Takuu atoll is also known as the Mortlock Islands.

their island.[11] Lacking both the political power to make their voices heard in the international community and the financial resources to improve their infrastructure, they might opt to remove the seawalls, relocate their houses, and hope for the best. Alternatively, they can take up the offer of the Bougainville Government and move to the mainland, where they will have to earn their living on a plantation.[12]

After the flooding, many of the islanders are discouraged enough to consider this option, but Satty is among those who refuse to be victims. He explains that '[l]istening to [Smither's] advice' has helped him decide what to do. It is not only the scientific knowledge of the outside experts he can draw on, however, but also more local knowledge that comes with experience. He recognises that '[o]ur ancestors were much wiser than the people today. They knew where they had to put the houses'. Accordingly, he starts rebuilding his thatched house on higher ground and advocates the demolition of the island's seawalls, so that its beaches can once again fulfil their protective function against king tides and storms. At the same time, he also understands that in a globalised world the agency of his community is limited and that local efforts alone cannot bring long-term solutions because global problems such as sea level rise cannot be solved locally. As long as the industrialised nations do not curb their emissions, the slow violence of climate change will continue and eat away at Takuu's protective beaches. It would take a great deal of eco-cosmopolitan solidarity among the rich and the poor in the world to solve the pressing problems of low-lying Nukutoa and the rest of the Takuu atoll. This is why Satty hopes that if 'somebody can see' that they have started helping themselves, 'somebody might be willing to assist' them in their efforts to save their homes from disappearing into the Pacific.

---

[11]   The Tuvaluans sold their internet country's '.tv' address at the height of the dotcom boom. They subsequently decided to spend 1.5 million dollars per year for a seat in the UN, a choice that signals their determination to become political actors on a global scale. Paul Lindsay's BBC-documentary *Before the Flood: Tuvalu* (2004) shows a powerful moment at the 1997 Climate Change Conference in Kyoto when the Tuvaluan Prime Minister Bikenibeu Paeniu reminded world leaders that for his people 'the whole issue of climate change … is not [of] economics and politics, but it is of life and death' (*Before the Flood*). The former president of the Maldives, Mohammed Nasheed, has been equally vocal about the need for the world to tackle climate change, so far without any meaningful consequences. There have also been attempts to raise awareness through cultural means. Nasheed's efforts are the subject of Jon Shenk's documentary *The Island President* (2011). Tuvalu's struggle against sea level rise is the topic of *Before the Flood*; the island also participated in the *Water Is Rising Project*, which combined traditional dance performances in fourteen US cities with information about sea level rise and its consequences for low-lying islands.

[12]   March has explained in an interview that if the people of Takuu had to relocate to a plantation on the mainland, they would not 'have the same access to go fishing or to garden the way that they garden [but] that's their fundamental way of life. But not only that, their cultural practices, their traditions and the rituals and everything that's related to their religious views and practices is all related to the land' (Chase).

It is one of March's achievements that she has made it possible for people all over the world to see both the problems of the Takuu people and the ways in which they are trying to cope with them while at the same time reminding the viewers of their own inevitable involvement in both the problem and the potential solutions. While the film provides comparatively little political and scientific context, its major strength is that it depicts the environmental perspective of the recipients of slow violence, who, as Nixon has stressed, are so often 'discounted as cultures possessing environmental practices and concerns of their own' (2). In their influential *Varieties of Environmentalism* (2000), Guha and Martinez-Alier have argued that the 'empty-belly' environmentalism of the global South is substantially different from the 'full-stomach' environmentalism of the North (xxi). Not only is the former often driven by destitution and despair in the face of 'visible ecological degradation' (17) but it also insists on the close relation between environmental problems and postcolonial globalisation and its resulting inequities. The 'struggles, of peasants, tribals and so on, are in a sense deeply conservatory (in the best sense of the word), refusing to exchange a world they know, and are in partial control over, for an uncertain and insecure future' (18). This form of conservational environmentalism is encapsulated in Satty's decision to rebuild his traditional house on higher ground and expressed in his staunch resolution that he will probably 'be the last one' to leave Nukutoa.[13]

There Once Was an Island ends with a sequence of shots that, once again, leads viewers into the transitional space of the island's eroded beaches with their lack of sand and fallen palm trees. In one of the last moments of the film Smithers asks viewers to imagine how it would feel to *them* to lose the places *they* hold dear and to then 'magnify that impact by ten times because this is all these people know. ... This is it. This is their world. And their world is being destroyed'. March connects this appeal for empathetic identification to John Hunter's call for a drastic reduction of emissions in the industrialised world 'in order to allow the developing world to raise its emissions' because 'otherwise they will not be able to lift themselves out of poverty'. The last words, however, belong to Satty, who suggests that 'somebody big must not look down. Somebody big should say: let's see what you've got. Let's get together and do something ... No matter how small you are ... you are still part of the world. If you lose something small in the world, you lose a lot'. The film thus documents how the local people have succeeded in expanding their environmental awareness, envisioning themselves not only 'as part of the global biosphere' but also 'as part of a planetary community' (Heise 62) that somehow must work together in order to solve global problems. Satty's solemn appeal for eco-cosmopolitan ethics and practice is followed by a sequence of peaceful and idyllic images of the island reminiscent of the opening shot, which give the viewer time to think about its implications.

---

[13]   Nixon reminds us that environmental protest by disenfranchised communities 'has frequently been incited by the threat of forced removal' (19).

Conclusion

Massey's understanding of geographical space as interactive insists on its openness to local and global forces, be they ecological, economic, political, cultural or some combination of these. *There Once Was an Island* impressively demonstrates how this is true for even the most remote and isolated locations and for spaces we tend to imagine as peaceful, pleasant and undisturbed, such as the beaches of a Pacific atoll. It is the excessive carbon emissions of highly industrialised countries in the North that indirectly cause the disappearance of Takuu's local beaches, and it is the islanders' own attempts to manage the related risks of flooding and coastal erosion that inadvertently lead to the worsening of the situation. As the German sociologist Ulrich Beck has shown, such 'unintended side effects' are inevitable 'concomitants of risk rationality' (14); even carefully considered mitigation measures often lead to new, unanticipated risks and hazards. The Takuu people's decision to build seawalls to protect their houses from the rising ocean leads to the accelerated erosion of their island's beaches. Without these sandy stretches of land, however, there is no natural protection left to stop the waves from washing away their few material possessions and, in the long run, their traditional Polynesian culture. It is a combination of abstract scientific expertise from the outside and recovered local knowledge that allows them to correct this misconception and the resulting ecological consequences, but this alone will not be enough to address the larger, global causes of their problem. This global dimension can only be addressed by a new form of eco-cosmopolitan solidarity that works against the many modes of 'slow violence' that Nixon sees at the heart of the past and the contemporary world order.

   One aim of March's environmental documentary is to help create such eco-cosmopolitan solidarity by raising awareness for Takuu's ecological problems and the islanders' perspective on climate change. March has explained that, because of their limited resources, the people of Takuu 'feel that they do not have a voice and we hope that through this film we will be able to give them one' (March). The decision to allow the islanders to speak for themselves, to tell their story to an international audience, makes the film itself an eco-cosmopolitan project, created jointly by the New Zealand filmmakers and their Polynesian protagonists.[14] March believes that her documentary 'has wide appeal because … it shares the characters' life experiences in a way that people everywhere can relate to and respect' (March). The global success of her film has proven her right. *There Once Was an Island* has been showered with awards and prizes, and it has been lauded by critics for its effective linking of local and global concerns that appeals to

---

   [14]   As film scholar Bill Nichols points out, documentary filmmakers often speak for the interests of 'the individuals whom they represent' (3). One of the central questions in this context is 'What responsibility do filmmakers have for the effect of their acts on the lives of those filmed' and how can they avoid exploiting the suffering of their subjects for the sake of a film? (6). March tried to deal with these ethical issues through a close cooperation with the islanders.

remarkably diverse audiences. Her decision to offer 'a character-driven story told in an observational cinematic style' (March) enables more affluent viewers to empathise and sympathise with Satty and the other people she portrays, inviting them to understand not only the environmentalism of the poor but also their own involvement in the slow, climate-change-related violence the islanders are subjected to.[15] If they are perceptive observers of their time and place, the wealthier among them will long ago have come to understand that their very lifestyle choices make them complicit in numerous forms of slow violence against countless groups of people around the world. Some of these viewers might even understand that what March shows in her film is indeed 'the microcosm of the macrocosm' (Gnanalingam), when Satty reminds them at the end of the film that '[i]f you lose something small in the world', you 'lose a lot', but we must also understand that the local, and to some perhaps irrelevant, fate of Takuu is only the first warning sign of a much greater, global problem that in the not-too-distant future will affect countless seashores and many densely populated urban areas. It is a development that resembles the little waves at the beginning of March's film that in fact foreshadow the dangerous king tide engulfing the island later on.

However, the fact that *There Once Was an Island* was shown at more than 120 film festivals and community screenings around the world from the Solomon Islands to Indonesia and from Tahiti to Hawaii (as well as to various indigenous communities elsewhere in the US) suggests that March's documentary is also a valuable source of information and inspiration for those who are more likely to be at the receiving end of slow violence.[16] Satty's final appeal that 'No matter how small you are … you are still part of the world' is a wake-up call not only for those who believe that there are no consequences for the perpetrators of environmental violence in a globalised world but also for those who are themselves subjected to such violence and who might not yet be aware of the option 'to get together and do something', as Satty puts it. The world today is warming at an alarming pace, and our growing awareness of a common, all-pervasive threat will hopefully help produce the much-needed solidarity that will allow us to tackle climate change effectively. The beach – that beautiful, vulnerable and constantly changing space made up of land and water – is a powerful reminder of that common, all-pervasive threat.

---

[15]   As Paul Slovic and Paul Västfjäll have shown, 'people are much more willing to aid identified individuals than unidentified or statistical victims' (393). The two psychologists observed a 'collapse of compassion' in cases where subjects were confronted with large-scale catastrophes with a high number of (abstract) casualties. Like Paul Farmer, they believe that 'images, narratives, and first-person testimony' can help us 'overcome our 'failure of imagination' in contemplating the fate of distant, suffering people' (395). This suggests that documentary films that focus on individuals who are the recipients of slow violence might in fact play a crucial role in the creation of pro-social behaviour on their behalf.

[16]   For a list of the dozens of small and tiny film festivals where *There Once Was an Island* was shown, see 'Festival Participation'.

Works Cited

Beck, Ulrich. *World at Risk*. Cambridge: Polity P, 2009.

Before the Flood: Tuvalu. Dir. Paul Lindsay. BBC Four, 2004. Film.

Chase, Andrea. Interview. 'There Once Was an Island – Filmmaker Briar March'. *Public Radio Exchange*. 9 Mar. 2012. Web. 7 Mar. 2013. <http://www.prx.org/pieces/75758>.

Davis, Richard, and Duncan Fitzgerald. *Beaches and Coasts*. London: Wiley-Blackwell, 2004.

'Festival Participation'. *There Once Was an Island*. Web. 6 Aug. 2014. <http://www.thereoncewasanisland.com/past-screening-list/>.

'Filmmaker Interview – Briar March'. *Florida Centre for Environmental Studies*. Web. 6 Aug. 2014. <http://www.ces.fau.edu/SLR2012/media/briar-march.php>.

Gnanalingam, Brannavan. 'Making *There Once Was an Island*'. *The Lumière Reader* 20 Aug. 2010. Web. 7 Mar. 2013. <http://lumiere.net.nz/index.php/making-there-once-was-an-island>.

Gorfinkel, Elena, and John David Rhodes. 'Introduction: The Matter of Places'. *Taking Place: Location and the Moving Image*. Ed. John David Rhodes and Elena Gorfinkel. Minneapolis: U of Minnesota P, 2011. vii–xxix.

Guha, Ramachandra, and Juan Martínez-Alier. *Varieties of Environmentalism: Essays North and South*. London: Earthscan, 1997.

Heise, Ursula. *Sense of Place and Sense of Planet: The Environmental Imagination of the Global*. Oxford: Oxford UP, 2008.

Hobbs, Carl. *The Beach Book: Science of the Shore*. New York: Columbia UP, 2012.

Huggan, Graham. 'Greening Postcolonialism: Ecocritical Perspectives'. *MFS Modern Fiction Studies* 50.3 (2004): 701–33.

Hughes, Helen. *Green Documentary: Environmental Documentary in the 21st Century*. Bristol: Intellect, 2014.

Hunter, John, Ian Allison and Tessa Jakszwicz. *ACE SLR Report Card Sea Level Rise 2012*. Hobart, Tasmania: Antarctic Climate & Ecosystems Cooperative Research Centre, 2012.

The Island President. Dir. Jon Shenk. Samuel Goldwyn Films, 2011. Film.

Mack, John. *The Sea: A Cultural History*. London: Reaktion, 2011.

March, Briar. 'Director's Statement'. *Press Kit There Once Was an Island*. 15 Oct. 2011. Web. 6 Aug. 2014. <http://www.thereoncewasanisland.com/media>.

Massey, Doreen B. *For Space*. London: Sage, 2005.

Nichols, Bill. *Introduction to Documentary*. Bloomington: Indiana UP, 2001.

Nixon, Rob. *Slow Violence and the Environmentalism of the Poor*. Cambridge, MA: Harvard UP, 2011.

Powell, Jacob. 'Breaking the Waves: *There Once Was an Island*'. *The Lumière Reader* 14 June 2010. Web. 18 Oct. 2011. <http://lumiere.net.nz/index.php/there-once-was-an-island>.

Plantinga, Carl. 'Documentary'. *The Routledge Companion to Philosophy and Film*. Ed. Paisly Livingston and Carl Plantinga. London: Routledge, 2005. 494–504.

Slovic, Paul, and Daniel Västfjäll. 'Affect, Moral Intuition, and Risk'. *Psychological Inquiry: An International Journal for the Advancement of Psychological Theory* 21.4 (2010): 387–98.

'Super-sized: Giant Taro'. *The Living Rainforest*. Web. 7 Mar. 2013. <http://www. livingrainforest.org/about-rainforests/super-sized-giant-taro>.

There Once Was an Island. Dir. Briar March. On the Level Productions, 2010. Film.

Water Is Rising Project. Web. 6 Aug. 2014. <http://www.waterisrising.com>.

Weik von Mossner, Alexa. 'The Human Face of Global Warming: Varieties of Eco-Cosmopolitanism in Climate Change Documentaries'. *Ecocriticism in English Studies*. Ed. Carmen Flys Junquera and Juan Ignacio Oliva. Special Issue of *Revista Canaria de Estudios Ingleses* 64 (April 2012): 145–60.

'What You Can Do'. *There Once Was an Island* Web. 6 Aug. 2014. <http://www. thereoncewasanisland.com/what-you-can-do/>.

Index

Note: Page numbers in **bold** type indicate illustrations